To Reggie ;-)
To help your while
away your convalescent
hours! Happy holidays!!
Ben, Leonore, Enid, Dean
Xmas 1975

CALIFORNIA

The Vanishing Dream

CALIFORNIA

The Vanishing Dream

MICHAEL DAVIE

Photographs by
CAMILLA SMITH

DODD, MEAD & COMPANY   NEW YORK

ISBN: 0-396-06534-1
Library of Congress Catalog Card Number: 72-3143

Printed in the United States of America
by Vail-Ballou Press, Inc., Binghamton, N. Y.

For Annabel, Simon and Emma

———————————————————————

Foreword

So leap with joy, be blithe and gay,
    Or weep my friends with sorrow.
What California is today,
    The rest will be tomorrow.
Richard Armour

MY first contact with California occurred at a dance in London, during the summer of 1951, when I found myself in the same "party" as a blonde girl named Honeybear Warren. Her father, then governor of California (he used his daughters, of whom there were several, each more beautiful than the last, to help him get elected) was also at the dance, but I did not talk to him, preferring Honeybear. She, as we circled the floor, gave me an impression of both her family and her state that was entirely favorable. I was accordingly not surprised when her father, promoted to the Supreme Court, turned out to be a great chief justice; and now, even after twenty years of riots, assassinations, and mass slayings, I still see California through a faint golden haze engendered among the pale London faces by the peach-fed Honeybear from Sacramento.

My first actual visit to California was in 1952, when I was the English member of a group of NATO journalists who were given a free tour of the United States by the State Department. The department hoped that, having accepted its bribe, we would write more favorably about America. Until we arrived in California, our program was formidably serious, packed with briefings on forgotten crises and "problem areas"; but as soon as we reached the west coast our State Department guides made it plain that we could now relax. Obviously, California was not a serious part of our education.

I recall the embarrassment with which the most intense of our guides explained that we were to have our photographs taken with Lizabeth Scott on a Paramount set (I still have her picture, though I have forgotten what he told us about America's policy toward Quemoy and Matsu). I also remember the lobsters that the U.S. government bought us on Fisherman's Wharf, in San Francisco. Nobody we met out there suggested that California was worth taking seriously, and perhaps at that time, it wasn't.

In Malibu, where we spent an evening together, Christopher Isherwood, the English writer, told me that what he liked best about California was the strange and unspoiled country within a half-hour drive of downtown Los Angeles. He also made an observation about the difference between Americans and Europeans. "Getting to know a European," he said, "is like making a landfall on an island with a narrow shore and mountains behind; but once you are over the mountains, you're friends for life. Americans have a very deep stretch of shore they let you into at once, and their mountains are much further back and very hard to cross." I thought, then, that Isherwood was like a man taking a long holiday among lotus-eaters; he was living a much less demanding life than his contemporaries in Europe, who had been through the war (he had left England for California in 1938) and who in 1952 were still struggling with its aftermath, both physically and spiritually. It was a forgivable error, coming as I had from a shabby and hard-pressed London to a tanned Isherwood in a bar beside the Pacific. Isherwood, I supposed, had been deeply involved in the politics of the thirties; yet now here he was drinking ice-cold Budweiser and writing for the movies. How could that be a serious way to live? Since then, I have learned that almost anyone who emigrates to California invites a similar reaction. Non-Californians refuse to take the place seriously. A girl photographer who recently moved from New York to Bolinas, north of San Francisco, told me she had felt compelled to lie to her friends about her motives. Her real reason for the transfer was that she wanted to work in a more demanding setting, but that would have seemed to her friends a ridiculous reason for going to California, so she told them she longed to surf, which they accepted as reasonable. And so she kept their esteem.

My own conversion to the idea that California was more than a playground occurred over lunch in the Redwood Room of the Clift Hotel in San Francisco. I had stopped off for a week to report the comic (as it seemed then) story of how a second-rate actor without a single day's governmental experience had become governor of California. After a day or two, however, I had an uneasy feeling that the explanation for Reagan's election was not simply that the voters were rewarding him for his performance in *Bonzo Goes To College.*

One local phenomenon struck me as especially weird and outside my experience: the hatred for the University of California that I encountered. Why, I wondered, would people hate a *university?*—especially a state-run university that was internationally renowned and virtually free to all comers, provided they were bright enough. At lunch, surrounded by the hundred-year-old redwood paneling, a Berkeley professor began to give me some clues. His own field of study was Africa and he had been raised on the east coast, so that, like myself, he was able to take an objective view of Californian phenomena. He had come to Berkeley after a stay in Ghana, where he had been treated with proper respect by the Africans, and he had at once been disconcerted by the hostility that he encountered from Californians. Education, he said, was the key issue in California because the educational system sorted out the sheep from the goats. The university was the ladder to success. Anyone, provided he was clever enough, could get on the ladder; and the system was so organized that a child soon knew whether or not he was going to get on the ladder. Parents learned very early which of their children were going places and which weren't going anywhere. The university had thus become the arbiter of every child's future. When the university rejected a child because he or she was not clever enough, the parents felt the decision was a verdict on themselves—as indeed it was. Not only the rejected children but also their parents had been adjudged failures by the university. There could be no excuses and no alibis. Hence the hatred.

Over the coffee, the professor had further thoughts. Back from his poor but happy Africans, he had been struck by Californians' generalized anxieties, which he was sure had helped to elect Governor Reagan. "The discontent," he said, "is a product of the affluence." This thought was new to me. Was it a *necessary* product? At that point I began to speculate whether perhaps California, far from being in some way more backward than the rest of the United States—less developed, less politicized, less highly structured socially—was actually on some kind of forward frontier, encountering the next wave of snags and troubles before other parts of the nation were fully aware they existed. "The future of industrial society is being decided here," said the professor as he left me, and I was sufficiently impressed to write down his dictum.

Next day, *Look* magazine printed an interview with Clark Kerr, the distinguished president of the University of California, whom Reagan had just helped to fire. Kerr, I saw with excitement, was thinking along almost the same lines as my professor. "Of all systems," Kerr had told *Look,* "the meritocratic system may be the hardest to run and may set up the most strains." But this was the very system to which all three political parties in Britain were committed! It was the system, for all I knew, to which every liberal political party in the Western world was committed. What were we all heading into?

Two days later, I was in the State Capitol at Sacramento, talking to the star of *Bonzo Goes To College* (the human star, that is). At a press conference that morning, Reagan had refused to reprieve a Negro murderer from the gas chamber, and despite his plum-colored sports jacket and glowing health he seemed introspective. He talked about Vietnam and the students and federal interference with states' rights, and then he paused. I said nothing. "Something," he said finally, "is basically wrong."

In this book I offer myself as a guide to what's going on in California, paying special attention to the themes and people that seem to me to have relevance far beyond California itself. As I slowly put the book together, I was more and more astonished to notice how developments that I had first come across in California cropped up a year or two later, like ground elder relentlessly pushing out its shoots, not only in the rest of the United States but in Britain, or Germany, or Japan, or France, or Scandinavia. The question I have constantly had in mind is this: if California represents the goal toward which a large part of the rest of mankind is also heading, some way behind—the goal of affluence, meritocracy, maximum economic growth, maximum technology—then what lessons does California contain for the rest of us?

The notion that came to dominate my wanderings, as they progressed, was that California really had been a perfect setting for man; yet, as the Governor had said, something basic had gone wrong. It was a Californian, Lincoln Steffens—the best reporter, if not always the wisest, that America has produced—who announced after visiting the Soviet Union, "I have seen the future, and it works." I began to feel that I had seen the future and it *didn't* work: that California, though full of marvels, had reached, or was about to reach, a kind of impasse—a kind of contradiction between the hopes of Californians and their actual circumstances—which was also characteristic, though less plainly, of people outside California. The impasse, or contradiction, was easier to spot in California simply because Californian society was newer and less intricate than society elsewhere. Who could ever know what animates New York?

So the book has a pretentious aim, but I have tried not to let it go to my head, aware that reporters, especially foreign reporters, are liable to get things wrong. The scheme of my reporting is simple: the background of the crisis; the crisis itself; what happens next? I end by asking what has to be done if California is to steer clear of future disasters and show the rest of us how to cash in on modern affluence and technology—instead of being damaged by them, or even destroyed.

Contents

CALIFORNIA

The Vanishing Dream

CHAPTER 1

The New El Dorado

W HATEVER may be thought of man's impact on California, the place undeniably embodies the fulfillment of his most basic longings. To millions of people who have never been there, and to some who have, California represents the modern version of the Land of Cockaigne: the daydream that man has always had at the back of his mind of a land of unlimited possibilities, of money, sun, leisure, and freedom; a place where his shoddy and guilt-ridden past could be traded in for a clean and liberated future.

Deanna Durbin and Robert Paige made the point in a film called "Can't Help Singing" in 1945:

> In this new El Dorado there's free avocado
> For everyone
> And there's none that weighs under a ton
> In this fabulous clime
>
> We have luscious persimmon
> And ditto our women
> Who never run
> When there's work or romance to be done
>
> So we say to each friend who may seek
>   journey's end we commend
> California

> Where the rain doesn't rain it just
>   dribbles champagne
> California
> Where romance is the theme of the day.
> From San Pedro to Fresno
> No maiden there says no
> In harvest time:
> For in gay California
> Everything's more tremendous, titanic,
>   stupendous,
> The climate is better
> The ocean is wetter
> The mountains are higher
> The deserts are drier
> The hills have more splendor
> The girls have more gender
> Cali – for – ni – ay!

A lot of things happened both to California and to pop songs in the next twenty-five years; nevertheless in 1970 the rock groups were still happily singing, in "California Highway," that "until ya been there ya ain't been nowhere." The California myth is nothing if not persistent.

It is also a very old myth, for California seemed special from its earliest beginnings, and the El Dorado theme was built into the roots of its history. Even the man who invented the name, a Spanish romance writer in the early sixteenth century, mentioned gold. He sited California, an imaginary island, "on the right hand of the Indies, very close to the Terrestial Paradise," and described it as "entirely populated by Amazon women of strong and hardy bodies [another recurring theme] whose arms were all of gold and so was the harness of the wild beasts they tamed and rode. For in the whole island there was no metal but gold." It was partly the Spaniards' search for gold and their pursuit of the legend of El Dorado, the golden man, of which they had heard from the Indians, that stimulated the whole Spanish exploration of the new world. The Spaniards conquered Mexico and Peru and pushed up into California, but they did not find El Dorado.

Two hundred years later, however, the legend came true. John Sutter, whose "fort" now stands neatly whitewashed and reconstructed in the suburbs of Sacramento, wrote to his family in the 1840s: "Man can fashion this place into a Paradise." Sutter had arrived in California after fleeing a debtors' prison in Switzerland, and the feudal empire he subsequently carved out for himself encouraged an optimistic point of view. But even Sutter did not foresee the abruptness with which the gates of Paradise would be flung open. He owned a sawmill at Coloma, on the southern branch of the American River, a tributary of the Sacramento, and employed there a man named Marshall.

> It was a rainy afternoon when Mr. Marshall arrived at my office in the Fort, very wet. . . . He told me then that he had some important and interesting news that he wished to communicate secretly to me, and wished me to go with him to a place where we should not be disturbed, and where no listeners could come and hear what we had to say. I went with him to my private room; he requested me to lock the door. I complied, but told him at the same time, there was nobody in the house except the clerk, who was in his office in a different part of the house. After requesting something of me which my servant brought and then left the room, I forgot to lock the door, and it happened that the door was opened by the clerk just at the moment when Marshall took a rag from his pocket, showing me the yellow metal. He had about 2 oz. of it; but how quick Mr. Marshall put the yellow metal in his pocket again can hardly be described.

Next morning, Sutter went to his mill.

> About half way on the road I saw at a distance a human being crawling out from the brush-wood. When I came nearer I found it was Marshall, very wet. . . . We went to the tail-race of the mill. . . . Small pieces of gold could be seen remaining on

> the bottom of the clean washed bed rock. I went
> into the race and picked up several pieces. I have
> had a heavy ring made of this gold, with my fam-
> ily's coat of arms engraved on the outside, and on
> the inside is engraved, "The first gold discovered
> in January 1848." [1]

Thus the gold rush, and the great migration, and modern Californian history began. It is significant that the man credited with
actually precipitating the gold rush was not the worldly Sutter,
who was trying to keep the find quiet, but a supposedly un-
worldly Mormon: a man who had transported 238 other Mormons from the east in order to found what he hoped would be a
new Mormon empire in the west. This man was Sam Brannan,
and before he went to San Francisco he had edited a Mormon
paper in New York. He heard the rumors about California's marvels at a time when the Mormon community, though growing
rapidly, was running into state hostility and mob violence in the
eastern states; California, he told his readers, was "the portion of
the new world which God made his choice above all others." Having landed in San Francisco, Brannan and his fellows (whose arrival doubled the local population) founded a community called
New Hope; but what came true was an old hope: sudden wealth.
According to the legend, it was Brannan who, hearing the rumors
coming out of Sutter's sawmill on the Mormon network, went up
there to investigate; and it was he who broadcast the news to the
world by running through the streets of San Francisco shouting
"Gold! Gold! Gold! Gold from the American River!" Whether or
not this shout ever got shouted, it is certain that Brannan and his
fellow Mormons were in at the very start of the gold rush; and
their greed overcame their religious principles. To Brigham
Young, the leader of the main Mormon community, by this time
settled in Salt Lake City, gold was for paving the streets: man
would get his reward not on earth but in heaven. Brannan took a
different view—he must have thought that God had known about
the gold when he made California His choice—and Brigham
Young consequently read him out of the Church: probably the

last time any Californian has been expelled from a church for being too rich. The New Hope Mormons' lust for gold was stronger than their fear of God, or, at least, stronger than their fear of Brigham Young.

For Brigham Young, the opening of the west was a heaven-sent opportunity to break with the corruptions of the Old World. He went west in the same spirit that the original Pilgrims went to New England: he wanted to build a kingdom of God on virgin land. But Brigham Young never got to California. The Californian ideal was different, partly because of the discovery of gold: it included not only the notion of a new start, but also the notion of new money. No other place in the world has ever been opened up so fast with such a simple lever: greed. California is the only society ever founded entirely on respect for money, which is one reason why it is now the richest segment of the surface of the globe, and why Californians are the richest people that have ever lived. There have been no Brigham Youngs to hold them back. California has allowed the get-rich-quick instinct to flourish openly, undisguised and unrestrained.

A BRIEF HISTORY

To understand how the gold rush fits into the history of California, it is best to follow the example of the old Spaniard who invented the name and think of it as an island, cut off to the west by the Pacific and to the east by the mountains of the Sierras. California was discovered by Spaniards in the early sixteenth century, but for the next three centuries practically nothing happened, mainly because it was an extremely hard place to get to. On the thousand miles of the Pacific coast there were no more than three good harbors; and the Sierras, though they slope down toward the coast with relative gentleness, present to the east a colossal wall of granite.

There is evidence that California is the oldest inhabited part of the Americas. A chemist at the University of California, Dr. Rainer Berger, carried out the carbon-14 age-dating test in 1969 on a human skull dug up at Laguna Beach and announced that the skull belonged to a woman—he deduced the gender from "the daintier shape of the eye sockets"—who was 17,000 years old. "We are now satisfied that we have the oldest direct evidence yet established of human presence in the two Americas," said Dr. Berger. Apart from humans, California has some antique wild life. The few Californian condors still surviving are descended from the prehistoric monsters with an eighteen-foot wingspan that lived in the Anza-Borrego Desert a million years ago.

Otherwise, California is practically brand-new. As late as 1768 the *Encyclopaedia Britannica* called it "a large country of the West Indies" and wasn't sure whether it was a peninsula or an island. San Diego, when celebrating its two-hundredth birthday in 1969, had trouble finding a handful of buildings more than fifty years old, let alone two hundred. (Though the city boasts a date palm allegedly planted by Fr. Junipero Serra in 1769.) Perhaps because they feel their state to be so new, Californians often try to connect themselves with the Spanish past, calling motels "El Dorado" or "El Conquistador," and conscientiously pronouncing La Jolla as "La Hoya," thus confusing strangers. There are other links with the past: descendants of the old Spanish land-owning families still live in proud isolation near Los Angeles; and the Spanish Colonial style has inspired much Los Angeles architecture. But for all practical purposes, modern California history begins in 1841 with the arrival of the first sizable group to reach California overland from the east.

One terrible episode that occurred five years later illustrates both the hardships involved in settling California and the recentness of its development. In April, 1846, a group of ninety, including thirty children, called the Donner Party, set off from Illinois for California, a journey of some 2000 miles. On October 25 they began the ascent of the Sierra Nevada, California's eastern wall; a week later they were lost in the snows. Behind them, the desert trail was strewn with their mahogany beds, bureaus, rockers, and musical instruments. To try to force a way across the pass, an advance guard of ten men, five women, and two Indian guides set out on homemade snowshoes; but after six days, snowblind and without food, they realized they could go no further. A Mexican herdsman died; so did an Irishman named Patrick Dolan, who had sold his farm in Iowa for a wagon, four oxen, and two cows; so did a fourteen-year-old boy. Lying at the bottom of a twelve-foot hole in the snow, the rest of the party, in George R. Stewart's account, "stripped the flesh from the bodies, roasted what they needed to eat, and dried the rest for carrying with them." The boy's sister had to watch her brother's heart being broiled and eaten.[2]

Thirty-three days after they had left the main expedition the survivors of the advance guard dragged themselves into a camp on the California side of the mountains. When a rescue party finally reached the main body, stranded still among the snows, they heard stories of unimaginable horror. One rescuer learned that the last of his children had been taken to bed with a scholarly German named Lewis Keseberg, and that next morning the child was dead. Keseberg had "hung the body in sight, inside the cabin, on the wall," and then had eaten it.[3] Eight of the women who survived their pioneer journey were still alive as recently as 1920. (Time and again the history of the west proves that women endure hardship better than men.)

The year of the Donner Party, 1846, may be taken as a turning point in California's development, for that year also saw the outbreak of the war between Mexico and the United States. Before 1846, all that had happened since the discovery of California by the Spaniards was that the Spaniards had been ejected by the Mexicans (apart from some extraordinary feats of exploration and, near the end of the eighteenth century, the planting of a chain of mission stations by the lame Franciscan priest Fr. Junipero Serra: whence all the popular songs about mission bells). Then in 1848, following the Mexican War, the United States, in the most massive and most successful imperial annexation in modern history, acquired vast stretches of the west, including virtually the whole of California.

From then on, the development of California (remembering that the population in 1848 was no more than 14,000) can be seen entirely in terms of improved transportation. The first overland settlers had struggled through on horses or mules, or on foot. Then came the wagon, developed largely by Presbyterian missionaries; and, with the wagon, mass emigration became possible.

The gold at Sutter's mill was found in January, 1848. Eight months later, a San Franciscan wrote an alarmed dispatch to the State Department in Washington: "Should this gold continue as represented, this town, and others, will be depopulated. The *Star* newspaper has but one man left. A merchant, lately from China, has even lost his Chinese servants. Should the excitement continue through the year, and the whale-ships visit San Francisco, I think they will lose most all their crews." In December, 1848, President Polk made a speech referring to the "abundance of gold" in California. That really did it. "The miners came in '49, the whores in '51, and when they got together they produced the native son," says the old song. By the end of 1852, the new State of California contained a quarter of a million inhabitants—fifteen times as many as at the beginning of 1848. By 1860, the figure was up to 380,000. Most of this astonishing migration, scarcely matched in recorded statistical history, was made possible by the wagon.

After the wagon, the railway. The stage coaches of the California Stage Company, the handcarts of the Mormons, and the heroes of the Pony Express mail service (New York to San Francisco in ten days) played their part in putting the west in touch with the east; but it was the linkup between the Union Pacific and the Central Pacific railroads in 1869 that joined east and west "with iron." When Leland Stanford, the first Republican governor of California as well as a director of the Central Pacific, drove in the famous linking spike at Promontory Point, north of Great Salt Lake, California at last was open to all comers. "To San Francisco in less than Four Days, avoiding the Dangers of the Sea!" said a Union Pacific poster. "Travelers for Pleasure, Health or Business Will find a Trip over the Rocky Mountains Healthy and Pleasant. GOLD, SILVER AND OTHER MINERS! Now is the time to seek your Fortunes."

It was the railway that stimulated the second great wave of emigration and opened up vast areas of the new state to settlement. It was the men who built the railway who made the colossal fortunes that have filled California with amazing art collections and palaces that mimic the Taj Mahal. And it was these men who ran the state for the next forty years as if it were their personal property (which much of it was).

After the railway, the motor car. By 1915 it was possible to drive all the way across the continent on a hard surface. During the next quarter of a century, the dominance of the transcontinental railways slowly declined. Today, they are disappearing. The Californian Zephyr, with its glass-domed observation cars, which used to run from San Francisco to Chicago, shut down just over a century after the triumphant linkup of 1869.

It was by car that the Midwesterners poured into the state in the 1920s; and it was by car that the Dust Bowl refugees of Steinbeck's *Grapes of Wrath* traveled during the 1930s. And the great W. C. Fields, in "It's a Gift," was en route to California in a car laden with furniture and family when he took a wrong turn into a private park, mounted a lawn, knocked over a statue of Venus, and, surveying the shattered fragments, drawled in an aggrieved tone: "Ran right in front of the car." Fields, after he arrived in California to take up the derelict orange grove that he had been sold by a con man back east, was lucky; he was bought out for a huge profit and was last seen disdaining the orange juice and fixing himself a jugful of Martinis. Most of the other refugees from the Depression, the "Okies" and the "Arkies," from Oklahoma and Arkansas, were less fortunate—at least at first. But the luck of many of them turned with World War II, when California not only became a great military base for the war against Japan—as it subsequently became a base for the war in Vietnam —but also acquired a string of brand-new industries. World War II also brought in from the South the Negroes of Watts and Oakland, who now constitute one of the state's most urgent problems.

MIGRATION BY AIR

After the car, the airlines. On a recent flight to Los Angeles from New York, I found myself sitting next to a technician from the Radio Corporation of America. He was wearing a Zapata moustache, beads, and a white polo-necked sweater, and told me he was thinking of emigrating to California. He was, he said, dissatisfied with life on the east coast. His hero was the "old British guy" Bertrand Russell, and he felt that the ideals of the good life which he had read about in Russell's writings were far indeed from being attainable in the Bronx, where he lived. He earned good money, he conceded, but he squandered it, and the waste made him feel sour and dissatisfied. California, he considered, might enable him not only to earn more money but to spend it in a more satisfying manner. After he had told me his thoughts, we settled down, somewhere over Utah, to read the "Inflight Magazine for America's Most Important Travelers," which happened to contain an article extolling California in much the same kind of prose used by the writer of the old Central Pacific railway posters. We read about Death Valley, the second hottest place in the world, and about the giant redwoods. We learned, what we had not known before, that there had been a forty-percent increase in California's strawberry sales to the east coast during the preceding year, because the fruit could now be flown by refrigerated aircraft from California's mist-kissed, sun-dipped produce farms direct, still fresh, to Mrs. American Homemaker. The final sentence of the article read: "Los Angeles is the American dream distilled." By the time the RCA man had finished the piece, he seemed, I thought, even more determined to emigrate: an airborne, 1970 variety of migrant stirred by much the same kind of feelings and much the same kind of booster literature that had been drawing men across the American continent since word first came through about the "terrestrial paradise" in the west.

Thus for a hundred years California has been the ultimate

frontier of the Western world: the stopping place of man's strange westering urge. For one hundred years, in boom and depression, people have been pouring into the state at an average rate of 3000 a week. Five years ago, California overtook New York as the most populous state in the union, and the gap is going to get wider and wider, even though the net annual immigration figure has recently declined. By 1980, when the state's population is expected to reach twenty-four million, one in every ten Americans will live in California; by the year 2000, one in every five. These are the figures, the key to California's history and to its future:

1848	14,000
1900	1,490,000
1920	3,554,000
1930	5,711,000
1940	6,950,000
1950	10,586,000
1960	15,717,000
1970	19,697,000
1980	24,000,000

In 1967, a survey showed that three out of every four Californians came from somewhere else—all of them in search of a better future. For the fact is that, like it or not, California has come to represent in some degree the type of society and region in which a substantial part of mankind would like to live—El Dorado, with a generally excellent climate, great wealth, new industries, new jobs, endless supplies of surf, sun, and sex. No classes. No questions asked. Space. Opportunities. Easy living. Oil, oranges, a technical hub of the world, and more higher education for more people than Britain, for instance, will achieve by the end of the century.

Some people of course, hate California, including a growing number of Californians. Clouds have obscured the Californian sun during the past few years, as they have dimmed the promise of the United States in general. Nevertheless, the myth of the west as a whole and of California in particular still retains an exceptional magnetism. One pronounced theme among both left-wing opponents and right-wing supporters of Governor Reagan is that in California, of all places, things *ought* to be better than they are, given man's advantages there—that California, of all places, ought somehow to be free of the divisions and complexities that trouble the rest of the less favored world. What hope is there for the future of mankind, people would say to me, if even the Californian dream turns permanently sour?

CALIFORNIA AS THE FUTURE

Naturally, your internal questions are extremely interesting to us, because in a material technical sense the United States is some years ahead of us. The problems of America today may very well be ours tomorrow: pollution, technological unemployment, social inequality in spite of welfare.

Sweden's prime minister, Olaf Palme,
in an interview with THE NEW YORK TIMES,
October, 1969.

Before World War II, most Europeans assumed that Americans were a race apart. The politics of Americans seemed often corrupt and childish, their army ill-disciplined and amateurish, and their universities second-rate. Their social customs seemed especially bizarre. They wore white dinner jackets, fussed over central heating, ate ice cream in winter, lived on credit, wore "male jewelry," and "male toiletries," and insisted on ice in their drinks. After the war, it slowly dawned on Europe that Americans might not be so different after all. It was partly a matter of money. Postwar America was still much richer than postwar Europe—John Foster Dulles in 1954 called it "a Paradise compared to most of the world"—but postwar Europe was much richer than prewar Europe. Businessmen were the first to notice the similarities, as American firms gradually began to invade overseas markets with what had earlier been thought of as purely American products.

To take a minor but typical example: Yardley's of London, founded in 1770, had been aware for decades that English husbands occasionally used the Yardley's Lavender Water bought by their wives; but until the American Old Spice after-shave lotion began to be successfully promoted in Britain, Yardley's had never imagined that Englishmen, like Americans, could be persuaded to buy "male toiletries." In the 1950s, Lord Thomson of Fleet, the North American newspaper tycoon, moved to Britain and made a fortune there largely because, as he freely admitted, he worked on the fixed assumption—long before any Briton accepted it—that what succeeded in America would ultimately succeed in Europe. He assumed that since commercial television, large Sunday newspapers, and yellow pages in telephone directories were successful in North America, then so they would be in sleepy Britain. As Europe became more affluent, it became plain that Europe plus North America was in fact one single market, with everyone inside it equally susceptible to motels, ballpoint pens, color television, and Barbie dolls.

Affluence, it turns out, induces the same material ambitions everywhere, or can be made to do so by a good advertising agency. Given this fact, European businessmen now instinctively look to the United States not only to find out how to run their business, but also, because it is richer and invents new needs first, to see what will happen next in Europe. East-coast American businessmen, in their turn, keep an eye on California, because it is the richest state in the union. It is as if the energy and experimental fervor that went into the making of the west, now that the frontier is closed, have begun to bounce back off the west coast into the rest of the United States. Californians, I found, are convinced that some such fertilizing process is occurring, much more so than people in the east, who often treat any suggestion that Californians *lead* the United States as a typical western megalomaniac fantasy.

Of course, a lot of things that happen in Los Angeles will never happen in Denver or New York, let alone Stockholm. Even so, an extraordinary number of customs that we now take for granted, and problems that most alarm us, started in California. The state's reputation as a trend-setter, which it invented itself, has lately become more and more convincing. A few years ago, Californians could claim that they had invented the idea of buying special clothes for "leisure wear." They could also point to their invention of the idea of eating salad separately from the main dish. But now it begins to seem as if almost all the really big social and political questions that affect the Western world began to show themselves first in California. San Francisco schoolteachers were at their wits' end about the high proportion of children taking drugs at least a year before the same anxiety hit New York teachers, and at least two years before the same problem appalled Crawley, Sussex. The 1964 student revolt at Berkeley was not the first student revolt in the United States, or even the first at Berkeley; but it was the first big one, fully deserving its reputation as the harbinger of all the rebellions that flared up subsequently across the Western world. Again, the backlash that these student revolts produced—the resentment, for instance, shown by taxpayers toward students—first showed itself in California.

The inferno that consumed parts of the Negro ghetto of Watts, Los Angeles, in the late summer of 1965, when thirty-four people lost their lives and more than a thousand were wounded, was the forerunner of other big city riots across the United States, and a warning of race troubles in Britain. Politically, too, California seems in some respects out in front. The weakness of the two great political parties was a feature of life in California long before they began to break up in the rest of the nation; the anti-machine politics of California, where people constantly vote across party lines, has lately reached even New York, where the Democratic Party, which used to control both the city and the state, now controls neither. The number of American voters who now classify themselves, in polls, as independents, rises all the time, following a trend long evident in California.[4] Politicians in California were the first to employ pollsters and public-relations firms in their campaigns, immediately after World War II. Television was being exploited as the most effective way to reach an urban electorate in California long before "the selling of the president" in 1968.

The list continues. Hippies, after first appearing in California, have now reached Moscow and Laos. Group sex among married couples, or "swinging," which appears to have started in California during the midsixties (a bar called "The Swing" was opened in suburban Studio City, Los Angeles, in 1966), was regarded as a novelty in 1971 in Paris, where it was known as *partouze*.[5] In the summer of 1967, I was told at Berkeley that industry was beginning to get worried because the brightest students, who in earlier years would have sought jobs with the big corporations, were saying that they did not want to become part of the business establishment; two years later, the Shell Oil Company held a seminar on the same theme in Europe, and it started with a film made on the Stanford campus, to illustrate the way things were going. Again: "law and order" paid off as a campaign slogan in California two years before it was successfully taken up by Nixon in 1968, and four years before it was suddenly injected into the Conservative Party's electioneering tactics in Britain during 1970. Yet again: pollution, which east-coast politicans such as Senator Muskie identified as a hopeful theme in 1969 and which became a fashionable European preoccupation in 1970, first came of age as a serious political issue in California.[6]

The concern now being expressed everywhere in the industrialized world about conservation issues and environment problems is an amplification of what Californian conservationists have been saying for decades.[7] The new anxiety about overpopulation was dramatized and turned into something like a national crusade by a fierce young biologist from Stanford, Dr. Paul Ehrlich.

Naturally, there are limits to the "California: Window of the Future" idea. But it is not clear where they should be drawn. One might have thought that a Californian specialty such as the private swimming pool was a luxury that would never be copied in Britain, except by the very rich. Yet a recent advertisement in the *Illustrated London News,* a middle-class journal, was selling heated swimming pools to Britons on the argument that since traffic made it increasingly irksome and time-wasting to get to the sea, a sensible person would bring the beach into his own garden: think of the saving on Father's nerves and petrol! Salesmen of swimming pools in California have been making a living off this argument for decades. When I told a Beverly Hills lady that I was staying in a motel in Santa Monica because I liked being on the ocean, she was amazed: "Why," she said, "that's no reason for staying in a *motel*. All the hotels in Beverly Hills have got *pools*."

The reason why California does indeed seem to prefigure the future for the rest of us is partly because it is new. The novelty means that California has a thin skin, so that you can see relatively easily what is going on. And the experimental nature of the society makes it easier, also, to see what modern man is really after.

CHAPTER 2

America Breaks Free

> [The frontier] was free from the influence of European ideas and institutions. The men of the "Western World" turned their backs upon the Atlantic Ocean, and with a grim energy and self-reliance began to build up a society free from the dominance of ancient forms.
>
> *Frederick Jackson Turner,*
> THE FRONTIER IN AMERICAN HISTORY (*1903*)

> All hail, thou Western World! By Heaven
>   designed
> Th' example bright, to renovate mankind.
>
> *Timothy Dwight,*
> GREENFIELD HILL—A POEM (*1794*)

> Aristocracy links everybody, from peasant to king, in one long chain: democracy breaks the chain and frees each link.
>
> *Alexis de Tocqueville,*
> DEMOCRACY IN AMERICA (*1835*)

IN California, man has thrown aside his chains with more abandon than anywhere else in the world. It happens that besides visiting California at intervals over the past two decades, I was also making regular trips to Australia. The two places have much in common. Both might be called "frontier societies." Both have been opened up in the past hundred and fifty years by extraordinary physical feats of exploration and a prolonged battle with na-

17

ture. Both have experienced a gold rush, stimulating migration. Both have been settled, in the main, by what a European would call working-class migrants. But Australia, though a working-class paradise by comparison with, say, northeast England, where many Australian migrants came from, is nevertheless much more inhibited than California. The marks of the old chains are still visible. The Irish Catholic influence, for example, remains powerful; books are officially banned in conservative Melbourne that no one in conservative Orange County would think twice about displaying on the coffee table. Even in Sydney, the most Californian city in Australia, pressures toward social conformity are strong. The difference between two social systems is accurately reflected in the way the inhabitants of the two places treat their surroundings. In Australia, the popular imagination is released only by fits and starts. A man will suddenly deck out his bungalow in amazing yellows and reds; a city council will paint a park bench with every wooden slat a different color. But you still feel a degree of restraint in Australia, a hint of Liverpool back streets, as if people are mentally living behind lace curtains. The Australians who established the character of the country did not want to break with their homeland, whether it was England or Ireland. In California, on the other hand—where from the beginning there was a potent mix of nationalities—all restraint has been thrown off. It is as if the entire place is a huge holiday camp. Ordinary people in California have been entirely unrestrained by town planners, or by notions of "good taste." They have had no feeling of having to conform to any outside esthetic pattern or standards. The result is that the whole state, especially southern California, is strewn with amazing objects, signs, and artifacts. A hacienda stands next to a miniature Glamis Castle. Ice-cream parlors are shaped like elephants. Huge windmills, advertising coffee shops, float against the sky. Gas stations identify themselves at night with rotating lozenges of light three stories high. Motels are constructed on themes that are often wildly at odds with their environment: I stayed at one, the Three Kings Motel, that served meals in the King Lear Room. At the new Century Plaza Hotel in Los Angeles, which is built, for no evident reason, on a boomerang curve, the flunkies who hurry out to drive the cars away to an underground garage are dressed in the scarlet and gold uniforms of beefeaters at the Tower of London.

This west-coast freedom of expression is not new; it started in a quiet way with the railway barons and their mansions on Nob Hill, San Francisco. Its trail can be picked up again in a comparatively elderly Los Angeles hotel, whose spacious foyer features a reproduction of the reredos of Burgos Cathedral, in Spain. The apotheosis of this freedom, however, is San Simeon, William Randolph Hearst's castle on top of the tawny hills behind San Luis Obispo. Here is the prototype of southern Californian building —an extravaganza so grandiose, so extreme, that it has passed beyond any architectural-magazine categories of "vulgar" or "out-of-character."

There are two items of interior decor at San Simeon that show how far Hearst and his lady interior decorator had passed beyond any thought of convention and were indulging an entirely random fantasy of homemaking. In the principal sitting room, which is about the size of a tennis court, the seats ranged all around the walls are genuine medieval choir stalls. The stone doorway that leads into the pool room comes from a twelfth-century English monastery. Hearst, sitting down to dinner in sneakers, with the sauce bottle prominent among the Queen Anne silver, had detached himself entirely from any considerations of what was or was not an appropriate way of spending money. A rose pergola a mile long—a feature of the San Simeon garden—would perhaps be generally accepted as a reasonable addition to a mansion among the California hills. Polar bears would not; but Hearst had them, trucking their ice up daily from San Luis Obispo.

The spirit of San Simeon today pervades southern California. It is the spirit of a monster pop-art show, staged by the kind of people who have hitherto been silent in western history.

THE NEW SOCIETY

The kind of society that has emerged in this bizarre setting was not foreseen by the early promoters. No theme in American history has so excited the nation's imagination as the westward expansion to the Pacific. Partly, the excitement reflected the stay-at-home's admiration for the pioneer. Men in cities naturally felt a wistful yearning for the free life of the hero who paved the way into the wilderness while being, as Daniel Boone allegedly was, "happier in his log cabin, with a loin of venison and his ramrod for a spit, than he would have been amid the greatest profusion of modern luxuries." [1]

It was originally hoped that the efforts of the pioneer heroes would produce a Utopia, an agricultural paradise. The Hero would map out the land; the Honest Farmer would follow; and eventually the whole west would be dotted with smiling homesteads, each farm owned by the man who worked it, and all the owners together—the independence and honesty of their characters strengthened by their free way of life—upholding a simple, ideal form of frontier democracy.

This hope never had any chance of being realized. The Californian freeway driver who now zooms past gleaming agribusiness factories surrounded by miles of tomatoes or lettuce may idly suppose that it is only recently, with the coming of twentieth-century technology, that big operators have engulfed the small farmer. In fact, Californian agriculture has been dominated by such men for a long time. Abel Stearns, a Massachusetts Yankee, arrived in Monterey in 1829, when there were barely two hundred Americans in the whole of California: forty years later, he owned more than two hundred square miles of land. One of his ranchos was bought after his death by a syndicate of San Francisco financiers—among them Sam Brannan, the man who announced the gold rush. Against such heavyweight competition, the small farmer had little chance.

Also, agricultural technology reached California earlier than it did elsewhere, which biased development in favor of large-scale ownership. A combine harvester was operating in California in 1854. As early as 1871, Henry George, then an unknown printer in San Francisco, was complaining about the concentration of land in the hands of a few. He predicted that "the steam plow and the steam wagon [would] develop, perhaps, in agriculture the same tendencies to concentration which the power loom and the trip hammer have developed in manufacturing." [2] And he was right. By 1880, a combine driven by a steam tractor was cutting swathes fifty feet wide through the California grain fields; and around the same time a California newspaper estimated that five men controlled four million acres of the state.

So the original dream of a garden of the west, a paradise of small farmers, faded away. But the politicians and propagandists had a second dream. They hoped that a new America would be born in the west which would be cut off from the debilitating influences of Europe. A European, at least, may well conclude that this hope has been realized. In California, the European traveler cannot fail to be struck by the absence of the political, social, and religious arrangements that the rest of America derived from Europe. Institutions that have grown up elsewhere in the United States have here scarcely taken hold, because the population has grown so fast. "California is very loosely glued together," said an economics professor. When I asked the editor of the *Los Angeles Times,* Nick Williams, to answer for me John Gunther's favorite reporter's question—"Who runs the place?"—he was silent for fully ten seconds and then said gloomily, "No one."

By comparison with, say, New York, Californian barriers to social mobility are low and easily crossed. The educational system is expressly designed to confer the benefits of higher education on as many people as possible. Traditional religious barriers—between Protestant and Catholic, or Christian and Jew—scarcely exist. Even the political machines are weak and ineffectual, unable to keep pace with the people flooding in. The social structure is kept loose by exceptional affluence and exceptional mobility. It is as if, after centuries of being cooped up in school, the American people have here burst yelling into the playground.[3]

MATERIALISM

We are easy to manage, a gregarious people,
Full of sentiment, clever at mechanics, and we love our luxuries.

Robinson Jeffers

To make so much money that you won't, that you don't, "mind," don't mind anything—that is absolutely, I think, the main American formula.

Henry James, THE AMERICAN SCENE

If I can't take it with me, I'm not going.

Jack Warner of Warner Bros.

The novel, and quintessentially American, society that is struggling out of its chrysalis in California has been based on a breach with Europe, the release of the little man, and the notion of getting as rich as possible as quickly as possible. It would be hard to prove that Californians are more materialistic than anyone else, but probably no one would disagree that, since they belong to the richest society the world has ever known, the naked drive to materialism can best be studied among them. The acquisitive urge is the only characteristic that most Californians have in common. Even the hippies who most fiercely reject "materialist values" sometimes turn out to have powerful, if camouflaged, materialist drives. Californian salesmen, I found, even refer to the "hippie market." "If the Volkswagen is the hippies' car," said a Ford man in San Francisco, "then we must get a slice of the hippie market." Members of the longshoremen's union, the ILWU, once the most left-wing union in the country, are now in the middle-class earnings bracket; an ordinary member can make up to $15,000 a year, and the elite, the supercargo men, can earn as much as $25,000, an income that compares favorably with that of a rising executive in a big corporation. Despite these stunning rates of pay, the union keeps demanding, and getting, large raises. What do they want the money for, I asked one of their members? "Oh," he said, "another color television, lawn-sprinklers, gingerbread for the house, perhaps a piece of land for a vacation home, membership in a country club."

Here are some other points that struck me about Californian affluence—trends which should soon be visible elsewhere:

1. A growing willingness to pay for exclusiveness. A night club in San Francisco has an entrance fee of $3000. The ILWU country club entrance fee is $1000.

Jules Stein, the multimillionaire chief of Universal Pictures, owned a vacant block of land on Wilshire Boulevard. He worried for a long time about how to make the most of it. Finally, he hit on the answer. He built an imposing entrance gate, hired a uniformed gatekeeper, gave the piece of ground an imposing title, and then charged an astronomically high price for the privilege of parking there. Money rolled in.

2. The more affluence, the more credit. California floats on credit. "DENTAL PLATES with all the credit you need. No money down. Two years to pay. All branches of dentistry: dental plates, bridgework, X-rays, inlays, fillings, crowns, extractions, free parking. Dr. Beauchamp, credit dentist."

3. Affluence and garbage. Aerojet General, originally a spin-off from Caltech, is working on "sanitary landfills," in which human sewage, instead of going through a sewage farm, is compacted down so hard that "you can build playgrounds or golf courses on top." "If the compacting is done properly," an Aerojet man told me, "there is no odor. But you can't build high." [4]

4. The insoluble problem of affluence turns out to be parking. In central Los Angeles, every business building must provide one parking space to every 1000 feet of office space. Apartment blocks must provide one space for each habitable room. Portable parking garages, six stories high, can be put up in three weeks and taken down in five days. One third of downtown Los Angeles is given over to parking lots. People telling you how to get to their

office invariably advise you where you will be able to park when you get there. Often, you can't. It is only a matter of time until the downtown area is effectively strangled by the lack of sufficient parking, according to the Los Angeles Citizens Advisory Council.

5. Any luxury is capable of further "improvement." Spare tires are no longer regular equipment on all new automobiles because some manufacturers claim to supply tires that run for fifty miles after being punctured.

The principle of endless improvement is illustrated by what is happening to swimming pools. First, there was the regular oblong pool; it might be small, in a backyard, or it might be big and surrounded by Greek and Roman temples, as at Hearst's San Simeon; but the basic pool was rectangular. Then the manufacturers began to construct pools of different shapes; a salesman in Orange County told me that pools were now "standard equipment" for the middle class, which meant practically everyone in Orange County, and that pools came in "forty-eight different molds," or shapes, which gives a lot of variety. That, you might suppose, about concludes the possible development of the swimming pool. But now California has come up with "two-part pools." The big pool is for actual swimming; the smaller, auxiliary pool is either for the children, or simply to look at, or it is "a therapeutic whirlpool." One house in Bel Air, for instance, has a satellite pool seven feet across by two feet deep, big enough for four bathers. You sit on a circular bench set sixteen inches below the water level; the water can be heated to 105 degrees. Seven jets around the circumference of the pool circulate "aerated water designed to massage the body." You recline on the bench up to your chin, being massaged.

At Ralph Stolkin's house in Palm Springs, the premier pool is built into the desert, with a beach made of small pebbles set in epoxy—part of the new idea is to construct the pool in an irregular shape, so that it blends into the landscape and looks like a lake. The secondary pool is indoors, in the middle of the house, and is "mainly to look at."

THE LOS ANGELES RICH

Freedom from scruple, from sympathy, honesty
and regard for life may, within fairly wide limits,
be said to further the success of the individual in
the pecuniary culture.

Thorstein Veblen, sometime Stanford professor

At the top of the materialist pyramid of California sit the Los
Angeles rich, accumulators of the most notable huge new fortunes
in present-day America. They live, many of them, in Beverly
Hills, Bel Air, and Brentwood, the most beautiful suburbs on
earth, their colonial or Tudor or Spanish houses buried among
flowering shrubs in a climate and lushness reminiscent of Ceylon,
and separated from the neighbors by driveways and constantly-wa-
tered lawns. Here, the freeways have been kept at a distance. The
speed limit is twenty miles an hour, and cars move quietly down
wide roads flanked by palm trees. At night, these suburbs are as
quiet as the desert.

On the summit of Beverly Hills, reached by a steep winding
track that leads only to the homes of the exceptionally rich, is a
low rambling house that looks down on the endless city. Up here,
it is as if one were suspended in a balloon, above the chains of
tiny lights, or, sometimes, a dangerous yellow bank of smog. A
dinner party, among English eighteenth-century furniture and
sporting prints. Fine silver, chateau-bottled wines, Filipino servants, and a French chef. Stray remarks, collected over four hours,
from the mainly middle-aged or elderly guests.

"Jack Benny always opens our banks."

"I said, 'You must have a million dollars worth of pictures in
here'; and he said, 'Three million, dammit!' "

"Is that your pale green Rolls? Such a pretty color for a car."

"You'll hate me for saying this, but Los Angeles is very
groupy."

"I'm going to stay at the Ritz before they pull it down. I used to stay there when I was young and wash my sheepdogs in the bath; they didn't like it a bit."

"Well, I know what I think about *Acapulco*."

"I asked the waiter to put the steak in a bag and when he came back with the bag he said, 'Oh, Mrs. Jessel, wouldn't your little dog like some pumpernickel and gherkins?' Just like a Sardi's waiter: he'd never think of asking *you* whether *you'd* like some pumpernickel and gherkins."

"He's been very unlucky with his wives."

"Nymphomania in fact is a very, very rare condition."

"I'm sure romantic love is coming back. This quick business is on the way out."

"He was very rich, as you know, and his son raped and killed quite an old woman; at the hearing the old guy said, 'Oh well, boys will be boys.' "

"Oh, he had another wife in there, did he?"

"He loses a quarter of a million dollars gambling every winter. But that's his limit."

This conversation seemed quite different from other rich conversation. Normally, people with old money like to talk as if money doesn't matter, or even exist. People with new money like to talk shop, having got into the habit of thinking shop in order to make the money. The Beverly Hills rich did neither; they seemed to be on some plateau of their own, assuming that the money would keep coming in, not feeling any need to be discreet or deprecating about it, accepting the freakish effects that wealth can have on people's lives, and above all seeming quite detached from the city they all lived in, as if on vacation. They behaved like people who had cut loose from all the old moral and economic problems and were floating in a private stratosphere where discretion, taste, modesty, hypocrisy, restraint, and social purpose no longer had any relevance.

HOW THE RICH GET STATUS

Out here you're competing with the champs.
Howard Ahmanson

Roy and I and the rest of the people don't work
for money. There are other things.
Charles B. Thornton of Litton Industries

One sign of the social muddle of southern California is that the
rich find it difficult to achieve the social status that elsewhere follows automatically from the possession of big money. To some extent, this is a general American problem. In England, a rich man
can acquire a title, and thus feel that his work or business has
been given social recognition. In the United States, if a man does
not become an ambassador, there are few ways for him to receive
public approval. Rich Americans have therefore been driven to
invent their own system of social status; and the system can be
seen in its most elemental form in Los Angeles.

The key man in the system is the director of the local art gallery, in this case Mr. Kenneth Donahue of the Los Angeles
County Museum. The museum is large and new and still somewhat empty. Donahue, a dark, bespectacled, cheerful man, works
surrounded by art books in a room with big windows looking
onto the museum lawns.

It was Donahue who explained to me the way buying pictures
has become a key to great social prestige. The communications
system, he said, had had a lot to do with it. For years, *Time* and
Life have had good art coverage, often showing important national figures, such as Nelson Rockefeller, surrounded by their art
trophies, so that people got the idea that that was the sort of
thing that rich and important people did with their money.
Vogue, too, was influential: the magazine, said Donahue, is
bought by people seeking status, and he recalled how, when he
had been on the staff of the Museum of Modern Art in New

York, *Vogue* was alway coming around to the museum to take fashion pictures against modern art backgrounds. This too helped spread the idea that status and art were connected.

Meanwhile, art itself was booming. After 1933, when Hitler came to power in Germany, the cream of the German art historians moved to the United States. Before their arrival, art was virtually a monopoly of Harvard and Princeton. But the Germans went west, and their diaspora was followed by a proliferation of museums. "Thus," said Donahue, "you got a combination of art scholarship, art institutions, and a popular interest in art expressed through the magazines."

Donahue turned to Los Angeles. "Out here," he said, "you've got a tremendous amount of new money. In San Francisco, though there are a lot of civilized and even rich people there, they don't buy pictures: they take you to the window, show you the view of the bay and say, 'Why do we need pictures when we've got such a beautiful city to look at?' But Los Angeles is not so beautiful. And the people here need reassurance about their wealth more than they do in San Francisco."

I asked Donahue to leave the generalizations and get down to the details. How did the system actually operate? The key point, he explained, was that social prestige arose from a connection with the museum, and the closer the connection, the greater the prestige. The museum was in search of money—he himself had his eye on a target of $36 million—and the rich were in search of prestige, so there was a deal to be made. "I was a little bit shocked when I first came out here," he added, "but I've got used to the vulgarity by now; and it's all in a good cause. The first principle is that it is easier to get money for buildings than it is for the actual paintings. If you give the money for a big building, you get your name on it in big letters; whereas if you give a picture you only get your name on a brass plate underneath, in little letters. If you give $2 million, you get a building named after you. If you give $125,000, you get your name on an inside room. That is the scale.

"We reward everyone who gives us money. If they give us

$25,000 they are asked to absolutely everything—all the openings, all the parties—and are sent copies of all museum publications and catalogs free of charge. If they give $5000 we haven't room to invite them to all the openings; but everyone gets something. You'll see a list of names being carved on a wall now of people who've given us money. That doesn't include the people who gave us $5000, of course. Naturally, not everybody wants to support the museum, and some people like to give money toward, for instance, a symphony orchestra; but backing a symphony orchestra doesn't command the same social prestige as donating a building or a room to the museum. By the way, because a man has his name on a room, that doesn't give him any say about what goes into it. We are just on the verge of buying this picture now"—he handed me a photograph of a Dutch portrait—"getting it very cheap, as a matter of fact, and it's going into the room of a man who may very well not like it at all.

"We have three buildings—the Ahmanson Building, the Bing Building, and the one we're in now, which has no name yet. Ahmanson was head of the biggest savings and loan bank in the country, and Anna Bing Aerol is the widow of Leo Bing, who owned a great many apartment houses in New York. She is an enchanting lady who has an enormous income, lives quite modestly, and thinks it her duty, and finds it her pleasure, to give away her entire income every year. She gives a lot to children's education, but the museum gets a great deal also. She came into my office here the other day and said she was feeling low, adding that when most women felt low they went out and perhaps bought a hat: but she already had a hat and what really gave *her* pleasure was writing checks; so she sat down and wrote me a check for $50,000, and said that made her feel much better.

"The donor of this building we're in unfortunately went bankrupt, so we're about to put it up for sale, as it were. Oh yes, there are plenty of people who'd like their name on it. In fact there's a line a mile long. I should also mention the Norton Simon Plaza: he paid a great deal for that."

Donahue went on to explain that prestige also attached to private art collections. But these were not like European or east-coast collections, because few Los Angelenos bought old masters: indeed, he could think of only two people, Edward Carter and Norton Simon, who bought old masters at all. "By far the most popular paintings to buy are the Impressionists. You must remember that the art tradition of the past was either religious, aristocratic, or humanist. The religious tradition means very little to buyers out here: if they see a Madonna and Child, it doesn't have reverberations in their mind: it's simply a picture of a lady holding a baby. The aristocratic tradition doesn't mean much either. People look at some aristocratic painting and think to themselves, 'Well, that's very nice, but totally irrelevant to me.' The humanist tradition certainly came to the United States—through people like Jefferson, for instance—and it may have reached San Francisco; but it didn't get down here to Los Angeles.

"Part of the attraction of Impressionist pictures is they are almost all optimistic. Besides, the people in Impressionist paintings are engaged in jobs which the collectors out here can understand. If they're looking at a Cézanne, in which the painter has been interested in the structure of an object, that is something a businessman or manufacturer can appreciate, because he too is interested in the structure of objects, and Americans are practical people who like to see how things work and how things are made. And, of course, the Impressionists have greatly improved their price over the years, which is not a point likely to be lost on a rich man.

"In many cases, the rich start buying for prestige or even for speculative reasons, but very often they come really to like the pictures. You might note the case of Norton Simon. Here is a rich man who spends more time with pictures than most directors of museums, who have a lot of administrative work to do, and as much as most curators. He's got his own business organized now and is really very deeply involved with art, especially art between about 1850 and 1910. He's gradually coming more and more up to date: at the moment he's talking with great excitement about early Picassos."

Donahue paused and looked out the window; on the grass, a pair of lovers lay entwined. "There is a powerful feeling in the community that this is *their* museum," he said. "Our attendance figure, in the entire United States, is second only to New York. There is a very strong feeling that Los Angeles must develop into a big and important cultural center. That, and the amount of money available, make it like living in Florence in the fifteenth century."

A PASSION FOR REPLICAS

For all this new freedom and prosperity, Californians have paid a price. They have so surrounded themselves with the man-made clutter of an affluent society, and become so dependent on it, that the lives of even quite ordinary people sometimes seem, like the lives of the Beverly Hills rich, distinctly cut off from reality.

For me, this cut-offness has come to be symbolized by the local passion for fake materials and replicas. True, this is an international trend; the wife of a former British Minister of Technology has been known to plant plastic flowers in the front garden of her London house. But in southern California the trend has gone so far that it is as if some basic change has taken place in the attitude of the citizens to external reality. Constantly, if one keeps one's eyes open, things turn out to be distorted and different from what they seem. The blazing log fire in the restaurant of the expensive and beautiful Bel Air Hotel—which resembles a millionaire's tropical villa—turns out to be actually gas, with fake logs. At the aforementioned Century Plaza, which again is no flophouse, the flowers in the corridors and foyers are made of plastic, as are some of the displays in the hotel flower shop. The litter baskets at Forest Lawn Memorial Park, the famous cemetery, are actually concrete made to look like tree stumps. One could multiply examples indefinitely: gnarled old beams of plastic, mosaic floors of vinyl, leather chairs that are not leather, stucco that is not stucco, linen that is really rayon. No good brick for building is obtainable in southern California, an architect told me; technology has produced something that looks like brick but is really vinyl.

The most elaborate example of this passion for replicas is the Palace of Living Art, which is attached to the Movieland Wax Museum, not far from Disneyland in Orange County. Set back a little from the highway, the Movieland Museum itself is unremarkable, featuring wax scenes from famous movies. It was started by a Mr. Parkinson, who made his money from sleeping pills, and was so successful that he added on the Palace of Living Art. Outside the Palace there is a startlingly white reproduction of Michelangelo's giant David, of which the original is in Florence; but this by no means prepares the visitor for what is inside. Mr. Parkinson's ambitious aim is to bring old masterpieces to "life" in wax, and he has sought to realize it by filling his "museum" with reproductions of the world's best-known works of art and then reproducing the subject matter of each masterpiece in wax nearby. For instance, there on a wall hangs a reproduction of Whistler's portrait of his mother; in an adjacent booth is the lady herself, in wax, dressed and posed exactly as in the portrait. But because Mr. Parkinson wanted to show the whole room in which she sits, although only part of the room is visible in Whistler's portrait, he has had to imagine what the rest of the room was like. So, in Mr. Parkinson's realization of the painting, Mrs. Whistler is seated cosily in front of a bright fire that glows with electrically-lit coals.

Our guide was a fair girl wearing a plum-colored uniform. She spoke in low tones, as if in church, and was evidently in awe both of the exhibits and of her employer, whom she described as "a public benefactor." Because of the Palace, she explained, Californians would no longer need to travel abroad to see the world's masterpieces and could thus save money. Mr. Parkinson himself, she said, had spared no expense to make the exhibits as true to life as possible; the wax bride and bridegroom in "The Marriage of Giovanni Arnolfini," by Van Eyck, had been clothed at a total cost of $6600 ($2800 for Giovanni's clothes, and $3800 for his wife's). Parkinson's imagination had in some cases led him to alter the masterpieces to suit his own tastes, it emerged. Michelangelo's Moses, in the Rome original, has a chip out of his knee, but the Moses in the Palace of Living Art does not, because "Mr. Parkinson wanted him perfect." In front of Ingres' "Odalisque," the guide explained that the girl in the painting was ill-proportioned; the eyes and the arm were wrong, and one leg, if extended, would be much longer than the other. Further, the Odalisque had only four toes, "but we thought she had enough wrong with her already, so in the wax we've given her five toes." The waxen Michelangelo David indoors, instead of being colossal, as in the original, was boy-sized, with lifelike hair on his body and blue veins in his bare feet. "People can't get over the veins," said the guide, and we believed her. Then there was the famous statue of the boy with a thorn in his foot. "Everyone loves this one," said the guide; "we put a real thorn in his foot for the first couple of months after we opened, but people kept taking it out, so we stopped." The dress of the wax statue of Romney's pink girl was ruffled lightly by a concealed wind machine. At one booth, Mr. Parkinson had taken off completely and had created a tableau of Don Quixote and Sancho Panza leading what looked very like a real horse and a real donkey. The girl evidently felt these animals to be especially bizarre, as we did, for she described them as "kinda spooky" and told us she had once been going to touch them, but "couldn't get up the courage." So thoroughly was the girl caught up in the spirit of the Palace that she seemed to have lost all sense of what was real and what was not. She said of the Winged Victory of Samothrace that it "was found in a thousand pieces and reconstructed," as if the actual object before her had been pieced together.

Perhaps the two most memorable sights in the Palace are the Venus de Milo and the Mona Lisa. Beside a marble reproduction of the Venus stands a waxen naked girl—fair-haired, blue-eyed—with complete arms and especially realistic nipples; she looks like a well-brought-up topless waitress from North Beach, San Francisco. Beside the reproduction of the Mona Lisa, Mr. Parkinson has created a wax statue of Leonardo at work at his easel, looking like some gaffer just in from the hayfield, while the Mona Lisa poses on a chair before him, smiling.

CUTTING LOOSE FROM EUROPE

> The West has kept itself free and independent while the East has been caught and spoiled with many of the flirting follies of Europe.
>
> *Oscar Wilde*

Besides a certain unreality which I take to be characteristic of California society, the break with the past has also produced symptoms indicating that the citizens are not quite certain, these days, what it is that a Californian is supposed to be. They are Americans, of course—I am talking here about the mass, not the new rebels—though they feel they are not quite the same as other Americans. They feel the same kind of suspicion of easterners that easterners often feel about them. The easterners consider themselves superior and believe that they set the standards of excellence for the nation; this, of course, gives Californians feelings of inferiority. Los Angelenos, I found, often refer to their city as "out here," as in, "of course, we don't have much theater, out here"; or "I'm afraid we don't change for dinner, out here."

Californians are much more detached from Europe than any other part of the United States, but they have not entirely cut adrift. The purchase of the humdrum old London Bridge by a small city in Arizona struck most Londoners as an example of Western American eccentricity—but it struck me as a moving attempt to use a monument from the old world to give an extra dimension to the new. An even more striking example of entanglement with the last European tendrils is the fate of the Cunard transatlantic liner, the *Queen Mary*. This fine old ship, which made her maiden voyage in 1937, was bought by the city of Long Beach thirty years later, in 1967, for one and a quarter million pounds. From the accounts of the purchase in the English papers, I could find no explanation of why a Los Angeles suburb should want a rusty old English ship; if the city wanted a "hotel and convention complex," why did it not simply build one from scratch?

Some time later, still puzzled by this question, I went to Long Beach to visit the *Queen,* which I knew from her days on the Atlantic.

She was lying at Pier E, stripped of two of her three funnels, like a gigantic wounded animal. In a union dispute after she docked, the land-based unions claimed that since she could no longer go to sea she had become a building, and was thus under their jurisdiction, while the maritime unions argued that anyone could see she was still a ship. Personally, I would have classified her as a building: an inert mass, with the innards being ripped out, but still capable of arousing a distinctly melancholy feeling, among the dirt and the stacks of dusty ping-pong tables.

It is no fluke that the *Queen Mary* has ended up in Long Beach. Administratively, Long Beach is a city, but geographically it belongs to the Los Angeles sprawl. According to the Rand McNally guide to the state, there have been two events in the history of Long Beach: the first occurred in 1921, when oil was discovered, and the second was in 1938, when Wrong Way Corrigan made what the guide calls his "strange" flight. These entries demonstrate how short of history the city really is, because what was strange about Corrigan's flight was that he took off from New York *aiming* at Long Beach, but actually landed in Dublin.

That leaves Long Beach with only one historic event, the oil strike; and you first become aware of the consequences of this, miles from the city itself. You drive past scores of giant orange pumps pecking at the empty lands behind the beach, like the toy birds which, when balanced on the rim of a glass of water, dip and drink indefinitely. Then you notice the oil rigs out at sea (camouflaged to resemble, at night, lighted apartment blocks). Then you smell the oil. Finally you reach the waterfront, an unhappy mess of run-down bars and vast ship repair yards.

Long Beach, because of the oil, is one of the richest places in

California. The offshore oilfield is about the largest ever exploited by the U.S. petroleum industry, and the Long beach municipality gets a substantial cut that will bring in, over the next fifteen years, something like $235,000,000. This sum, by law, must be spent on improving the waterfront.

Faced with the awful task of spending all that money, the city called in a firm of consultants, who later reported that what the city certainly needed was a symbol, so that people would know they were in Long Beach and not somewhere else in the Los Angeles area. Knowing where you are in Los Angeles is a problem that puzzles everybody. But the *Queen Mary* is like the Eiffel Tower: tie *her* up in Long Beach, and you really have a landmark.

Once the city had bought the ship, their plans expanded to meet the size of their purchase. As Michelangelo's Vatican became the centerpiece of Bernini's reconstruction of Rome, so the *Queen Mary*—despite a string of financial rows and crises—is becoming the hub of a monster waterfront reclamation project that will include the world's largest man-made pier, oil derricks disguised as palm trees, 43 acres of "support area" with underground parking, a 420-acre marina with mooring for up to 5000 small boats, and what are described as "international villages of the type the *Queen Mary* visited"—like, perhaps, New York.

At no stage have Long Beach officials publicly doubted the earning power of their extraordinary purchase. In a hut on the jetty belonging to the Queen Mary Department of the City of Long Beach, I met Mr. Hal E. Martin, a distracted man with a quiff of hair and spectacles, who was wearing a silver *Queen Mary* tie clip. Among the items in his office were a book on modern marketing research, a handbook of financial mathematics, and an adding machine.

No sooner had Mr. Martin greeted me than, in response to a skeptical question about the drawing power of the city's buy, he went to work with his adding machine. Before long, he had covered several sheets of yellow paper with figures proving, to my satisfaction, that the ship would recover her cost of conversion—at

that time optimistically estimated at some $25 million—in twelve
or fourteen years and would thereafter make a substantial profit.

"You have to analyze the market penetrations of similar attractions," he told me as his pencil flew over the yellow paper, "such
as Knott's Berry Farm and Disneyland. The *Queen Mary* will
have three attractions of her own: the tours, the museums, and
the commercial enterprises—the hotel and restaurants. You will
see that from tours alone I estimate a low of 1,350,000 and a high
of 2,000,000 visitors a year. The restaurants will be a great draw;
the ship will be just a gorgeous place for fine dining. And the
convention bookings are extremely solid.

"Conventions, as you may not know, are a tremendous and
growing market in the United States, for there are literally thousands of organizations that hold meetings every year and are always looking for somewhere new to go. The *Queen Mary* will
be ideal for conventions of 500 to 1000; and what could be more
enchanting? It will also be ideal for banquets, like the local
high-school banquet. Before long, as you can see from these
figures, I could be hitting, very conservatively, three million
visitors a year. That's a lot, though not as many as Disneyland.
However, the enthusiasm is tremendous. In the first three or
four months after she arrived I had 10,000 letters from people
wanting jobs or asking about opening shops on board."

Here a colleague of Mr. Martin's, also from the Queen Mary
Department, broke in to explain that the old liner meant almost
as much to Americans as she did to the British: not only to the international set, but to the thousands of GIs who sailed in her during the war when she was a troopship. In fact, there was a GI in
Long Beach who had been aboard when she sliced a cruiser in
half—H.M.S. *Curacao*—during a black night in the Atlantic.
"The life of the *Queen Mary* will never be seen again. And we
want to keep the image of great service: the living image of the
1930s."

As we boarded the ship, which rang with distant sounds of
hammering and drilling, Mr. Martin explained how this aim was
to be achieved. "The superstructure, obviously, we don't touch.

The rest is undergoing a major modification without touching the integrity of the *Queen*. The six lower decks, the engine room, and the boiler room are being gutted, apart from one propulsion unit which we're keeping. We've built a box with a glass floor, through which visitors will be able to see an eighteen-foot propeller slowly rotating. People will obviously be impressed.

"The degutting will give us 400,000 square feet of building equivalent, and will make room for museums. One of these will be a Museum of the Sea, with an all-round view of 360 degrees: you will descend deeper and deeper into the ocean, as it were, seeing big whales and porpoises. Then there will be Heritage Hall, illustrating the history of Man and the Sea, going back to the galleons and the Phoenicians. There will also be a Horizons Hall, again multilevel, which will tell the story of past and present explorations; and finally a museum of the *Queen Mary* and of Cunard. Incidentally, Cunard left us 200,000 pieces of dirty linen. And cockroaches! The ship was full of them."

Mr. Martin showed me into a former first-class cabin. "We will have only four hundred hotel rooms aboard, because only a third of the old cabins are suitable. These four hundred are being restored to their pristine state, same furnishings exactly, just as they were when she made her maiden voyage. We will, naturally, install air-conditioning throughout."

Footsteps echoing, we walked through the huge main dining room and the lounge, where first-class passengers used to take tea to the music of a palm-court orchestra. Mr. Martin explained that the dining room was not suitable for dining and instead would be used for conventions, with closed-circuit television. We walked through the galley. "Not the most modern equipment," said Mr. Martin. "That notice always amuses me," he added, pointing to a sign on an empty wire cage that read "First-Class Fruit Room." "It implies there's a *second*-class fruit room."

We went into the Verandah Grill, full of chrome and thirties murals. "The kids call it camp," said Mr. Martin. "We'll keep *this,* of course. We have some old menus, and we'll print some new ones. Put it all together and it's mother. You know what impresses people about this ship? Its size, for *then,* and the woods. The woods are just gorgeous."

He next ushered me into a large suite, which he said was the one favored by the Duke and Duchess of Windsor. Now it was a makeshift office, strewn with architect's plans. On deck, there was a view across the shipyards to a dark gray aircraft carrier in from Vietnam. "All this paintwork will be sand-blasted and repainted," said Mr. Martin, examining part of it. "Your British sailors: they weren't the neatest. And the funnels! They were practically rusted through!" He looked at a line of rivets. "We might color the nuts up a bit," he said reflectively.

He explained the route the tours would take, and how, with 15,000 people aboard, the ship would be really crowded. Restrooms, he said, would be built along the route, and some companionways would be converted into escalators, though retaining the appearance of companionways. As we passed the lifeboats he remarked that, during tours, the boats would be raised and lowered every ten minutes, "with the klaxons going."

On one of the upper decks, Mr. Martin showed me where the world's largest outdoor ice-cream parlor was to be built, with a British theme: Alice in Wonderland. Ice cream would be served by the Mad Hatter, or Alice, or the March Hare. "For the kids," Mr. Martin explained. "I think it'll be exciting."

I asked whether the ship still had the imposing signed photograph of Queen Mary herself, which I remembered from the old days. "No," he replied, "Cunard wouldn't let us have that or the royal standard. They said they were the property of the royal family. They also removed the plaque of Queen Mary, but we have had a replica made and I don't think anyone will notice the difference."

The last place we visited was the captain's quarters. Here, I was told, a panel was to be removed and glass inserted, so that people could look inside and see the captain and some of his officers, in wax. "We'll buy the regular store mannequins, but we'll get some nice, sculptured heads done specially. We're getting the uniforms through a uniform agency."

On our way ashore, I had a final surprise: a live English remnant of the crew, Mr. Jack Lowe, a comfortable-looking man wearing a cap with a merchant navy badge. He had been aboard the *Queen Mary* for twenty-one years, he told us, looking after generators and pumps, and he was one of two crew members who had stayed behind to help Long Beach. He conceded, after thinking about it, that he did find it a bit depressing to watch dockyard workers ripping out the equipment he had cherished for so long, but anything was better than the ship going for scrap. Did he live aboard? we asked him. "Not likely!" he replied.

Back on the jetty, after Mr. Martin had hurried away to his office, I stood for a while contemplating the old ship, sifting through my impressions. How impassioned and full of zeal the Americans were! How matter-of-fact, by comparison, was Mr. Lowe! And the Americans' attitude toward their prize: could Englishmen, nowadays, bring to a task of this magnitude such a strange mixture of sentimentality and commercial hard-headedness? Perhaps only at the height of their power could nations be so unselfconsciously absurd and so effective at the same time: like the British building St. Pancras railway station to resemble a Gothic cathedral.

And the ubiquitous Californian passion for replicas—the Tudor houses and the Spanish haciendas, the eighteenth-century candy shops and the Dutch windmills, the replica of Independence Hall at Knott's Berry Farm and the replica at Forest Lawn Cemetery of the church where Gray wrote his Elegy. And now a "replica" of the *Queen Mary*: I could now understand, I thought, what this passion for replicas signified. It must be connected with Los Angeles's growth in half a century from not much more than a village to the second largest city area in the world, and with the fact that this growth represented the most massive example in modern history of a people's attempt to escape to a better life. I reflected on the Americans' two attempts to slough off the past: first, when they founded the nation on the shores of the Atlantic, and, second, when they conquered the west and established themselves on the shores of the Pacific. To a remarkable degree, Californians had indeed left the past behind; yet they still apparently felt the need sometimes—perhaps barely consciously—to recreate the past, here and there, including the European past, and to have it dotted about to refer to. The *Queen Mary*, I thought, fitted into this pattern. A big municipal sign in midtown announced: "Long Beach, the Home of the *Queen Mary*;" and new apartment blocks on Ocean Boulevard had started "Queen Mary Clubs," which residents could join for three dollars a year. The old ship was going to end up very differently from the way she had really been back in the thirties; but even so, she was clearly meeting an important need. She was helping the people of Long Beach to find an identity.

NORTH AND SOUTH

> In the north, the women wear gloves. In the south, they dress like tarts.
>
> *Leo Rosten*

The exuberant affluence, the social breakthroughs, and the cultural uncertainty of California are much more noticeable in the southern half of the state than in the north; but the north increasingly takes its cue from Los Angeles. Down there, among the smog and the billboards, is unquestionably the state's dynamo.

The two halves of the state are, as everyone constantly remarks, very different. Partly it is a matter of climate, partly a matter of geography; it is partly that California is both very big and peculiarly elongated, and partly that the north was populated and developed before the south. The division goes deep into history. Under the Mexicans, the southern half revolted against the north. At the very first constitutional convention in 1849, before California was admitted to statehood, the southern delegates tried to divide the area in two. The north, they thought, should become a state at once, and the south a territory. Being landowners from the agricultural part of the terrain, they could see no reason why they should pay taxes to meet the expenses of a state government, when all they themselves needed was a territorial government whose costs would be largely met by Washington. Since then, there have been numerous proposals for splitting the state, and the issue is as alive today as ever.

Socially, the two parts of the state are quite different. At a time when the women of Paris and New York had long since abandoned hats and gloves, the smart women of San Francisco and even the models in the windows of I. Magnin's store were still decked out in elaborate accessories. The bouffant hairdo was a feature of smart San Francisco life long after it had been abandoned in Newark, New Jersey. The reason for the formality is that the well-to-do in San Francisco believe they have a mission to set the social tone of the west coast. They look down on southern California and think it is up to them as San Franciscans to maintain an outpost of civilized society—by which they mean a society whose standards of civilization are derived from Europe. "They actually have an inferiority complex about Europe," said an English girl, long resident in San Francisco and familiar with its upper reaches. The proof of it, she said, was that a con man from London had climbed rapidly to the apex of San Francisco society entirely on the strength of his British accent and his knowledge of the social ropes, picked up from his father, a West End waiter. The reason why Europeans visiting the United States invariably find San Francisco the most agreeable American city is, no doubt, precisely because of all American cities it is the least American and the most European. As in a European city, the social structure is clearly visible.

Sir Denis Brogan, of Cambridge, England, has pointed out that of all cities in the United States, San Francisco has the most *rentiers,* not counting St. Petersburg (Florida) or Santa Barbara; they are often civilized and always rich; and they do not have to work because the money rolls in automatically. These fortunate people, in many cases, belong to the families that have given San Francisco its public-spirited and cultivated tone; it was the private benefactions of such families that helped propel Berkeley and Stanford so rapidly into the top rank of American universi-ties. Like the cable cars, traditional social features survive: old la-dies in thick-walled mansions overlooking the bay; families like the Hearsts, still with newspaper interests; young men who have made the grand tour of Europe, waiting to take over family firms. The San Francisco *haut monde* is most clearly visible at the opera, where, once a week during the season, the cream of the city dress in evening finery and assemble, everyone knowing everyone, among the chandeliers and champagne of the Opera House, like the privileged members of a Ruritanian court. Some of the opera-goers have an overdeveloped sense of propriety that is positively English. Not long ago, in order to raise money for the opera (the pride taken by grand San Franciscans in local culture sometimes stops short of actually supporting it with cash) some well-wishers organized a fund-raising and publicity-promoting evening which involved dancing at a discotheque. One of the opera's senior council members was pushed out on to the floor by a girl fund-raiser, and was appalled next morning when his photograph, in what he regarded as an undignified posture, appeared in the local paper. He found the notion of such publicity, even if it raised money, "abhorrent," he said. This is not an attitude one would be likely to encounter in Los Angeles.

But the tide is running against him, and against the whole of traditional San Francisco. The old character of the city is being undermined—from within by angry youth and militant blacks, who reject everything that San Francisco, in its role as the Queen of the Coast, has stood for, and from without by the breakers roll-ing in from Los Angeles. Until recently, San Francisco by and large ran the state; but it no longer does.

The turning point came in 1964. In that year the University Regents—the nearest, someone once said, that California gets to an aristocracy—looked at two political documents. One was a list of Rockefeller's liberal Republican backers, and the other a list of Goldwater's. "We knew every single name on the Rockefeller list," Clark Kerr, the former university chancellor, told me, "but we knew not one person on Goldwater's." The Goldwater backers all came from southern California, where the migrants who had arrived during the twenties and thirties, and subsequently prospered, had joined with the men who had made big personal fortunes—such as Henry Salvatori, in oil—and combined to give the state an entirely new, right-wing power base. Governor Reagan's victory, two years later, confirmed the trend.

There are other signs of the brash new southern California battering at the gates. "San Francisco used to be a special place," remarked an agriculturalist at Davis, "but look at Oakland now: it *is* Los Angeles." Culturally, despite the famous opera, San Francisco is relatively dead. The best painters have moved to Los Angeles; the star west-coast conductor, Zubin Mehta, conducts the Los Angeles symphony orchestra; Stravinsky, who lived for years in Los Angeles, had nothing to do with San Francisco music. For a week in San Francisco I stayed at the old Claremont Hotel, the great white wooden structure that stands up in the hills behind Berkeley and is a landmark for the city of San Francisco itself. The hotel was empty, the carpets frayed, the swimming pool stained and cracked, and the huge restaurant with a view over the whole city had been converted into a bleak help-yourself cafeteria. The desk-clerk told me that the owners were waiting for the lease to fall in, so that they could build something more profitable and up-to-date, like motels or a housing development. Before long, you may be sure, the old gardens of the Claremont will be like a slice of suburban Los Angeles.

For there is nothing, it appears, in the European-derived San Francisco tradition which is virile enough to withstand the chaotic but powerful thrust coming up from the south. What alarms those San Franciscans who dislike Los Angeles is not simply the prospective impact of a more vulgar society. Their principal anxiety is caused by the ever-louder hum and whine of advancing modern technology, which they fear will breach and distort their civilized enclave as it has already distorted, in their opinion, not only Los Angeles but most of the rest of the state.

CHAPTER 3

Technology Sets the Pace

The scientific achievement of the United States is moving at a rate we all ought to marvel at. Think of the astonishing constellation of talent, particularly in the physical sciences, all down the California coast, from Berkeley and Stanford to Pasadena and Los Angeles. There is nothing like that concentration of talent anywhere in the world. It sometimes surprises Europeans to realize how much of the pure science of the entire West is being carried out in the United States. Curiously enough, it often surprises Americans too. At a guess, the figure is something like eighty percent, and might easily be higher.

C. P. Snow

We must ask the bat-eyed priests of technology what on earth they think they are doing.

Lewis Mumford

ONE peculiarity about California as the world champion of science and technology (the only contenders for the title are Cambridge, Mass. and Adademogorodok in the Soviet Union) is that the buildings, laboratories, and centers in which the work proceeds can often seem invisible. Firms engaged in secret or dangerous work are tucked away in the hills or deserts; and the great technocratic centers on the Pacific coast north of Los Angeles appear as a series of anonymous square blocks. The most important building in California, and perhaps in the United States—the Lawrence Radiation Laboratory in Berkeley—occupies, it is true, a dominating site in the hills above the campus; but it fits well into the landscape and looks like a modern art gallery. At the Rand Corporation, the famous think-tank of technologists, they reckon they are inventing new ways of thinking about all kinds of technical matters, ranging from intercontinental ballistic missiles and earth satellites to second-strike nuclear capability and the military potential of Russia and China, to say nothing of the uses of computers. But all this goes on in a low Spanish-style building that is half monastery, half motel—with cell-like offices but also with patios and parking, right opposite the pier in the beach atmosphere of Santa Monica, where the mothers are bursting out of their shorts, the ice-cream wrappings lie thick in the gutters, and a Holiday Inn offers "all you can eat for $2.45."

The Aerospace Corporation occupies an equally odd site. The corporation, the main intellectual center for the most spectacular technology of the modern world—namely, missiles and satellites —employs 1900 scientists and engineers. It is very close to the Los Angeles airport, which is convenient for the staff, since it facilitates their constant commuting to White Sands or Honolulu or Washington. But the main approach road to the corporation is crossed by some old Santa Fe railway tracks, and the antique freight cars often come trundling slowly through at the very time the space engineers are driving to work, making them wait in line, boiling with frustration. A little further down the highway is one of the peculiar unfinished parts of Los Angeles, with dirt banks, scrubby fields, and a dilapidated stall selling strawberries.

Both Rand and the Aerospace Corporation conform to expectations more on the inside than the outside; to enter, you must acquire a pass. The Aerospace Corporation contains a beautiful low quadrangle in the middle, like a twentieth-century cloister. The Rand corridors are full of purposeful-looking men, striding up and down, wearing crisp white shirts. Even so, there are incongruities. In the lobby, where soft Musak plays, the only literature offered the waiting visitor is a stack of old copies of *Sports Illustrated*.

One day as I was coming out of Rand a bald, extremely fat man (not Herman Kahn) was going in; he was wearing a seersucker jacket, very baggy gray flannel trousers, and a pair of startlingly white tennis shoes.

Thus the playground side of Californian life merges with the technological, a circumstance which, as we shall see, has important consequences.

ERNEST O. LAWRENCE

How did it happen that California, at one time best known for oranges and movies, has turned into the world's scientific headquarters? The answer is, partly, that the opening up of the west was from the beginning closely linked with the advance of science. America's first big concentration of scientists, the U.S. Geological Survey—one of the most formidable scientific bureaus ever known—grew out of the Federal Survey of the Rocky Mountains. The first mass-produced technocrats were the result of the Morrill Act of 1862, which was expressly designed to open up the western frontier by doling out grants of land to colleges on condition that they undertook technical training. The University of California was chartered as a result of the Morrill Act, and its first building, South Hall on the Berkeley campus, was a chemistry laboratory. Long before the turn of the century, Berkeley had started to attract some of the nation's leading scientists, especially during the term of office of the university's second president, John Le Conte, who was famous for his work on electricity.

But the key figure in California's scientific progress, and arguably the most important man in the history of twentieth-century California, was Ernest O. Lawrence. At Berkeley during the 1930s, the young Lawrence used a windowpane, some sealing wax, and pieces of old brass to build a cyclotron, a device which "was to physics what Galileo's telescope had been to astronomy." In the early forties, Lawrence inspired the research that demonstrated the utility of plutonium as the explosive ingredient in a nuclear weapon. Because of Lawrence, plutonium was born at Berkeley, on February 23, 1941, "during the early stormy hours under the eaves of Gilman Hall."

He was deeply involved in the building of both the atomic bomb and the hydrogen bomb. It was his lobbying that led to the establishment of the Compton Committee on the eve of America's entry into World War II; in the fall of 1941, the committee reported the possibility of building "a fission bomb of superlatively destructive power." When the atomic-bomb project began in earnest, Lawrence became director of the process for producing uranium-235; and the Los Alamos Scientific Laboratory, which built and tested the bomb, became an adjunct of the University of California. After the war, together with his colleagues Edward Teller, Luis Alvarez, and Wendell M. Latimer, all from the Berkeley Radiation Laboratory, Lawrence led the right wing of nuclear science, those who successfully advocated the development of the hydrogen bomb in response to Russia's development of "conventional" nuclear weapons. (The most celebrated opponent of the H-bomb, J. Robert Oppenheimer, used to sit at Lawrence's feet during the thirties, at the Monday evening meetings of the Physics Journal Club in Berkeley's Le Conte Hall).

Before the war, little public money went into science. But after the war the federal tap was turned full on, and the cash has never stopped flowing since. Luis Alvarez has recalled that at Berkeley, before the war, "when we finished with a part, we carefully unsoldered the connections and put everything back on the shelf;" but after the war, "we ran it with a big barrel of greenbacks." [1] California got the money largely because after 1945 Lawrence's protégés took up key positions in the new scientific establishment in Washington that was handing out the huge sums of money needed for research. Sometimes they were handing it out to other former pupils of Lawrence. In 1953, a brilliant young graduate from Lawrence's lab, W. H. K. Panofsky, became director of Stanford's High Energy Physics Laboratory; four years later he submitted to the Atomic Energy Commission his "Proposal For a Two Mile Linear Accelerator." California, however, was not the only part of the United States that wanted a monster accelerator;

so did the midwest, in order that it, too, could get into high-energy physics. The subsequent battle was a classic of scientific infighting, but it was the fast footwork of the Californians that won the verdict and the $100 million for the Stanford accelerator. The chairman of the Atomic Energy Commission when this decision was taken was the tall and gloomy Glenn T. Seaborg, a loyal Californian.[2] He was still chairman of the AEC when the Lawrence Radiation Laboratory was asked to design the most expensive scientific installation in history, the 200-bev accelerator whose cost was estimated, as of 1967, at $340 million.

No other state has received anything approaching such largesse. At the height of the Stanford accelerator battle, figures were published to show that California's universities, aerospace firms, and electronics firms were getting no less than 34.6 percent of *all* federal expenditure for research and development, a total of over $4.9 billion, or an average of $315.14 for each inhabitant of the state. Missouri, which led the midwest queue for handouts, enjoyed a mere 2.7 percent of the total. Even Massachusetts, for all its cluster of famous electronics industries on Route 128, as well as Harvard and M.I.T., had only 4 percent. Gasps of envy and loud complaints from other states followed the publication of these figures. It made no difference to California. In 1969, the Pentagon alone gave California almost $2.3 billion, or 36.3 percent, of its total expenditure on R and D. The National Aeronautics and Space Administration in the same year awarded California 34 percent of its big contracts—well over $1 billion. After 1969, to California's great pain, less money flowed in from Washington as space and defense programs were cut back; even so, California was still, by normal standards, or the standards of other states, enjoying a federally financed bonanza, centering around technology.[3]

THE BONANZA

Thanks largely to these massive injections of capital from Washington, California has done better than any place else in achieving the main goal of all modern governments, including Communist governments: namely, to get as rich as possible as rapidly as possible.

Californians are richer than anyone else has ever been, having raced past New York back in 1965. They buy more goods than anyone else; they sell more abroad than any other state; their speed of growth is unparalleled. The value of Californian manufacturing was under $4 billion in 1947, but up to $21 billion by 1966.

The growth of manufacturing over the past twenty years represents a massive shift away from an economy previously dominated by agriculture and oil. Another equally massive shift is on the way. At the end of 1969, manufacturing was the biggest employer, but by 1980 the largest source of jobs will be the service industries—a nationwide trend that will be still more marked in California—followed by trade and government, with manufacturing in fourth place. One main reason for this shift is the ever-increasing expansion of new research and development activities. R and D will get stronger still with the state's heavy concentration of "industries of the future," which include the aerospace concerns and the aircraft firms, as well as newcomers like marine sciences and oceanography, concentrated at Long Beach, San Diego, and between Monterey and Morro Bay.

The weakness of the Californian economy is its overreliance on defense industries and federally supported projects, with the result that a cut in space and defense programs in Washington can cause instant havoc in California, as happened in 1970. These cuts produced the first real alarm that California has known since World War II, with the very people who have been most crucial in producing California's wealth—the middle-class technocrats—demonstrating in angry groups against President Nixon, carrying placards reading "Jobs Not Rhetoric." [4] But the change in emphasis from a government-supported to a private economy has already begun, though it still has a long way to go. The 1970 shake-out may help this process, since the people who found themselves suddenly out of work will be driven to invent new private businesses in order to keep going.

Despite the traumas of 1970–71, some California businessmen are beginning to perceive an even richer future for the state. They see the lands round the Pacific Rim—California, Japan (expected by Herman Kahn of the Hudson Institute to overtake the United States as an industrial nation by the year 2000), Australia (with its huge mineral resources), and South Korea (where Seoul is growing faster than any other metropolis in the world)— combining to turn the Pacific into an inland sea for international trade and developing a new circle of wealth and influence. As time goes by, California becomes less and less like one state among fifty, and more and more like a separate nation.

Sheer wealth is California's most obvious asset, but it has other advantages. Roaming round the State Capitol in Sacramento, I called one day on Jesse Unruh, a leader of the Democratic opposition to Governor Reagan, and found in his anteroom a member of that uniquely American breed of efficient young legislative assistants who often, in my experience, know more about what's afoot in the United States than anyone else. They are often more intelligent than their bosses, and less blinkered by egotism. Around Sacramento, I had not been deeply impressed by the politicians I had met. I had been made especially gloomy by the evening drinking sessions in the Clipper Ship Bar of the Senator Hotel. The blonde waitresses, with their piled-up hair, their silver toenails, black net stockings and skirts up to their bottoms, displayed their pants when they leaned over the legislators with the drinks; and the legislators talked more and more loudly and expressed increasingly alarming views about the state they were supposed to run. One evening when I was there, a group began to discuss the grape strike organized by Cesar Chavez. It became plain that none of them was familiar even with the rudiments of the dispute, but that did not prevent them from talking of the Mexicans involved in tones of contempt. "Your agricultural workers are bums," one of them said. "These people make sixty-five dollars a day picking grapes: I talked to one of the owners." Another legislator added that Chavez had "been in Commie outfits."

None of this was remotely true. The regulars in the bar also displayed an unappealing moral outlook, mixing salacity with prudishness. They would tell dirty jokes and peer up the waitresses' skirts, while complaining about the alleged sexual laxness of blacks and Mexicans. One evening, a legislator became especially incensed about a sculpture exhibition which at that time was causing a scandal. He had been to the show and was appalled: "There were lifesize statues of positions that are illegal in your own *bedroom*," he said.

Unruh's assistant, whose name was Jack C. Cruse, conceded that the caliber of Sacramento's politicians was not all it might be; but he argued nevertheless that California was in advance of the rest of the United States. He ran down the list of assets:

1. An unmatched educational system, especially higher education, and especially the seventy or so community colleges, or junior colleges, which offer two-year courses of mainly vocational training, at very low tuition fees and are open to almost any high-school graduate.
2. The best system of highways and communications in the United States.
3. Cleaner local government and widespread use of the city-manager system.
4. Newer buildings and therefore better houses and offices.
5. Scandal-free state government.
6. A high standard of economic opportunity, stemming principally from the educational system.

He did not attribute all of California's advantages to good government. He thought the role of the climate, in attracting both people and industry, had been "basic." [5] Nor did he regard Californian society as perfect; he was worried that the resurgent right wing might be set on tearing down some of the advanced welfare systems of the state, and he was sure that the problem of the minorities would not be easily solved. Basically, though, he was an optimist. "We have solved the problem of production here," he said. "Now we need to solve the problem of distribution. That's all. Of course, it would take a lot of pressure to do it, but this is the state where it could be done, if anywhere. It could happen here. It could be a superstate and a model for everyone else—if only modern technology can be cashed in."

There is much to be said for Cruse's boosterlike view of the state. Conditions of life that Californians take for granted can astonish an outsider. A man on the staff of the Aerospace Corporation told me that there were 635 pupils in his son's school— Westchester High School, which is part of the Los Angeles school system—and no less than 83 percent of them were going on to college. It is true that there are unpleasant Chinese ghettos in San Francisco, and the black and Mexican ghettos of Los Angeles would cause general shame in a society with a livelier conscience than California's. But the only time I felt myself to be among really poor people in California was among the Mexican grape-pickers. An English girl from a poor family in Liverpool, whom I came across in Los Angeles, told me she was lodging with some theoretically poor whites who struck *her*, by Liverpool slum standards, as comparatively rich. When they bought a refrigerator they bought a new one; and they were not irresponsible. Cruse was probably right when he said that Californians by and large enjoy better conditions of life than any large mass of people in history. Their trouble is that the technology which has produced the bonanza is throwing these conditions of life out of gear.

EFFECTS OF THE AUTOMOBILE

The improvement in city conditions by the general adoption of the motor-car can hardly be overestimated. Streets clean, dustless and odorless, with light rubber-tired vehicles moving swiftly and noiselessly over their smooth expanse, would eliminate a greater part of the nervousness, distraction, and strain of modern metropolitan life.
SCIENTIFIC AMERICAN, *1899*

Despite California's enthusiastic embrace of technology, many of its consequences are not normally experienced by the citizens, though there can be sudden, alarming reminders of what is going on. In the fall of 1970, the last item on the San Francisco Channel 7 news, delivered by a cheery announcer, ran as follows: "If you saw a bright glow in the western sky tonight don't worry—we found out it was an intercontinental missile fired from Vandenberg Air Force Base down the coast."

Nuclear missiles may be the most alarming product of the technologists; but the most important, more so in California than anywhere else, are automobiles. Strangely enough, not all Californians at first welcomed the automobile. Wilshire Boulevard has a kink in it because one obstinate landowner refused to sell and let the highway drive straight through. Since then, the automobile has had it all its own way, but the full social consequences of this fact have scarcely yet been assessed. Almost every other aspect of life in California is exhaustively studied by sociologists, but no one has yet written a standard work on the effect of the car on the lives of the people. Perhaps it will have to be written by an outside observer, not an American, for the same reason that a foreigner, R. N. Salaman, was needed to interpret, in a classic work, the history of Ireland in terms of the potato.

An Englishman at Berkeley, Leslie Wilkins, who is professor of criminology, speculated about the effect of the car along these lines:

"California," he said, "contains a far greater variety of people than England, although England has a class system and California is supposed not to have one. The rich in California are richer, and the poor are poorer. Yet despite the much greater variety of people in California, and the theoretical equality of everyone, Californians have much less experience of variety than people have in England. Americans, and even Californians, have no real word for 'eccentric'; they talk in a pejorative way about 'nuts,' 'kooks,' or 'screwballs,' whereas in England an eccentric is regarded as a perfectly honorable person.

"Consider Californian living conditions: you have black ghettos, but you also have white ghettos, with the middle class all living in houses of very similar value. This is where the car comes in, for it increases this isolation. You move from place to place in your steel box, not encountering anyone else. Public transport on the other hand is a strong integrating factor; on a bus or subway train you come into contact with a random selection of other people—hear them talk, perhaps talk to them, smell them, brush against them, are part of them. But in California there isn't any public transport to speak of. People haven't accommodated to density because even in the cities isolation is still maintained by the automobiles. In Los Angeles, who walks? And once you are in the car, you are isolated. That means you don't have so much information about other people; and lack of information tends to lead to prejudicial stereotyping of others.

"Compare a village culture, which can integrate the village idiot with the squire. If you move the village idiot into an urban environment he has to be incarcerated, whereas in his village everyone knows him and has enough information about him to keep him out of jail. One characteristic of California is that in the urban areas small incidents build up very rapidly into large incidents, which may well be related to the narrow range of information some groups of people have about other groups of people; and for this mutual ignorance the car is partly responsible."

The most famous example of isolation in Los Angeles has been the Negro district of Watts. When the 1965 race riots broke out, the worst in American history (34 dead, 4000 arrested, 200 buildings destroyed at a cost of $16 million), the curfew area was the size of the whole of San Francisco; yet few whites had ever visited Watts (except possibly to view the Watts Towers); and many black residents, because they had no cars and there was virtually no public transportation, had considerable difficulty in visiting other parts of Los Angeles. Hence the shortage of work in Watts; hence the shortage of social services (at the time of the riots there was no hospital in the area); hence the cut-off between the Watts residents and the police (even five years later few, if any, of the police dealing with Watts actually lived in the district). It was symbolic that the riot started after an incident involving two policemen on the highway patrol; they knew nothing about the area and had no idea of the possible consequences of their arrest of a Watts black; they were two men who stepped out of their steel box to deal with a stranger in a totally unfamiliar territory. In Watts, the transportation arrangements tended to isolate and immobilize an entire community. But the lack of a car is a serious social disadvantage everywhere. The people waiting at bus stops are the dispossessed.

The automobile can produce eccentric as well as socially damaging results. Recently in Los Angeles the Valley Community Church started experimenting with "drive-in worship" in an "outdoor worship area." According to the minister, the Reverend A. Ray, the arrangement had many advantages:

1. People should be encouraged to worship in their normal setting, and their normal setting these days is a car.
2. It is a help to invalids and the aged.
3. It encourages people who cannot bear crowds.
4. It gets away from the conventional notion that you have to be inside a conventional church building in order to engage in worship.
5. It allows possibly shy potential worshipers to window-shop and see whether they like a particular church's offering without embarrassment.
6. It allows parents with a baby to bring him along without worrying that it might disturb other worshipers.
7. It allows those with personal sorrows to be entirely alone.
8. It encourages people to come to church who might otherwise be wearing what they consider the "wrong" clothes.
9. It offers "a change of pace."

Undoubtedly, too, the automobile has had a profound effect on the stability of the average Californian family. As a fellow in Bakersfield said to me: "My son treats our home like a hotel, because he has a car. He can be a hundred miles away before his mother realizes he's gone out." But the most serious social effect of the automobile is its impact on the old notion of the neighborhood. There is little communal feeling anywhere in California, and it would not be surprising if a correlation could be worked out between this lack of communal feeling and the incidence of the automobile. If you can reach people twenty miles away in twenty minutes, why bother to know the neighbors? In Los Angeles, especially, there are few neighborhood organizations, and thus none of the sense of identity and communal feeling that those organizations provide. Talking on this theme, a girl reporter on the *Los Angeles Times* told me that her colleagues thought that *Couples*, the John Updike novel about a small New England town, was funny: "They couldn't imagine knowing the neighbors well enough to sleep with them." In Los Angeles, she added, "neighborliness doesn't make sense any more."

THE ROLE OF THE FREEWAYS

According to Dr. Jacob Bronowski, a scientist-philosopher who is resident at the Salk Institute of Biology in La Jolla, the two great Californian achievements are the system of higher education and the freeways, an example of California's technological pioneering. He ascribes the excellence of the freeway system partly to the fact that California gets little rain and scarcely any frost, which means that the road surface is relatively cheap and easy to maintain. Most Californians, like Bronowski, think well of the freeways; and there are even a few who consider the crossover systems (for instance, the San Diego–Santa Monica interchange) engineering feats of actual beauty, and express delight at the way the automobiles endlessly join and separate at different levels, like corpuscles in serpentine concrete arteries.

For a New Yorker or a Londoner, used to driving at ten miles an hour and to frequent stops and starts, getting onto the Californian freeways can be highly exhilarating. There is a positive physical satisfaction to be had from moving smoothly along in a shoal of cars all traveling at the same speed, shifting into the right lane and precisely selecting the most advantageous exit out of seventeen on the way from San Francisco to Oakland, or flowing through the Los Angeles system at a steady sixty, reading the signs correctly, taking the off-ramp at precisely the ordained speed, arriving at point B at the exact time you had calculated when you left point A. There are, however, snags. One mistake, one wrong exit, and you may be lost for hours, ejected from the lavishly signposted freeways into the anonymous no-man's-land of the rest of Los Angeles where every street looks similar, and the signs, to a stranger, have no meaning. Such mishaps can happen to anyone, not just to people from out of town. One night, going from Beverly Hills to a downtown social occasion in a chauffeur-driven car, with two people who had both lived in Los Angeles for decades and who were both concentrating hard on finding the way, we got lost twice; twice the great Cadillac glided confidently off the freeway and came to a humiliated and bewildered halt in a neighborhood that neither chauffeur nor passengers could recognize. A still worse hazard is to find yourself sandwiched among evenly-moving traffic and suddenly realize you are going in the wrong direction. Almost all Californians boast of their freeway system, but some fear it. It is not unusual to meet people, especially women, who never go on the freeways at all if they can avoid it. And whenever it rains, the freeways are dangerous; accustomed to dry surfaces, many Los Angeles drivers have little idea how to drive on a wet road, and they brake and skid as if on ice. Besides, though freeway fans do not like to admit it, the freeways can jam; and a freeway jam is awe-inspiring, like the beginning of a science-fiction story about the day a city died. As with the automobile itself, the system works in favor of the alert and fit, and against the timorous or incompetent. Those who use it well and easily live in another world from those who do not. One girl told me how she thought she had taken some nondriving out-of-towners to the L.A. railway station; by mistake, however, she had dropped them, plus a pile of baggage, at a church (an understandable mistake in Los Angeles, where the appearance of a building is not necessarily a guide to its function). The wretched travelers, she heard later, had been stranded for hours.

For the most part, however, the freeways work so well even in Los Angeles that most Los Angelenos assume that an infinite number of cars can readily be accommodated, as the need arises, simply by the construction of more freeways. This is an illusion. Despite extensive improvements to the freeways during the past ten years, peak-hour travel times in L.A. have not improved at all. The fact is, as the traffic engineers are beginning to find out, in a city like Los Angeles it is simply impossible to build enough freeways. The effect of the freeway system is not so much to solve the problems of the cities as to shift the problems elsewhere. The former mayor of Boston, John F. Collins, who later became professor of urban affairs at M.I.T., has remarked that "we can't afford to permit people to flee to suburbia, separated by twenty-five miles of highway from the problems of the core city;" but in Los Angeles, where this process has gone further than anywhere else in the U.S., there is not a hope that it can ever be reversed. Los Angeles, indeed, is so far along that not only is the core city decaying because people have fled from it to suburbia, but parts of the suburbia to which they fled have decayed too. For instance, Venice—an extraordinary shantytown on tidewater canals near Santa Monica —is now so full of hippies and panhandlers that the city, including the developers, has had to mount a major campaign in order to recapture the area for the suburbanites.[6] The freeways spread the problems out, eat up the land, and reduce the tax base of the cities. (In Bakersfield, for instance, the supermarkets, to which almost all the customers travel by car, are carefully sited just outside the city limits to avoid the city tax.)

Despite general enthusiasm, the freeways are for these reasons starting to produce enemies. One of the angriest is a grizzled and eloquent man named Sam Wood, who used to work in state planning but is now in the forefront, through his magazine *Cry California,* of the attempt to save what's left of the beauties of the state. He told me that California had had three- and four-lane highways since the thirties, but the concrete didn't really start to flow until 1956, when in a program billed as "the greatest public-works project in history" President Eisenhower got Congress to finance a 42,500-mile interstate highway system at a cost of $27 billion.

"Because the original idea was that the interstate system was needed partly for defense reasons, shifting troops and so forth, the federal government pays ninety percent of the cost and the state only ten percent," Wood explained. "So, naturally, everyone loves the freeway. In Oregon and Washington they've used freeways to tie the cities together; and that was the original aim of the interstate program—to build a network of freeways connecting all the big population centers. But in California they've used freeways to solve the problem of congestion inside the cities. The freeways in Sacramento have cut the city off from the river, which could have been a recreational area and a great local amenity. Sacramento is the freeway junction of the state: every freeway goes right through it. The Division of Highways in this state is an absolutely sacrosanct part of the bureaucracy. The highways people don't have to go through the state legislature, yet they have two or three million dollars of state money to spend, besides some four to six million dollars of federal money. There is no legislative control over them. When Governor Brown was in office I remember going to him to complain about one particular freeway, and he said there wasn't a thing he could do. 'I can't control that damn division,' he said. 'If they wanted to drive a road right through Capitol Plaza, I couldn't stop them. They do as they damn please.' They want a freeway alongside Lake Tahoe. And the bay next to it. They'd run it right across the bay. They never give up. They wanted to build a freeway on Route 1 by the ocean, along those big cliffs south of Monterey. They want a ten- or twelve-lane highway along San Francisco Bay. They drive 'em straight through towns.

"The Highway Division is in politics all over the state, because each county decides about roads for itself. You don't have a *plan* for California; freeway building is not related to anything else. There's supposed to be a highway commission of laymen to recommend routes, but only between A and B, not where they actually go. And of course no one wants to build underground railways or rapid-transit systems when you can get freeways for virtually nothing. Los Angeles desperately needs a rapid-transit system, but they continue to build freeways.[7] Every metropolitan area in the world has some form of rapid-transit system except California. In California, if you don't have a car you can't get to work.

"By 1980, we'll have as many cars as we have people now, twenty million. We've already got twelve or thirteen million. I've got three cars myself: one for me, for my wife, one for my son. It's out of control. You know they even want to put a freeway through one of the national parks? They say, 'Well, this land isn't being used anyway: it's just a park!' There's no overall cost-benefit system; they don't take into account, for instance, the cost to the farmer whose land the freeway goes through. It's all calculated on the savings per mile to the automobile driver, which is a very narrow base for working out the economics."

Indignant freeway opponents like Wood are beginning to gather support. Having allowed the freeways to curl into the center of San Francisco in a series of specially ugly loops on concrete stilts, the citizens finally struck, complaining about noise and pollution, the destruction of homes, and the ruin of historic neighborhoods; as a result, they held up 17.4 miles of proposed expressway construction. The controversy is being repeated elsewhere; and at the beginning of 1970 the Federal Highway Administration in Washington estimated that, nationwide, 128.4 miles of construction were being held up by local disputes. In other words, the interstate system is dumping traffic into the cities faster than the cities can handle it—if they can handle it at all. More roads generate more traffic which generates more roads which smash the cities to pieces. The scale of the highway assault on the cities is best seen from the federal figures: with California well to the fore, the States' Highway Commissioners have worked out that they "need" to spend $320 billion during the next fifteen years to cope with the expected total of 143.5 million cars, 38.5 million more than today: which means doubling the present rate of spending. Of this colossal sum, the cities "need" $123 billion. What the cities will look like after that, nobody knows; but it is highly improbable that this avalanche of technological expenditure will make them into places that people want to live in.

AGRICULTURAL TECHNOLOGY

The technology of the automobile is changing the family and the neighborhood. The technology of the freeway is altering old notions of the city. And along with these changes, old ideas of rural life are on the way out, undermined by the technology of agriculture.

From the way some people in California complain about the way housing and freeways are eating up the most productive land, it is easy to get an exaggerated idea of the decline in Californian agriculture. In fact, the total space occupied by cities is still relatively small: it was 2.4 percent of the total area of the state in 1958, and it is expected to grow to only 4 percent by 1975. Thirty-six million of the state's hundred million acres are still used for farming; and California still easily leads all other states in farm production (it outranks Iowa, its nearest competitor, by more than $500 million a year) and produces nearly half the fruit and vegetables eaten in the United States.

California has long led the nation (and thus the world) in the mechanization of agriculture. Machines used to be developed for such needs as cultivating the soil or for cutting irrigation systems. But the machine technocrats now are increasingly concentrating their inventiveness on the crops themselves, which sometimes involves changing the character of particular fruits and vegetables.

Consider the fate of the familiar tomato. Until 1964, California tomatoes were customarily picked by Mexican immigrant workers, the *braceros,* who came over the border in season. In 1964, following complaints from Mexico about the disruptive effect of the *bracero* system on family life—and from American unions about its depressing effect on labor prices—the U.S. Congress, despite predictions of doom from the growers, effectively stopped the program. At that point the California farmers, who hitherto had found it cheaper to use men than machines, turned for help to the agricultural engineers at the Davis campus of the University of California. The engineers designed a machine that picked tomatoes by lifting up the vine and shaking it. That was efficient, but it was not efficient enough; because the fruit ripened on different days, the machines had to go through the fields three or four times to harvest all the tomatoes. The solution was to put every plant on exactly the same timetable. A mowing machine went through as soon as the plants sprouted, trimming the tops off all the plants; at once the plants began to branch, and later they all bore fruit simultaneously.

That solved the picking problem but created a packing problem. Tomatoes, like all California produce, were traditionally packed in a field box, which held fifty-six pounds; but the new machines picked the tomatoes faster than they could be packed in the old field boxes. So the engineers invented a "bulk bin," which was much larger. But then the tomatoes, raining down into the big bin, tended to get squashed; so, as a man at Davis explained to me, "we had to design a tomato to fit the bin: a tomato with a tougher skin, easier to handle, and—to save space—not so round: in fact, a tough, oblong tomato." Even that isn't the final solution of the problem. The stalk at the end of each tomato, when the tomatoes are packed in a bin, may pierce the skin of its neighbor; so now Davis is trying to develop a tomato which, when harvested, leaves its stalk on the plant.

Besides altering the product, the agricultural technocrats are constantly at work on the related task of reducing the number of agricultural jobs—especially the humbler jobs, and those done by the workers who are becoming unionized and demanding more money. Work is in progress on breeding a more uniform carrot, because too many women are involved in carrot packing. In the old days, people liked to buy carrots with the bushy green tops intact, as an indicator of freshness. But the bushy tops took up freight space, so the growers took to chopping the tops off with a mowing machine before the harvest; and customers became used to buying carrots, their tops sliced off, in a plastic bag. But they did not like buying carrots of different sizes in the same bag; they thought they were being cheated. So now, before the carrots are packaged, an army of women sorts them into piles of the same size. This work is badly paid, and, as a man at Davis said, "each woman is devoting her energy to a futile occupation. If we can get carrots to grow at exactly the same length, diameter, and color, we can do away with all these women."

As farming becomes more technical, it naturally requires more capital, and the small farmer—like the farm worker—finds it harder and harder to survive. Small farms have been decreasing in number all over the United States, in spite of federal programs to keep them going, and nowhere has the decline been faster than in California. Between 1950 and 1970 the number of small California farms was halved. Thought is now being given—by the Bank of America, for instance—to how they can be abolished altogether. The Bank considers that one of the obstacles to total abolition is sheer sentiment—"the romanticism with which many Americans view the small family farm as remembered from the days of their youth." Abolish the small farm, says the Bank of America, and the big farms, freed from federally imposed restraints, will be able to become more efficient. How is the death sentence to be carried out? Perhaps, says the bank, by paying small farmers an annual income on condition that they run down their farms and take other jobs.

Talking to Californian agriculturalists, I constantly came across the assumption that agriculture nowadays is like any other industry: they used the word "agribusiness" to distinguish their modern practices from mere old-fashioned "farming." They seemed to take it for granted that farming, like other industries, should lend itself to greater output produced more rapidly. But in the past few years, there has been increasing anxiety about the damaging side effects of this enthusiastic industrialization. Parts of California have still not recovered from the use of arsenic in fruit orchards in the last century. Since the publication of Rachel Carson's book, *Silent Spring*, both the agricultural industry and the academics have been paying far more attention to the results of pesticides. Now the soil experts are expressing anxiety about the effect of technology on the soil itself.

Speaking at a Berkeley seminar, an emeritus professor of soils did some arithmetic and pointed out that each man in the world is ultimately dependent on one arable acre. The chain of life, with man at the end of it, starts with this acre of soil: the mix of plants, the microbes, the actual earth. Man now, with his chemicals and pesticides, has started interfering with this natural mix. He himself may scarcely realize what he is doing, but animals, it turns out, can distinguish between "natural" and "unnatural" foods, even if man cannot. Given a choice, cattle always eat hay grown in soil with the least chemical content (rabbits and hogs are equally discriminating). Thus the alarming question is posed: if man is interfering with the bottom of his food chain, the soil itself, and if he is feeding animals on artifically treated foods even though they prefer natural foods, what is he doing to his own prospects of healthy living, at the end of the chain?

The best agriculturalists, of course, are aware of these and similar fears; and some of them try to avoid the dangers. They know now, for instance, that the leveling of land and the creation of ever bigger fields removes the natural habitat of the predators; they know that the crucial bumblebee is disappearing, as are many other insects, along with the swamps, small woods, and hedgerows. The new practice is to leave small enclaves intact when harvesting a field, so that the predators can lodge in them and move to the new crop when it has grown; the enclave, in its turn, can be cut. But the long-range effect of this practice, and other modern farming methods, is quite obscure. Why do the pilots of crop-spraying aircraft in California have so many automobile accidents? Why were so many apparently healthy young farm workers found unfit, when examined, for service in Vietnam?

Were pesticides responsible?

In California supermarkets, the piles of shining and uniform fruit and vegetables look magnificent. Yet there are complaints about quality. Do the tomatoes taste the way they used to? The food editor of the *San Francisco Chronicle* told me that the yolks of eggs from the new chicken factories always seem to break. There are fears, too, that eventually the range of fruit and vegetables available will be decided, not so much by what people want to eat, as by what the machines can best handle. Already, the fumes of one nonagricultural machine, the automobile, have driven certain crops out of the Los Angeles area: spinach was the first to go, its leaves spoiled by brown spots, and the same has happened to celery, beets, and romaine lettuce. An economist from International Harvester, Dr. L. S. Fife, says that crops which cannot be mechanized will disappear as common commodities. Even if the crops can be mechanized, they will be cultivated more and more either to be frozen or to go into cans. "The person who likes fresh vegetables and fruit," I was told at Davis, "is going to have a hard time of it."

Undoubtedly, California points the way ahead for agricultural activities elsewhere. In Europe, one of the main ideas behind the Common Market is to abolish the small peasants and turn the continent over to large-scale cultivation: to replace all the one-man, twenty-five-cow farms with three-man farms of five hundred cows. But it is important to be clear about the price to be paid for super-efficient agriculture—quite apart from ecological considerations. It would be absurd to lament the disappearance of laborers' jobs in California; there is no dignity in grading carrots or in picking grapes under a blazing sun among the pesticides. But something fundamental is at stake. For everyone, the land represents an anchor and a spiritual resource. Technology is destroying a traditional form of civilization—the man on the land—and obliterating the rural images that even the most urban man needs. In California, much of the country now possesses neither the drama of a natural wilderness nor the soothing qualities of a man-made rural landscape. Rows of lettuce, or even avocados, stretching to the horizon can be as bleak to contemplate as a stretch of empty freeway. Even the orange groves, with their shapely round trees, are threatened—where they survive—with flat butch haircuts.

HENRY ADAMS' WARNING

The opening of the west not only produced a formidable scientific drive, but also evoked the most plangent nineteenth-century prophetic utterances about the perils of science: those of Henry Adams. In the 1860s he visited the geologists who, under the supervision of his friend Clarence King, were surveying the mineral resources of the western United States. "They held under their hammers a thousand miles of mineral country with all its riddles to solve, and its stores of possible wealth to make. They felt the future in their hands," he wrote. "I tell you these are great times. Man has mounted science and is now run away with. I firmly believe that before many centuries more, science will be the master of man. The engines he will have invented will be beyond his strength to control. Some day science may have the existence of mankind in its power, and the human race commit suicide by blowing up the world."

The rumble of alarm sounded by Adams was lost among the general nineteenth-century euphoria at the progress of science and technology. It is only since World War II, and especially since science has fulfilled Adams' prophecy by having "the existence of mankind in its power"—a process greatly helped by scientists from Berkeley—that the general public has slowly realized that the basic question of what man wants to do with his remarkable powers has not been fully answered, least of all by scientists and technocrats.

Adams wrote of the new technocrats: "The work of domestic progress is done by masses of mechanical power—steam, electric, furnace, or others—which have to be controlled by a score or two of individuals who have shown capacity to manage it. The work of internal government has become the task of controlling these men, who are socially as remote as heathen gods, alone worth knowing, but never known, and who could tell nothing of political value if one skinned them alive. Most of them have nothing to tell, but are forces as dumb as their dynamos, absorbed in the development or economy of power." [8]

One important reason for California's technological leadership is that the climate helps to attract the best people to work there. The trouble is that the climate is so good that it takes a strong-minded person to think seriously outside his office about the purpose of the work he does inside it, or to reflect on anything much beyond surfing or tennis or the golden California girls. Even at Berkeley, the premier intellectual institution of the state, visiting professors have been known to complain that the faculty spends too little time working, too much time gardening, and often sneaks off early on long weekends.

California is a great producer and consumer of science and technology, but expends comparatively little energy, even now that the crisis caused by these twins is plain, in thinking systematically about their effects.[9] Yet technology is now the main agent of change and the principal arbiter of the social order. It has indubitably brought benefits to California, as we have seen; but it has also disrupted a society that was already rootless. It is undermining one of man's traditional ways of living: in the country, on the soil. It is changing dramatically his social life: the life of the family, man's relations with his neighbors. And, having made possible the growth of big cities, through the provision of cheap energy, it is now profoundly affecting the way man lives in cities, as we shall see in detail in the next chapter.

CHAPTER 4

The End of the City

> I am convinced that, after the fundamental question of preserving peace, it is the form and organization of urban areas that is now looming up as the greatest social challenge for the world for the rest of this century.
>
> *Colin Buchanan, Professor of Transport,*
> *Imperial College, London*

BECAUSE Southern California is so loosely organized, so spacious, so affluent, and so unplanned, it is the one place in the world where it is possible to see how the mass of people, given the chance to decide for themselves, really want to live. Largely because of modern technology, the majority of them seem to have concluded that they do not want to live in cities. They are, so to speak, voting with their wheels. Elsewhere, especially in the United States, town planners are struggling to adapt traditional cities to modern pressures: trying to work out how to fit everyone in, whether to build high or low, how to fend off the private cars and improve public transportation, how to pump new life into decaying city cores. In southern California, the plans and the planners, as well as traditional cities, scarcely exist. Jane Jacobs, the diagnostician of urban diseases, has said that either the car will destroy the city, or the city will have to fight back and defeat the car. In southern California, the car was declared the victor before the city climbed into the ring. Los Angeles is the first giant city to have grown up since the invention of the car; and the car has turned it into a metropolis of an entirely new kind. Other cities have ways of warning a visitor that he is approaching: railway lines, bigger road signs, fingers of housing pushing out into the surrounding country, a factory in a field. But you can find yourself in Los Angeles scarcely knowing whether you have arrived or not: traveling south on the main freeway from San Francisco, the Los Angeles city-limits sign appears, without warning, when the road slices between two ragged brown hills. Even in the central city, there are few landmarks by which even residents can get their bearings, apart from the hump of Beverly Hills and the forlorn huddle of larger buildings known as "downtown Los Angeles."

The heart of Los Angeles is simply a vast expanse of low buildings, gas stations, and parking lots, strewn across a huge saucer edged by what the poet Karl Shapiro called "dry purple mountains." There is no concentrated business district, no special residential area; even Hollywood does not exist. The famous gibe about Los Angeles being a series of suburbs in search of a city is no longer accurate; the search, half-hearted even twenty years ago, has been abandoned. The suburbs do not press inward to the city center, wherever that may be, but outward into the empty spaces, up into the mountains, down the coast to San Diego, further and further into the San Fernando Valley. Without the freeway signs, few people would be able to find their way around Los Angeles at all. Seen from the air, the freeways clamp down over the houses, as a British conservationist has written, "like a Crown-of-Thorns starfish devouring the living thin layer of coral on a tropical reef." When Los Angelenos are not on the move—unless they are very rich, resident in Brentwood or Bel Air, or very poor, for instance in Watts—they mostly live hemmed into the interstices between the rivers of concrete, as dependent on cars as Venetians upon *vaporettos*.

Few Los Angelenos object to the dominance of the automobile. One way to reduce its power would be to build a public-transportation system; but only the old, the poor, and the crippled do not

own cars; of the rest, only a minority think that public transportation would make Los Angeles more civilized.[1] A particularly detailed proposal for such a system was decisively defeated in a
referendum in November, 1968—despite a propaganda campaign
with pamphlets showing drawings of relaxed, happy newspaper-
reading Los Angelenos being whisked about the smogless city in
stainless-steel tubes. In other cities of the Western world, it is
sometimes hoped that the day will come when the ordinary mo-
torist will revolt against the automobile, and sacrifice some of the
freedom it gives him in order to launch a counterattack on its
effects—on the noise, the pollution, and the relentless voracity
with which it consumes space for parking lots and gas stations.
Some Europeans, watching what is happening to Rome, for instance, where the cars jamming the Via del Corso drown even
Italian sidewalk conversation, say hopefully that Europeans are
still in the adolescent stage of car-worship. This stage will gradually give way to the stage of automobile maturity, when they realize that the car is merely a means of transportation. Judging by
Los Angeles, where the car has been a commonplace much longer
than it has been in Europe, that day is a long way off. Californians may *drive* with a relaxed lack of competitiveness that is still
unusual in Europe, but that is as much because Californians take
the car for granted as because of the strict and efficient highway
patrols. But the car in California remains an important social
asset: as one rich young Los Angeleno said, "You can spend an
extra $200,000 on a house, and where does it show? But spend
$15,000 on a B.M.W. and every head turns to look!" Still more
important, the car in Los Angeles is the essential passport to a
mode of living in which the city, as traditionally conceived, has
little, if any, place: it is the main technological item that is making the city out of date and prefiguring the end of the city altogether. Who wants cities? The answer is, in the one place where
people are free to choose: practically nobody.

True, a small group of rich people in Los Angeles has lately
tried to impose a more metropolitan flavor on what some of them
privately regard as a hick town. Mrs. Chandler, the dominating

spirit of the powerful *Los Angeles Times* empire—a lady and an institution that few Los Angelenos would wish to affront—has in the past few years put both her own social influence and the power of her newspaper behind an attempt to construct a species of cultural heart for the city.

But if you peer into this nucleus you can see how feeble the forces of urbanity really are. There stand Mrs. Chandler's Music Center and the Ahmanson Theater, a shade flashy for some tastes, even in Los Angeles, but both plainly metropolitan artifacts, with appropriate standards of music and drama. Nearby are the new Bunker Hill Towers, expensive high-rise apartments. Some locals anticipate that these apartments will in time prove to be the greatest white elephant in the history of Los Angeles, precisely because, apart from proximity to the Music Center and City Hall, they offer no geographical advantage of any kind; and they are no competition for apartments elsewhere, which are not only cheaper but have pools, shrubs, and patios. Nor is it easy to see any social (in the broad sense) advantage in living downtown; the street life around the Music Center after dark is no livelier than it is in the outermost suburbs. In other urban centers, where the automobile is less taken for granted, or where the streets are habitually jammed by traffic, there might be advantages in being within walking distance of the equivalent of City Hall, the *Los Angeles Times,* and the Music Center. But the inhabitants of Bunker Hill Towers would no more think of going on foot to City Hall, despite its proximity, than of walking to San Diego; and once in the car, you might as well drive ten miles in fifteen minutes as half a mile in five. So the argument of convenience for downtown living is not strong. Meanwhile, half a mile from the Music Center (a very short distance, in Los Angeles), poor blacks are moving into some fine houses—as fine as the eighteenth-century houses of Georgetown in Washington, D.C., or the brownstones of Philadelphia—that have been abandoned by whites. If there is any part of Los Angeles that one might expect to be exerting general urban pull, it is this area; but in fact it is attracting only a handful of rich business people and blacks—two minority groups who do not communicate with each other, and who have no real reason to be where they are rather than anywhere else.

The need for a city in California is, quite simply, disappearing. Historically, cities met a need for protection, for a power center, for social life and entertainment, and for trade. Most American cities, if they do not supply all these needs, still supply at least some of them. Los Angeles does not. A selling point emphasized by salesmen of new housing developments is that these provide better protection against vandals and rioters than the city itself. So they do. Nor does living in Los Angeles have any relevance to the exercise of political power. Governor Reagan's kitchen cabinet of Los Angeles businessmen can be in touch with him as effectively from Palm Springs—by telephone, or, if necessary, by private plane—as from Wilshire Boulevard. Anyone who seeks a private word with Mayor Yorty would be wiser to take him off for a weekend cruise than hang about his outer office. The power circles in California are as dispersed as every other circle. As for social life and entertainment, Los Angeles is one of the few cities in the world where, because of the automobile, social life no longer centers on the neighborhood.

People move to southern California—surveys invariably show —partly for the climate, partly to take part in the prosperity of the state, and partly to be successful. When they get there, they find that southern California does not have a recognized hierarchy of success; there is no social ladder to climb. In San Francisco, you can still make a name in the neighborhood by being on the school board, or by running for office, or by being a success in business. Even a journalist can achieve social recognition. Herb Caen, the columnist, proves it. In Los Angeles, few people know anybody who is not on television; even Mrs. Chandler is not a name to conjure with in the bowling centers of the San Fernando Valley. For most new arrivals the only means of demonstrating— both to the folks back home and to themselves—that the move to California was a wise decision is by buying as expensive a house as they can afford, a visible proof of success, and by taking advantage of the great outdoors. For all these purposes—personal safety, good housing, fresh air, and often, even for a well-paid job —residence in the city is no advantage. Indeed, the closer you live to the geographical center of Los Angeles, the harder these aims may be to achieve.

What is true of individuals is becoming true of firms: the city is losing its point for them, too.[2] After the Watts riots, whites learned with surprise that part of their city was visibly decaying, breeding unemployment and violence; so they decided that Watts must be renewed, above all by introducing some enlivening industry. But businessmen now seem inclined to think that there may not be much point in the idea after all. Thomas Paine, who was a general manager for General Electric in the peaceful town of Santa Barbara before he became deputy administrator of NASA, said recently: "We should make reasonable efforts to improve things in the ghetto, but fundamentally we are dealing with an obsolete urban area—the streets, sewers, transportation. To bring a modern factory into that and expect it to compete with a factory out on the crossroads of a couple of superhighways is pretty unrealistic. The alternative would be to move people out to the suburban part of the city, where there are some clean houses near some factories that offer job opportunities after we give them some training. I don't expect this to happen overnight, but it *is* happening. It *is* going to happen, and in our long-range planning it seems to me that speeding it up is a sound direction to go. Let's make the exits bigger and the aisles wider. We should look at the city, and state, as a geographic social system which will encourage people to do what they want to do. There are institutions that have become, and institutions that are becoming. Cities are inherently the second. They never should be finished. Americans are criticized by Europeans as being in a throwaway society. We should be criticized; but only because we build too permanently. We should make things with fairly short useful lives so we can rearrange our structures to meet the needs of living people. Our big office buildings are artifacts of the paper-and-typewriter society, and already we see the writing on the wall in the magnetic blips of microwave communication that will put these buildings out of date." The evidence from all over the United States is that the modern city cannot be made to work; the evidence from California is still more dramatic: that the city has lost its point.

WHAT DO PEOPLE REALLY WANT?

Given the chance, people want to live in houses with plenty of space, and they are ready to abandon the city to get them. This is a trait especially noticed by Americans from eastern cities who move to the west coast. One reporter from an eastern paper was amazed, after moving to the *Los Angeles Times,* to discover that whereas her colleagues on the New York paper almost all lived in apartments in Brooklyn, in Los Angeles they all lived in houses, many of them a long way from the *Times* office.

"Space is very, very important to everyone, I find," the girl told me. "They are not interested in urban living. It is hard for them to conceive of someone who likes there to be people on the streets at eight o'clock at night. I unconsciously sought out an area where that happens, but for the same money I pay for an apartment, my colleagues rent a house out in Hacienda Heights. Even the apartments here are not apartments at all in the eastern sense. In west Los Angeles there are these streets, like Barrington Avenue, of garden apartments, two stories at the most, very shrubby, with balconies and lawns and a pool, so that even life in an apartment isn't urban living as I understand it. Eventually Los Angeles may have to become a city like the others, but I don't know anyone who wants it. One reason many people seek space is for their children. Parents think it is almost immoral to live in a place where the kids can't play the stereo as loud as they want, or where they don't have a private pool."

So the citizens move further and further out, seeking space, and business encourages the centrifugal migration. Aerospace plants are moving into San Bernardino, seventy miles east of central Los Angeles, and the employees are perfectly content to go with the plant, and to have their place of living determined by their place of work, because they know that the suburban environment in which they have lived hitherto will be reproduced wherever the plants are built. They will not object to having to move further away from the city, because they rarely use the city. The *Times*, at least, is certain that the spread will continue: they have an Orange County edition, and a huge plant in Costa Mesa.

In other cities, one characteristic of urban life that might counter this spread, drawing people to the center, is entertainment; but a Los Angeles youth can find the same pleasures in Anaheim as in the city itself. The satellite suburbs of Los Angeles are rich enough to construct their own entertainment centers, so that life can be just as much (or as little) cosmopolitan in one part of the "urban area" as in any other.

THE NEW CITIES

Whole new communities in California are being planned, built, and sold by private entrepreneurs on the proposition that escape from the anxieties of the times is both desirable and possible. The American dream may have gone sour in the old style of city, but it can be recaptured in the new, where people with enough cash for the down payment on a house can buy shelter from the changes that have spoiled life elsewhere. The trend of the times seems to be that people have tried out cities, don't like them, and now want to retreat to a new kind of one-class supervillage. Two advertisements, typical of many, illustrate the trend:

> BEING CREATED NOW: ORANGE
> COUNTY'S ONLY TOWN
> WITH WATER AND WOODS
>
> Lake Forest will be different. A place where your children will grow up remembering happy hours, sailing, swimming, hiking. Here, life will

be easy. You'll know your neighbors by first names. You'll walk down to the Village Center, with its quaint shops, a restaurant, bank, supermarket, and offices. Your home in the Village will be close to your own private recreation center . . . the Lake Forest Swim and Racquet Club . . . where you'll swim, play tennis, meet friends, or set sail on a sparkling lake from the docks of your own private marina. You'll enjoy an afternoon stroll through a tall, green forest. And your children will walk to their own new school. Lake Forest . . . "the little town with water and woods" . . . the only town of its kind in Orange County. Come today, and be counted among the first families of Lake Forest.

THE CITY THAT NEVER LETS THE COUNTRY OUT OF ITS SIGHT: WESTLAKE

Twenty years ago, if you had wandered about this big and gentle valley, you'd have seen it dotted with great, gnarled live oaks, patriarchs of their kind. Whispering streamlets meandering their bright and aimless way through wide-stretched meadows. Grazing horses. Softly rolling hillocks and grassy landswells. All of it held in a protective ring of giant hills, under a sky so fresh and clear you could almost see the other side of the universe.

You can still see it, exactly the same, today. None of it has changed. Only now, Westlake is here. A new kind of city. A different kind of city. What makes it different is that this city didn't push the country out of the picture. This city moved in carefully, so it wouldn't disturb the centuries-old beauty of the area.

The country around Westlake justifies the advertisement's boast: wide-screen California at its best. The "city" occupies eighteen square miles, with winding roads, neat groups of spruce and comfortable houses, and, in the middle, a man-made lake of 150 acres—the crucial part of the plan. Each neighborhood is sharply distinguished from the next: the Island Homes (with a bridge to the mainland and a twenty-four-hour security guard) which sell for $53,000 to $73,000; the Foxmoor Homes, already equipped with carpets and lawn sprinklers; the Westlake Trails Estates, grouped near riding stables ("for people who don't want to kick the habit"). There is a golf course, floodlit at night, a motel, a neighborhood shopping center, putting greens, the most discreet gas station in California, and, on the fringes, carefully landscaped light-industry factories and a cemetery (Memorial Park), which sold off lots at specially reduced rates to early buyers. The developers of Westlake have taken great care with details, and the place possesses a manicured look far removed from the bleak and raw appearance of most new housing developments: some of the oak trees have been transplanted to strategic sites, a landscape architect has constructed small artificial islands in the lake, all telephone and power wires are buried underground, and television aerials are concealed. The houses are close together, yet do not overlook one another. Inside, each home seems like a *House and Garden* feature come true: gleaming kitchens with views to the mountains, picture windows, double garages, marble coffee tables, and manly family rooms with dart boards and colorful prints of the gun that won the west. Westlake has been so successfully geared to what people want, that on selling days eager buyers lined up outside the sales office long before it opened and, while waiting, were fed coffee and sandwiches by the staff.

None of this happened by chance; and the calculation behind it was explained to me by Mr. John L. Notter, the friendly, quick-witted, thirty-seven-year-old president of the American-Hawaiian Land Company that developed Westlake. The idea of buying this stretch of country, which had previously been a ranch, was the idea, he told me, of his boss, one of the richest men in the world, Daniel K. Ludwig, who owns more ships than Onassis and Niarchos combined and is head of the American-Hawaiian Steamship Company, of which Notter's company is a subsidiary. Ludwig, said Notter, has been diversifying more and more, espe-

cially into real estate, and believes the Westlake kind of development to be the wave of the future. He bought the land, told Notter his general idea, and left him to produce the master plan.
Notter was president of a savings and loan business at the age of
twenty-five, specializing in single-family construction loans, so he
had intimate knowledge, he explained, of how people really
wanted to live.

"People want a house to be good-looking: something to be
proud of and to show their friends," Notter said. "Inside, they
want it to be contemporary and pleasing, and they are ready to
pay as much as, if not a little more than, they can afford. You'll
notice that Westlake has no modern houses at all, because few
people want them. That's where Reston [a new town near Washington, D.C., which was planned with great imagination by Bob
Simon, but which was finally taken over by an oil company]
made a major error: trying to sell modern houses. My experience
is that if you're trying to sell a group of houses, one of which is
modern, the modern house is either the first or last to go; and if
it's the last to go, you end up lowering the price and having a lot
of trouble getting rid of it. We decided to build Westlake in as
traditional a manner as possible: lots of wood, brick, and plaster
—materials people can relate to memories of their childhood.
You'll notice that we have a number of Spanish traditional houses
—a Californian version of Spanish houses, that is. Of course, they
aren't really Spanish; in fact in Spain you don't find houses like
that at all. We put Spanish-type tiles on the houses: a very practical product, which helps to keep the houses cool. They cost a little
more than other roofing, but they are worth it.

"The lake idea is *very* important. A lot of new housing developments *claim* to have a lake, but only of 20 or 30 acres, if it's
there at all, and not in the least like this one—150 acres, landscaped, and one you can really go boating on. Especially in southern California, which is very dry, and especially in this part of the
San Fernando Valley, the value of water is indescribable; it makes
a great appeal to the imagination. For one thing, it allows people
to place themselves: they can describe their house as being, say, a

mile north of the lake. We were selling houses back in 1966, and the basic reason was the lake, though at that time it wasn't even there. Some of these developments *claim* they are going to have a big lake, but when the place gets built the lake has shriveled away to the size of a bath.

"We have avoided anything that looks like Los Angeles. For instance, you notice that the used-car lots on the edge of our city don't have the usual strings of flags and signs round them. This was a very major point with us, and it held up development of the automotive area for a year while we argued, until we finally won our point. We did the same with Standard Oil over the gas station, which has a tiled roof, no big signs, and doesn't look at all like the usual gas station. Standard Oil wanted a sign thirty-five feet high so that it could be seen from the freeway, but we fought them and eventually had our way. Most development companies couldn't afford to wait that long or to be that tough; but they haven't got the finance behind them that we have.

"Why aren't the gardens larger? People don't want gardens. The property taxes are so high that a garden becomes extremely expensive, and besides, people don't want the labor of keeping them up. As well, land is so expensive in California that it amounts to thirty percent of the total cost of the house, and sometimes thirty-five percent, so larger gardens would mean higher prices, which would make the houses that much more difficult to sell.

"Of course, Westlake is not really a city. Personally, I like the cosmopolitan urban style of living, but it simply isn't available in Los Angeles, including downtown. Unlike New York, say, we simply don't have a megalopolis where people live and work in the same groups of buildings and create a cosmopolitan urban atmosphere. A lot of people would probably like that kind of living, but a lot more would not, especially people with families. They prefer suburban living. What we have done at Westlake, because people have a lot of time on their hands, is to create as many recreational facilities as possible: riding, golf, tennis, swimming, boating. If you live in a city you have other ways of

spending your time: window-shopping, restaurants, night clubs, and the rest. There are other ways in which Westlake is not a city: we don't cater to the unmarried, and we don't have older folks.

"There's no question about it that people are attracted to West-lake, too, because it is a long way from any ghetto or riot areas. It's not that they don't want to live near minorities, but they do want to be well away from any violence. This is unquestionably a major selling point, though we never mention it. The people who come to Westlake sometimes say they want to be free from the idea that crowds of people might come running down the street breaking windows. That fear is a very very important factor in our society. We have absolutely no bar on Negroes coming to Westlake, of course, but we probably don't cater to that kind of market."

As Notter had said, Westlake has no old people, no modern ar-chitecture, and no Negroes. Besides, it has no poor, no billboards, no overhead wires, no television aerials, no works of art, no bars, no poolrooms, no weeds, no city center, no annoyances (no power boats on the lake, for instance), no vulgarity, no visible sex (un-less one counted the waitresses showing their pants in the West-lake Inn overlooking the golf course), no flashy nighttime scene. Both the developers and the inhabitants are evidently striving to create a form of community life—nearer to a daydream of village life in Europe than to city life in the United States—from which any source of unpleasantness has been so far as possible removed. In the Memorial Park, the white lifesize statue of Christ imported from Italy looks as unfamiliar with suffering as if he, too, were a satisfied Westlake homeowner. Undoubtedly, as the sales prove, Westlake is what people want. It is a gathering of like-minded people of similar incomes who are all seeking the same "way of life," revolving around the family, the home, and (what everyone mentioned) "the water." The pressure to conform must be very strong. The developers have provided everything: they have even decided the layout inside the houses (the master bedroom, the children's bedroom, the television table). Any deviation from the norm, indoors or out, would show. It struck me that the people of Westlake did not any longer want their ambience to be interesting or stimulating: they wanted it perfect: a safe and beautiful rest home, cut off from the pain of the world, for healthy people.

MOBILE HOMES

Not long ago, a California magazine published a feature about a Los Angeles family that resided permanently in their car. Every day the father would drive off to work, cast adrift the trailer containing his wife and children near a school, and collect them in the evening to take them home to the parking lot. The report was a joke; but only just. Nobody would be very surprised if such a freeway family existed. Already the mobile home and the "mobile village" are established and growing features of California life: a brand-new mode of existence stimulated by dislike and fear of cities. This trend was made possible by roads wide enough to take a mobile home and by a social structure in which people can afford a car plus trailer yet have too few roots to care where they settle —or whether they settle at all.

These mobile-home villages can be quite pretentious, with golf courses and community centers and twenty-four-hour security patrols. They sound, in advertisements, like the very place to pursue the California dream "among streams and pure mountain air." Many of them, however, are stuck loosely onto the edge of small towns, in limbo.

I visited one of these trailer villages at Woodland, not far from Sacramento. It was set in a flat, scrubland landscape beside a main road, opposite a railway yard. Some forty huge trailers—each one cream or pale tan or gray, each with its attendant car—were moored in three rows on asphalt. A large notice beside a miniature swimming pool read: "No lifeguard on duty today"; a girl wearing a bikini lolled on the edge of the pool, watching the traffic on the main road. Some of the trailers were forty-five feet long and many of them were growing TV aerials and white picket fences, doormats and telephone wires, slowly becoming less mobile, like stranded hulks that would never again put to sea. One of them, with *Crusader* painted on the side in Gothic letters, had two window boxes of pink geraniums; the lower part of the trailer had been boarded in, camouflaging the wheels and making it look like a small house, four windows along each side, one window at each end. It belonged, a notice read, to L. Hertel. Number 16 belonged to the Globkes: pale green. The next was *Flamingo*, a brighter green, with "The John Coffmans" carefully written on a triangular stone. Care had been taken: an oval concrete doormat had been placed at the foot of a short flight of steps that led up to a glass door halfway along the trailer; a china cat, a china boy, and a china rabbit looked out of the end window. Nearby, *Champion* was silver and pink. There were signs of life: a dark girl put away a hose; an old man wearing an undershirt dragged a mower out of a shed; a new trailer drove in, and a young man opened it and extracted a woman and child; from Aloha, Beaverton, Oregon. On the edge of the village there was a wire fence, a washing line, and an incinerator: "No garbage cans or bottles in this incinerator. Papers only." Beyond the wire lay a deserted fairground.

The owner's wife, Mrs. Flora, a buoyant gray-haired lady wearing flowered overalls, told me that the two outside rows of her park were for the "permanents," some of whom had been there since the park started fifteen years ago; the central row was for "overnighters." The trailers they built nowadays, she told me, were amazing: "You wouldn't believe what's in them: they are all self-contained, which means they've got lavatories, and inside it's like a little ship: little washbasins, television sets, dishwashers." Her own trailer was ten feet wide and fifty-five feet long, but the new trailers were twelve feet wide or, when expanded, twenty-four feet wide. Her trailer was, she assured me, a genuine mobile home; it could be packed up and got on the road in two days thanks to a mechanism whereby one complete room slid into the rest of the trailer like a concertina, leaving all the furniture still in place. Inside, her trailer appeared little different from any small, compact open-plan house, with fitted carpets, wood-paneled walls, pictures, a desk, and, in the kitchen, an eye-level grill. To one side, the trailer had a sunroom, with mesh windows in position to keep out the insects. Like the other homes, Mrs. Flora told me, her trailer was fully air-conditioned.

She and her husband had bought the park, which she sometimes referred to as a "mobile-home park," three years earlier, and very expensive it had been: $3000 per space. They owned space for forty-seven trailers in all; for the outside, or permanent, spaces, they charged $36 a month, exclusive of utilities such as electricity and telephone rentals, and $2.25 a night for the center spaces. Most of their tenants worked in Sacramento as nurses, schoolteachers, or small businessmen. Counting twelve children, the total population was well over one hundred. They gave little trouble, Mrs. Flora told me: "We have it in the agreement that we can move out people at thirty-days notice if we don't want them. We've only had to evict three people in our time. We had two girls here under false pretenses: one of them with an illegitimate child and the other one pregnant. We knew what was going on, so we asked them to leave; they went without causing any trouble."

Why, I asked, were people moving more and more into trailer homes? "A lot of the reason is that property taxes are so high," she replied. "On an average home of $25,000 to $30,000 you might pay $250 or $300: terrible, just ridiculous. But the taxes on a mobile home are practically nil." Another reason was the violence: "California should be such a good place to live in. But the violence—it's not only universal, it's worldwide. The kids are out of control—they've all got automobiles, and the drug-taking is terrible. I hear them in the fairground next door at two or three in the morning." With a mobile home, you could be up and away if the neighborhood became too rough; in any case, Mrs. Flora added emphatically, people nowadays liked to be mobile.

Some days after my visit to Mrs. Flora, I toured some new and especially magnificent mobile homes on sale in Orange County.

One of them was entirely ready to move into the moment the customer put down his deposit: carpets, furniture, pictures on the walls, and even, in the vases, fresh-cut flowers. Californians nowadays seem ready to buy a home that has been wholly furnished by someone else. At Westlake, I had heard of a lady in Woodland Hills nearby who had bought a house twelve years earlier and was now going to buy a new one fully equipped, rather than go to the trouble of replacing the carpets, dishwasher, and furnishings. Her former house, she said, was "worn out."

LIFE IN THE NEW SUBURBS

Mobile home parks and the new villages or "cities" like Westlake are the most novel domestic developments in southern California; but it is to the sprawling new suburbs, neither town nor country, that most people are moving. Like water finding its own level, Los Angeles is creeping down the coast toward San Diego, spreading through the San Fernando Valley and flowing on to the plateau below Hot Springs. There is little attempt to control the flood. One of the few places subject to coherent planning is the colossal Irvine Ranch, which survived as countryside longer than other land near Los Angeles because it was owned by a single family; it is now being turned into another satellite campus of the University of California. In an attempt to keep it rural, a strip beside the freeway that bisects the ranch is, in theory, to be kept free of development for thirty years; but as the editor of the *Los Angeles Times* remarked to me, "There won't be many orange groves still there in thirty years. How can you afford to raise citrus when values have risen so much that the citrus land is worth $1400 an acre?"

Out in the San Fernando Valley, life to a visitor seems strangely cut off. The people in their neat homes are often aerospace employees, with the accents of the midwest and the south; and they are often profoundly conservative. There is evidently something about involvement in technology that produces, not, as one might expect, elation about the future, but deep fears and suspicions, especially among technicians of the lower and middle ranks. Perhaps the reason for these anxieties is that the technicians have often made the grade entirely by their own efforts; they feel they possess only one skill, which at any moment may be devalued either by younger challengers or by an unpredictable change in government policy—a canceled appropriation in Washington that closes an aerospace plant in California—or by some new development in the technology itself. Senator Goldwater's son, who is more conservative than the senator himself, won a congressional seat in the valley precisely because of such people. They have very weak party loyalties, as studies of their voting behavior have shown, and will as soon vote Democratic as Republican. But they always vote as far right as possible. "We have so many Birch societies," a plaintive valley girl told me. "A lot of our neighbors are lower-middle class aerospace workers who have moved here from the south; conservative people who know they will have jobs provided only that things remain the same. People here are terrified: who knows of what? They are even frightened by the adoption of Negro children. A minister adopted one; he got anonymous telephone calls, and his children had rocks thrown at them on their way home from school."

In these valley communities, almost everyone is striving to lead as regular, stable, and line-holding a life as possible, to build private family fortresses that nothing will disturb. There is little community life: as one citizen of Granada Hills put it: "we are really just a·child-rearing community." Granada Hills, like most other Los Angeles suburbs, is little more than the name of a postoffice district and a name on the local Chamber of Commerce; it is hard to tell where the place begins or ends. Fifteen years ago or so, it was orange groves; and it has grown too fast for community sentiment to grow with it. "We have little sense of a neighborhood. People really don't have anything to belong to: there are the churches, and that's it."

In such communities, people are nervous of strangers. Outside San Francisco there is a suburb called Moraga—neat and new among low hills, middle-class, horses in the fields behind the houses, two cars in most garages. Into Moraga moved a man and his wife and their two children; he was Austrian-born and his wife was Australian, a trained social worker and the daughter of a clergyman. The man had been appointed to Berkeley as a visiting professor in the department of industrial relations. Before moving to Moraga, the family had been in Chile, where the man had worked on development for the UN. In Moraga, they found themselves being treated as social outcasts; their way of life was different. Unlike the other residents, they did not have a mailbox for the conservative local paper, the *Oakland Tribune*. They did not turn on their sprinklers every evening. Their car was not American, and they rarely washed it. They did not go to church on Sundays. The man habitually worked late; lights in the house were often on until two or three A.M. His wife, a strong character, had a few low-key (to her) arguments with other mothers about teaching methods at the local school.

When their lease ran out, the owner of the house sued them, on the ground that they had not looked after it properly. The man and his wife were astonished. The case went before a judge, and in court, neighbor after neighbor came forward and told lies in support of the owner. Yes, they had seen the house before and after the lease, and it had been spoiled. Yes, the children were quite unruly, always climbing in and out of the windows; the wife was a slattern, who had taken no trouble to keep the place up. The professor and his wife could scarcely believe the things they heard their former neighbors saying about them; and they lost the case. They felt as though they had been subjected to a kind of nonviolent lynching, run out of town because they marched to a (slightly) different drummer.

The life-style developing in such places as Moraga and the San Fernando Valley is characteristic of the whole trend of Californian life. It is very different from the life-style of a traditional city, or indeed of a traditional village.

The old city or village was socially comprehensive, including every class, and it was various, including every human type. The new Californian "urban areas" are socially exclusive, self-selected by income and taste, and spiritually uniform. An academic study shows what is happening. No less than three in five of all "housing units" in the metropolitan areas of California were built between 1940 and 1960; and new housing developments have the following characteristics:

1. Very few blacks, Mexicans, Japanese, or Chinese.
2. Very few older people.
3. High percentage of people under twenty.
4. Large average size of households.
5. Relatively few women in jobs.
6. Few poor or uneducated.
7. Very high percentage of single-family, owner-occupier residences.
8. Strikingly high auto availability.[3]

Historically, cities have been the breeding grounds of tolerance and liberty. It is no accident that the most traditional city in the west, San Francisco, has also been the west's principal source of radicalism and tolerance. By comparison, the new settlements—overwhelmingly white, middle-class, family-centered—are cut-off, fearful, and anxious about outsiders. The alternative to cities, in other words, turns out not to encourage the old civic virtues.

WHITTIER AND THE NIXONS

One small part of the vast Los Angeles sprawl that retains a distinct identity of its own is the place where Nixon grew up, the Quaker settlement of Whittier. On the perimeter, Whittier is the same as most of the rest of Los Angeles: straight roads, street signs, autopia. But the sprawl has been halted on Whittier's outskirts. The town was founded some eighty years ago by migrant New England Quakers who named it after John Greenleaf Whittier, the Quaker poet. They chose a site on low hills, with a distant glimpse of the Pacific, and the Quaker character survives: quiet and shady side streets with substantial houses, a university that "seeks to train men and women for Christian leadership," and, on the main street, opposite the principal Quaker church, the roomy, old-fashioned William Penn Hotel, where no liquor is served, and elderly ladies meet in the foyer during the long hot afternoons. Whittier even knows the size of its population—72,800 —and most of them go to church on Sundays. During World War II, it was one of the few California communities that felt confident enough to treat its Japanese citizens humanely; elsewhere they were herded into camps and, in many cases, financially ruined. Viewed from Whittier, the rest of Los Angeles seems gimcrack—with Whittier left behind slightly in another age, square and intensely respectable. Whittier College, a private institution, seems worlds away from, for instance, Berkeley or even the Santa Barbara campus: scarcely a long-haired student in sight, and the student body clean, large, and healthy. I asked one strapping girl carrying a tennis racket whether the students had ever rioted at Whittier. She looked startled: "Oh, no!" she said. "If they did, I'd run to my dormitory." The whole campus, with its trees and air of youthful high spirits, reminded me of one of the prewar Mickey Rooney pictures, all ready for the big graduation day of mortarboards and proud parents. It seems scarcely to have changed since Richard Nixon, born in Yorba Linda of a specially devout Quaker mother and a somewhat erratic father, was writing songs for the football team and enjoying a reputation as a big man on campus, admired for his eloquence in college debates. When Nixon graduated, Professor Upton (who is still at Whittier) wrote him this testimonial: "During the four years in which I have observed his rather prominent career at Whittier College he has displayed a rich sense of humor, human understanding, personal eloquence, and a marked ability to lead. He is intellectually honest, modest, and youthfully enthusiastic. If he has any handicap, it is his lack of sophistication." The testimonial, preserved in the Whittier library, is worth quoting because it neatly points to a striking difference between the older California and the new.

Nixon has always puzzled observers by being so unlike the common stereotype of Californians, having a distinctly sober attitude to life, no interest in the great outdoors, and nothing in him of the freewheeling, experimental side of California. Nixon has certainly employed, and still employs, the flashier type of Californian (such as Murray Chotiner, his former political manager and hatchet man) to help him on his political way. But the values of Whittier have survived in Nixon. He is a natural square, still doggedly poring over his briefs; and the source of his appeal to all those other "silent" Americans is his wish that the United States could recapture the values of Whittier, where the boys present their dates with camellias, and the big man on campus has scarcely heard of the S.D.S.

The local newspaper editor described Whittier to me as a place where "people are extremely interested in creating a community. Everyone works so hard to create a nice place to live. It's a lovely, lovely community." The Chamber of Commerce spokesman said: "Financially, it is very, very sound, partly due to the Quaker influence. We're different from most of the rest of Los Angeles: in the hills and away from the rat race, a stable, quiet community, with our prosperity based on the service industries and retail trades, not on the more modern kinds of wealth like aerospace and electronics."

However, the new life approaches. Nixon's father's store—the president, exaggerating his childhood poverty, likes to describe how he helped in the store: he keeps quiet about the fact that he got to Whittier on a scholarship endowed by his mother's family —has been torn down and replaced by a gas station, across the street from the Thrifty Mart. Still more ominous, in the hills at the back of Whittier College they are prospecting for oil. As a surviving enclave of traditional city living, even Whittier seems doomed.

CHAPTER 5

The Crisis of Values

> Armed with all the powers, enjoying all the
> wealth they owe to science, our societies are still
> trying to practice and to teach systems of values
> already destroyed at the roots by that very science.
>
> *Nobel Prizewinner Jacques Monod*

THE impact of technology on California is causing a fundamental and rapid change not only in cities but in almost all the conditions of life. While the state has been accumulating wealth and industries of the future, it has at the same time become deeply split. California's San Andreas earthquake fault is well known, but there has recently developed a kind of *social* San Andreas fault. Like the seismologists who sit on mountaintops monitoring the earth tremors, so now sociologists study the social rumblings and plot the outbreaks of student violence, the drug-taking, the acts of violence against (or by) the police, the race riots, and the rest. Everyone by now has his favorite list of reasons for the troubles, but though there is general agreement about the gravity of the phenomenon, there is none about the causes, and still less about the cure.

One preliminary point that can be confidently made about the crisis is that it plainly involves an assault on "old values" by people who are motivated by different or "new values."

But what exactly *is* the old life-style that is being disturbed and undermined? The whole subject is by now so confused, so buried under layers of analysis and prejudice, that it is hard to get it into perspective. Old and new clash nowadays in many ways: on the streets, in the ghettos, on the campus, inside nice homes at Pebble Beach, where the parents graciously entertain guests on the lawn while their children smoke pot in the pool. But the deepest conflicts in American life are often revealed most clearly in the courts, as a poultice brings a boil to a head. The case of Mark Painter, which concerned the fate of a small Californian boy, came before the Iowa Supreme Court in 1966, but it is still a classic illustration of the contrast between two ways of life, and illuminates the Californian scene like a flash of lightning.

Mark Painter was nearly five years old when his mother and little sister were killed in a car crash, in December, 1962. After other arrangements for the boy's care had proved unsatisfactory, his father, Harold Painter, a Californian, asked his wife's mother and father, a Mr. and Mrs. Bannister, to take care of Mark. In July, 1963, the Bannisters traveled to California and took Mark back to their farm in Iowa. Then in November, 1964, Mr. Painter remarried; at about that time, he indicated to the Bannisters that he wanted Mark back. The Bannisters refused, and legal proceedings began. Eventually, in 1966, the case reached the Iowa Supreme Court.

In handing down its decision, the court first reviewed Harold Painter's upbringing and attitudes to life. Painter was born in California. When he was two and a half his parents were divorced and he was placed in a foster home. Although he kept in touch with his parents, he considered his foster parents to be his family. He flunked out of high school and then out of a trade school—from lack of interest rather than lack of ability. He joined the navy at seventeen and did not like it. After getting an honorable discharge, he went to college under the G.I. Bill for two and a half years. Then he quit college. He worked on a newspaper in the state of Washington, then on another paper in Alaska, where he met his first wife. The marriage, everyone agreed, was happy.

In its judgment, the Iowa Supreme Court said it was "obvious that the Bannisters did not approve of their daughter's marriage to Harold Painter and did not want their grandson raised under his guidance. The philosophies of life are entirely different. As stated by the psychiatrist who examined Mr. Painter at the request of the Bannisters' attorneys: 'it is evident that there exists a large difference in ways of life and value-systems between the Bannisters and Mr. Painter, but there is no evidence that psychiatric instability is involved. Rather, these divergent life patterns seem to represent alternative normal adaptations.' "

The court then went on to discuss the opposed "philosophies" of Painter and the Bannisters, on the grounds that they had an "important" bearing on the case: "The Bannisters," said the court, "have provided Mark with a stable, dependable, conventional middle-class background, and an opportunity for a college education and profession, if he desires it. It provides a solid foundation and secure atmosphere. In the Painter home, Mark would have more freedom of conduct and thought, with an opportunity to develop his individual talents. It would be more exciting and challenging in some respects, but romantic, impractical and unstable."

Then the court gave its views on the Painter home: "Our conclusion as to the type of home Mr. Painter would offer is based on his Bohemian approach to finances and life in general. We feel there is much evidence that supports this conclusion. His main ambition is to be a freelance writer and photographer. He has had some articles and picture stories published, but the income from these efforts has been negligible. At the time of the accident, Jeanne (Mark's mother) was willingly working to support the family so Harold could devote more time to his writing and photography. In the ten years since he left college, he has changed jobs seven times. He was asked to leave two of them; two he quit because he didn't like the work; two because he wanted to devote more time to writing; and the rest for better pay. He was contemplating a move to Berkeley at the time of trial.

"The house in which Mr. Painter and his present wife live, compared with the well-kept Bannister home, exemplifies the contrasting ways of life. In his words 'it is a very old and beat up and lovely home'. They live in the rear part. The interior is inexpensively but tastefully decorated. The large yard, on a hill in the business district of Walnut Creek, California, is of uncut weeds and wild oats. The house 'is not painted on the outside because I do not want it painted. I am very fond of the wood on the outside of the house.' "

Next the court turned from Mr. Painter's unpainted house to his beliefs: "Mr. Painter is either an agnostic or atheist and has no concern for formal religious training. He has read a lot of Zen Buddhism and 'has been much influenced by it.' He is a political liberal and got into difficulty in a job at the University of Washington for his support of the activities of the American Civil Liberties Union in the university news bulletin.

"There were two funerals for his wife. One in the basement of his home in which he alone was present. He conducted the service and wrote her a long letter. The second at a church in Pullman was for the gratification of her friends. He attended in a sport shirt and sweater.

"These matters are not related as a criticism of Mr. Painter's conduct, way of life, or sense of values. An individual is free to choose his own values, within bounds, which are not exceeded here. They do serve, however, to support our conclusion as to the kind of life Mark would be exposed to in the Painter household. We believe it would be unstable, unconventional, arty, Bohemian, and probably intellectually stimulating."

In making its judgment, the Iowa Supreme Court knew that Mark's mother had made a will consigning the children to their father's care, as if she had anticipated that a struggle for them might develop between her parents and her husband in the event of her own death. "I am confident," she said in her will, "that he (Harold Painter) will faithfully provide for their care, and I wish him to have unfettered power to do so."

The Bannisters' case against Harold Painter was merely that he had unorthodox beliefs and preferred an intellectual life to tangible assets—for instance, he had quit a well-paid job because he did not find the work stimulating. Yet the court decided in favor of the Bannisters. Evidently the Iowa way of life of the grandparents seemed, to the Iowa Supreme Court, so superior to the Californian way of life of the father as to override all other considerations.

It is the Iowa way of life, as described in the Painter case, that is now reeling under the impact of those who do not accept its values.

TWO WORLDS

Coming from the outside, the extraordinary feature of the Californian social split is that it is not invisible, like most social change, but hits you in the eye. Just as you can see the San Andreas fault, a ravine in the ground, so you can see the social split. On one side, there is what might be called the World of Reagan —the governor spent much of his early life in Iowa. On the other side, there is the World of Berkeley. The gap between the two is now so wide that it is hard to imagine how it could ever be bridged. In November, 1970, I attended Governor Reagan's re-election victory party in Los Angeles. Four days later, I went to the opening of a big new art museum in Berkeley. The contrast between the two events, and the style of those attending them, was as extreme as if I had crossed from one civilization to another —as in some ways I had.

The Reagan party took place in the Century Plaza, which advertises itself as "the world's most beautiful hotel." It is the newest large hotel in Los Angeles, built on the old Twentieth Century Fox lot, and when the rebuilding on the site is finished it will be the centerpiece of the ambitious new Century City. It could scarcely be grander in conception. It stands on a street called the Avenue of the Stars. It towers up over the shining automobiles around its base in a giant curve, like a tautened bow. The bellboys who carry your bags to your room are dressed in the uniform of pre-Maoist Chinese, with baggy silken trousers and skullcaps. Inside, all is orange and gold, on an imperial scale: a vast entrance hall with escalators leading down to still vaster banqueting rooms and coffee shops and drugstores and jewelers and dress shops on the floor below. Here, I thought, is a fitting temple for the worship of the God of Growth. It seemed appropriate that the banquet for 3000 people given by the president of the United States to celebrate the safe return to earth of the first men to land on the moon should have taken place in this shrine. (In the World of Berkeley, the moon-shot had been regarded as an aberration. In the Filmore West, a temple of Berkeley culture, the slogan had been written up, "Astronauts! Where Are You *Going?"*)

I was escorted to my room on the fourteenth floor by one of the Chinese, and his manner, after he had put down my bag and switched on the outsize lamps, increased my sensation of being received into some bizarre court. "This room faces east and room service is available all night," he said. Then he bowed, silently pocketed my dollar, and withdrew.

After he had gone, I inspected the room and detected an obsession with temperature: another attempt, I thought, like the moon-shot, to control and subdue the natural environment. Los Angeles has a Mediterranean climate; even in January, in midwinter, the average daily high gets up into the sixties, and very rarely sinks below forty-five degrees. Yet not only had the room a thermostat, with a dial showing both actual and desired temperatures, but the extra-large sybarite's bed was covered by an electric blanket, also with a temperature control, graded from one to ten. Despite the spaciousness of the accommodation, there was no bath: only a shower. In the anteroom to the shower, however, the management had decreed a wider range of hotel-room accessories than I had ever before encountered. Viz.:

> A "shoe mitt"
> Two rolls of toilet paper, mounted side by side, each roll decorated with a floral design in orange-brown that picked up the decor of the room

A tissue holder, similarly decorated

A shower cap, with the compliments of the management

Calgon bath-oil beads

Trav Wonder Suds

A travel kit of safety pins, buttons, one needle, six cards of different colored thread, and two bandages

Ten towels

Two sorts of soap, one of them a "deodorant bath and beauty soap" giving "round-the-clock protection"

Cut off from the motorized city by fourteen floors, and soothed by the management's restoratives, I remembered what Henry James had had to say about the old Waldorf-Astoria in New York at the end of the century. Returning to the city after an absence of twenty years, James had pronounced the new stately homes of Manhattan to be "a record in the last analysis of individual loneliness"; neither the buildings nor the families who lived in them gave him a feeling of permanence. The family units could not be considered part of an organic, molded, and coherent society. In the luxury hotel, by contrast, he saw "a social order in positively stable equilibrium," fulfilling everything that people wanted. "It sat there, it walked and talked, and ate and drank, and listened and danced to music, and otherwise reveled and roamed, and bought and sold, and came and went there, all on its own splendid terms." [1]

To James, the "amazing hotel-world" demonstrated in its most concentrated and characteristic form the true spirit of America. It met all human wants and admitted everyone, provided they had the money and appeared to be "respectable." Above all, hotel life seemed American to James in its supreme gregariousness, by contrast with European notions of the private life.

So the Century Plaza seemed to me to express the concentrated spirit of Los Angeles, or, to be more precise, of Reagan's Los Angeles, where the old values of self-help, self-reliance, respect for the conventions—"respectability"—and, above all, money, were prized. Entrance to the Century Plaza, especially on a night when the governor himself was celebrating his victory over the forces of darkness, was a proof of identity; and the ability to pay thirty-six dollars, excluding service, for a hotel room, was certainly a proof of financial substance. That night, in a penthouse suite guarded with special care, Reagan and his associates held court: the men in extra-white or extra-colored shirts and well-pressed dark suits, and the women wearing makeup, elaborate hairstyles, and "evening dresses" set off by jewelry. Downstairs, in an enormous ballroom, the humbler Reaganites—many of them young—milled gregariously about, holding drinks, watching election results being put up on a board, listening to a sweating cheerleader on a platform backed by a traditional band with a traditional "bandleader" in a tuxedo. Almost every man in the room wore a tie; and the girls were dressed like Long Island debutantes, showing, I thought, the attentions of mothers dreaming of their own youth. All night I saw only one black and one man with long hair: both of them worked for CBS. Everyone present glowed with health or prosperity or both; they gazed around eagerly at their fellows, applauded the "television favorites" when they were introduced, and were ecstatic when the governor himself descended from the penthouse with Mrs. Reagan and addressed them. Poverty, doubt, confusion, Vietnam, students—all seemed a million miles away, or would have, had it not been for the wedge of six security men who, when the governor moved out of the ballroom, fell in behind him, presumably to prevent him from being shot in the back.

Four days later I attended the opening of the Berkeley Art Museum, a building as stark and angular, with its rough concrete walls and jutting interior platforms, as the Century Plaza is curved and plushy. Almost all the visitors to the museum wore their hair long, often to their shoulders; none of the men wore a tie, and few of the women wore brassieres. I had moments of genuine puzzlement when I could not tell the difference between the sexes. From the casual and entirely random character of their dress, I had the feeling that those present had burst some kind of clothes barrier. Many of the girls had evidently ceased entirely to think about the physical impression they made; it was not merely that they had not on this particular occasion tried to make themselves look pretty, but that they seemed to have permanently suppressed any of the emanations of femininity that girls naturally give off. Many of them seemed, in their sexlessness and shapelessness, to have achieved the Women's Lib aim of ceasing to be sexual objects. Nor was the casual dress contrived: it was genuinely casual, as if those present had been handed out garments, regardless of sex or size, by a blind old-clothes man. They had a peculiarly timeless look. Looking down from one of the jutting balconies was like seeing a nineteenth-century painting of immigrants—"Arrivals from Europe"—come alive, especially as many of the girls wore shawl-like garments around their shoulders. The only men I noticed who were dressed in any particular style were a couple of tall, black-bearded fellows wearing boots and frontier hats, as if they had just stepped off a wagon train. I saw only one woman who could have merged into the Reagan gathering without attracting attention; as she passed a Van Gogh I heard her say, "He's the one with the one ear, isn't he?" Unlike the Reaganites, who continued to shout happily to one another even when the band was playing, the Berkeley crowd talked little. Berkeley—the Berkeley always, I premise, of the rank outsider (as Henry James would say)—presents two faces: the first, anger and frustration when set against "pigs" or "fascists"; the other, as at the museum, of detached, even dreamy, gentleness and almost unnoticing tolerance. A dozen Berkeleyites in the Century Plaza ballroom would have caused, I am sure, instant alarm, as if serfs had broken into a Winter Palace soirée in Leningrad before the Russian Revolution; but a dozen Reaganites, dark-suited and white-shirted, would have caused no stir at all in the museum. What is extraordinary about the gap between the Reaganites and the Berkeleyites is that both groups belong not only to the same nation, state, and age-group, but to the same social class; yet their differences encompass not only beliefs, but life-style, habits, dress: everything. There is total cut-off. If Henry James is right in picking out gregariousness as a principal American characteristic, then what is striking is that the Reaganites were absolutely gregarious, but the Berkeleyites were not—were absolutely not. Gregariousness was precisely what they were rejecting, which is a much more fundamental difference between the two worlds than any of the more discussed, and more superficial, divisions, such as Vietnam or "permissiveness" or drugs.

CHARLES MANSON

No example of social disorder was more alarming or bewildering to Californians than the Charles Manson killings of the summer of 1969. When all the corpses had been counted it appeared that Manson and his followers, or "family," had been responsible for no less than nine murders: five at the home of Sharon Tate, a film actress, in Los Angeles; the wealthy La Bianca couple; Donald Shea, a stunt man and ranch hand, whose body was never found; and Gary Hinman, a musician, who was tortured, stabbed, slashed, shot and finally suffocated with a pillow, at a house in Malibu.

Why were the Manson killings so alarming? Murderous violence was scarcely a novelty in California. There are some eight hundred murders a year in Los Angeles County alone. The history of the west is full of violent solutions—labor union shootings, vigilante killings, Indian massacres. The undercurrent of violence in American life was most thoroughly idealized in Los Angeles itself, in the Western movie and the romanticized and admiring accounts of sadistic killers such as Jesse James or Bonnie and Clyde. Nor were Californians unfamiliar with bizarre murder. The movies had long been producing stories of crazed killers loose in the Californian landscape—James Cagney at large in the Sierras in *White Heat,* or the youth in a recent film who crouched with a rifle high up behind the screen at a drive-in theater, picking off the audience like fairground ducks. Not much more than a year earlier, Sirhan Sirhan had assassinated Robert

Kennedy in a Los Angeles hotel kitchen. (The Manson murders were followed by other unusual killings: the first ecological murder, when a young man killed his neighbors solely because they were consuming too many natural resources, and the uncharacteristic slaughter by a Mexican-American of a group of farmworkers north of Sacramento.)

But the Manson family's deeds seemed loaded with special significance. They appeared to be connected, though in ways not easy to pin down, with some of the most striking and (to the majority) least desirable social upheavals of the previous few years. Manson, though actually a jail-bird in his early thirties who had spent half his life behind bars, looked with his long hair and tangled beard the very stereotype of a hippie. He and his family lived in a commune. They traveled in a school bus, like Ken Kesey and his LSD freaks. According to their own accounts, they practiced extreme promiscuity. They took drugs: "I'm on a constant LSD trip," one member of the family, Susan Atkins, said. "I'm so high even now"—she was making a confession—"I'll never come down." They seemed like the ultimate drop-outs. In addition, their mode of living was touched with particularly western fantasy: their base was an old movie set, a secret desert hideout in Death Valley, as if they were a rebel band of cattle-rustlers, chased out of town by vigilantes, and now holed up—cut off by society and rejected by it—waiting to strike back. Manson was a criminal lunatic who attracted and dominated feeble-minded girls; yet at the same time he and his family set up nightmarish echoes of religious cult leaders, frontiersmen who considered themselves above the law, and nuns possessed by devils.

What evidently most appalled and mystified newspaper-readers in California during the trial was the revelation of Manson's power over his disciples. He had persuaded them to kill on his behalf at long range, and with scarcely paralleled brutality; yet even when on trial for their lives they had failed to come to their senses. And the disciples came from "nice homes"; they were, one might have said, "ordinary" girls. Manson's influence, whatever its origins, had staying power: "He is the King and I am his

Queen," said Susan Atkins. It was not surprising that the court-room should fail to impress Manson; he was far gone in fantasy, appearing almost daily in a new role. He came bearded, clean-shaven, in denims, in gold corduroy trousers, now docile, now threatening, now pleading guilty, now not guilty, at first with a cross on his forehead, later with a swastika, and finally welcoming both his imprisonment—a prison, he said, was where he felt most at home—and his sentence of death: "Are you kidding? The gas chamber? Death is permanent solitary confinement, and there's nothing I'd like more than that." It was not surprising that Man-son should remain out of touch with the real world, but it was shocking when the girls too failed to "come down." Among the grisly detritus left by the Manson killings, no detail was more dis-turbing than the behavior of the Manson girls when photographs of the Tate bodies were produced in court, the corpses linked by nylon ropes with a carving fork protruding from a dead man's stomach. The girls huddled together, giggling.

For explanation some went to Aldous Huxley. In *The Devils of Loudon* he wrote: "Assemble a mob of men and women pre-viously conditioned (by drugs, propaganda, alienation, etc.), treat them to amplified music, bright lights, and the oratory of a dema-gogue who (as demagogues always are) is simultaneously the ex-ploiter and the victim of herd intoxication, and in next to no time you can reduce them to a state of almost mindless subhu-manity." Huxley was writing not only about the possessed nuns of Loudon and the causes of religious hysteria, but also about mod-ern mass political hysteria.

Before the intoxication takes effect, the deluded group must first feel themselves to be separate from the mass of common hu-manity: they must consider themselves an elite. Political and reli-gious mass hysteria also involves an idea, which is invariably con-cerned with what Professor Norman Cohn has called "the pursuit of the millennium." Manson's fantasies evidently included the notion of a race war between blacks and whites, which he would promote and guide himself; he was a constant user of such words as "revolution" and "Armageddon."

To an outsider, it was precisely this separateness from society, the rootlessness of both killers and victims, which seemed peculiarly Californian. The Manson family lived far outside society; but so, it appears, did some of those they killed. I briefly met Sharon Tate at a party given by Mr. and Mrs. Kirk Douglas in 1968, and I recall her as a pale, beautiful girl who seemed a long way from home (her father was an English colonel), married to an expatriate Polish film director and living in a rented house. Rumors that circulated after the murders about the disorderliness of the Polanskis' life-style were no doubt exaggerated; but, in any case, it was not a style that recognized traditional restraints. A neighbor's verdict on the massacre was: "Live freaky, die freaky." One might say that both murderers and victims were casualties of the peculiarly insubstantial nature of Californian society, especially that of southern California—of Los Angeles, "the Nowhere City," where "no one has a past" and "nobody cares what you do." The recent writings of Professor Daniel Bell of Harvard are relevant here. He has described the United States today as "the divided society" in which a technocratic and industrial superstructure exists alongside a culture that seeks only the new, experimental and sensuous, and has rejected all traditional bourgeois notions of rationalism and sobriety. Instinct is all: "Impulse and pleasure alone are real and life-affirming." Few would deny that in Los Angeles, the most modern of cities, impulse and pleasure are enthroned. Professor Bell writes: "The post-modernist temper demands that what was previously played out in fantasy and imagination must be acted out in life as well. There is no distinction between art and life. Anything permitted in art is permitted in life as well." This is a change; hitherto, "whether demonic or murderous, the fantasies were expressed through the ordering principle of aesthetic forms."[2] Polanski's demonic fantasies were expressed through his films, notably *Rosemary's Baby,* in which an innocent girl is exploited by contemporary witches; other people in Los Angeles acted out similar fantasies in real life —the Alasteir Crowleyites are quite busy there. Very few taboos survive in Los Angeles: "Nobody cares what you do." For the

Manson family, there obviously was no taboo on murder.

Many Los Angelenos interpreted the resulting massacre as a revelation of, and verdict on, what they supposed to be the true nature of the hippie world. It was a simple-minded interpretation, though no one who had seen anything of the degradations of some forms of Californian hippiedom—in Venice, for instance, or in the mountains behind Big Sur where the combined effects of drugs and a virulent strain of venereal disease have caused some of the young people who roam that coast to sit on mountain-tops awaiting the end of the world—could affirm that there was no connection whatever between the hippie world and the massacre. During the trial the hippie world, as represented by the underground press, showed a certain tendency to sympathize with Manson, not for his crimes, but as the innocent victim of authority. The Los Angeles *Free Press* accused society of "inventing" an imaginary Manson—"a long-haired, oversexed, acid-gobbling bastard son of a teenage prostitute who thinks he's Jesus and was formerly arrested for white slavery"—so that it could, through this imaginary monster, try all rebels for their life-style. The Manson jury, said the *Free Press,* were "wolverines" out for vengeance.

The *Free Press* seemed disinclined to be appalled by the actions of Manson and his family. So did a young American with whom I discussed them in London; he in no way attempted to defend Manson, yet he could not entirely accept the notion that Manson was merely a criminal lunatic. Death, after all, wasn't so different from life, especially if you believed in some form of after-life; and Manson was "an amazing guy," as shown by his writings (ravings, in truth) published by the underground newspaper *Rolling Stone.*

Thus the murders reverberated. They demonstrated that even in Los Angeles one commandment survived: Thou shalt not kill. Incest, fornication in public, homosexual weddings, wife-swapping, black-mass rituals—these were okay. But not murder. Yet it appeared that not all members of the "adversary culture" could instinctively and wholeheartedly agree with "conventional" Los Angelenos even about the appropriate attitude to the murder of a pregnant girl—perhaps the most appalling event that any "conventional" person could imagine. The chaos of the event—documented chaos in the lives of the murderers, suspected chaos in the lives of the murdered—was thus reflected in the Los Angeleno reaction to it. It was another fragment of evidence of the dislocation of Californian society.

LOS BANOS

Reporting a foreign country, any journalist is liable to be seized by fears that he has got things entirely wrong. Attacked in this way by a feeling that I might be getting an exaggerated or distorted view of California's difficulties, since I had been talking to people mainly about problems, I decided one day to visit a small town chosen at random from the map, and to see what was happening to the old values there. The place I picked out was Los Banos, in the San Joaquin Valley, and I went there because I had no reason for going there.

Road signs and smog fell away as I drove through brown hills covered with cattle. It was a Saturday; there was little other traffic; and as I drove along, I began to be soothed by an agreeable sensation of great space and remoteness. But my first sight of the town depressed me, since it receives a stranger, as American towns are liable to do, by bombarding him with the same signs and billboards that he has left behind him in the last town. Away from the main street, however, I came upon a large village green, dotted with maples and set about with chairs and tables, with a swimming pool nearby. There was also a row of swings. They looked sturdy, and no children were about, so I climbed on one of them and swung to and fro; from the top I could see mountains. Near the swings was a museum, opened in 1968; inside was a gray-haired lady, evidently the curator, and an excessively noisy and garrulous old fellow wearing suspenders and an orange shirt who, as I entered, was bellowing about minerals and the pile of money he might have made if he hadn't been conned out of his last two thousand dollars by a woman he met in Eureka. The museum was not pretentious; almost anything local qualified for a place: photographs of debutantes, which gave the place an Andy Hardy flavor; a picture of a Farm Center Picnic at the San Luis Gonzaga Ranch, taken "about 1930"; a jar decorated with pieces of broken china picked out of the gutters of Chinatown, San Francisco, by Dolly Kays, a small girl from Los Banos, when the streets were sluiced down after the 1906 earthquake; a photograph of 186 geese killed with three shots from "the world's largest double-barreled shotgun"; World War I posters urging people to buy Liberty Bonds; elephant bones; and an Indian arrow.

Los Banos, the lady curator said, meant "the baths"; and the garrulous visitor interrupted to say that they were still there and still providing good fishing; a "colored fellow" had caught a catfish just the other day weighing five pounds: "it's a paradise up there." He sounded like a character out of *Huckleberry Finn*. The town had been founded, the lady went on, by a German butcher from San Francisco, who bought 500,000 acres of the region as a cattle ranch; the district was a convenient staging post between San Francisco, 120 miles to the northeast, and Los Angeles, 300 miles to the south. The butcher had died in 1916 (it was strange, to a European, to be in a town which seemed relatively old by local standards—with pleasant wooden frame houses in side streets under big trees—and then to learn that the "founder" had died as recently as 1916).[3]

What else, I asked? Well, people round about liked to shoot, especially duck and pheasant. They grew cotton, cantaloupes, and sugar beets. But what were the big events of the past twenty years? Well, there was the dam: a really big one, the San Luis Dam and the reservoir, the starting plunger pushed by President Kennedy; that enterprise had brought a lot of people in. The population now was 9943.

And how had life in Los Banos changed in the past ten years? (I was looking for signs of social revolution.) The lady seemed nonplussed. Things were much the same. Did the town still have debutantes? Yes, it certainly did. Anything else? There was a new junior high school: well, not a *new* junior high, but the old one had been renovated. What about pollution? Yes, there might be some pollution; sometimes the fish from the canal didn't taste right. Ah! She did remember one development in her lifetime: as children, she and her friends used to swim in the canals, and the banks then were grassy; now they were cement. That was a change.

I left the museum thinking that Los Banos was a rare, lucky, and socially unified community. Next I dropped by the offices of the *Los Banos Enterprise* and discovered at the back door the owner, editor, and publisher—bald, cheerful, and unshaven—chatting to a friend and carrying a small dog with a pink ribbon around its neck. He introduced himself as Frank Knebel and showed me his offices; and then told me that Los Banos was about to be hit by a tidal wave of growth and progress. The dam I had been hearing about was a key installation in the massive Californian Water Project, whereby water is being brought from the wet north of California to the dry and faster-growing south. The San Luis Reservoir was designed to store the future water supplies of Los Angeles. Not only that: the dam would eventually irrigate half a million now-arid acres. And not only that: Los Banos was about to become a crossroads in the middle of California: Interstate 5 when completed would cut straight down the center of the state like a spine and intersect with the east-west road 152. The intersection would be so conveniently sited between the two most heavily populated areas of California, San Francisco–Oakland and Los Angeles, that it would become a major warehousing center. Interstate 5 would really make Los Banos boom.

And how did the publisher feel about that? It turned out that he had lived through a similar experience once before. He had originally come to California as a cabin boy and had sailed into San Francisco when the Golden Gate Bridge was being built. Later, after World War II service in Europe, he had settled in Garden Grove and acquired a little newspaper, a wife, two sons, half an acre of land, and horses. Garden Grove was sixteen miles from Long Beach, the port of Los Angeles, with a view of Mount

Baldy to the east. There was a two-lane highway from Long Beach when he arrived; that was all. Then, during the late forties, the pressure started. Garden Grove grew from 2000 to 45,000 in three years. In 1951, the first tentacle reached out: the Santa Ana Freeway; and the subdividers were out ahead of the freeway. With the arrival of the freeway, the onslaught really got going. Garden Grove shot up to 120,000. In 1953, the town tried to become incorporated, in an attempt to protect itself, and failed; but in any case it would already have been too late.

In 1956 Mr. Knebel sold out his paper at a big profit and transfered his family to the peace of Los Banos. "Garden Grove was a beautiful, beautiful agricultural area. It made you sick, because it grew too fast. By the time I left, you never saw the mountains."

He talked of Los Banos. Yes, it *was* stable: seventy-five percent of the people were Portuguese and Italians: a trickle was still coming in from the Azores—and Catholics kept things stable. There was a sprinkling of old Mexican families: three to five percent. The Negro population had grown in the past two or three years; they had moved out of the Oakland ghetto to a chitlin'-packaging factory. There had been one incident at the high school, but race might not have been behind it. Really they had no race problem. Yet the social upheavals had reached them? "Yes: here too." A puzzling divorce had gone through in the last week: a young attorney and his wife. No one could quite see why it had happened. And his own family—his elder son was in Vietnam, a conservative, very interested in the paper; but the younger boy was twenty-one, wore his hair down to his shoulders, and, despite a university education, was now working as a fry-cook in another town. The other night he had come home and had been drinking beer when he suddenly pushed back his chair, shouted at his father, and stormed off up to his room. " 'What did I say?' I asked his mother. She didn't know. I have no idea what angers my own son. Why is there this difference between the two boys? I wish I knew. It's the same thing in other families."

Knebel displayed mixed feelings about the prospects for Los Banos. The boom, no doubt, will make him rich. Real estate will rocket. The population will expand. Yet he remembered the fate of Garden Grove and the view of the mountains: "These tremendous assets"—he meant the stability and amenities of Los Banos society—"can be dissipated very fast." He should know, I thought, if he's a survivor of Garden Grove. Before I left, Knebel reached into his desk drawer and presented me with a generous handful of red pencils—inscribed with a message saying, "Your best advertising is in the *Los Banos Enterprise*." If I come back in five years, I thought, he'll be handing out gold pens. Interstate 5: growth: the warehousing center of the San Joaquin Valley: well, I thought, too bad: it couldn't happen to a nicer place or a nicer guy.

AFFLUENCE IS NOT ENOUGH

The goals and values of most Californians are probably much closer to those of the Bannisters than to those of Harold Painter. The common man, as he has poured into the western playground, has turned out not to have the tastes and aspirations that his historic champions expected him to have. His drive toward self-improvement is noticeably weak; and the number of waterfront workers or airport employees who use their leisure and prosperity in order to devote themselves to cultural activities, as the socialists of the thirties hoped they would, is small. What has happened in California is that the common man, though leaving the old social and religious structure behind him as he pushed west, has nevertheless enthusiastically embraced the values of his old bourgeois oppressors. The ideas of Henry Ford I are in better standing in California, even now, than those of Jack London or Upton Sinclair. Unlike Harold Painter, the overwhelming majority of Californians have put tangible assets first. But it is becoming clear that affluence often produces severe dissatisfactions. Of course, almost all Californians want to be rich, or at least well off; but one of the commonest Californian experiences these days involves the discovery that affluence is not enough and that there is no necessary connection between affluence and contentment. Of all the instances I came across, the most poignant occurred near San Luis Obispo. I was driving idly down a winding, almost English country road with rolling farmland on either hand, when I saw the perfect house. It was set back a hundred yards from the road, with its own rickety white gate and rough track. It was new, small, and neat; single-story, with a big front window, like the bow of a ship, which pointed across a field and up a lush green hill to the horizon. Old trees grew around the house: there were no other buildings in sight. A blue Volkswagen stood at the door.

Curious and envious, I went to call. A gray-haired man in short sleeves welcomed me and took me in to meet his wife, also gray-haired, who was canning fruit. The house gleamed, with the kitchen, dining area, and sitting room all forming one big room: fitted carpets, fine kitchen equipment, a big television set, deep armchairs, central heating—they told me—in the ceiling, and the big window with the sunny Californian view. I thought to myself, as the woman sat me down at the kitchen table and gave me (no kidding) a slice of apple pie: "Here it is. This is what they all come to California for. This is the dream come true."

Mr. Gruber had been a bus driver in Los Angeles, who, when the time came for him to retire, had luckily been able to sell his house for an unexpectedly high price. He and his wife had decided that after so long in a city they would retire to the country; in her Los Angeles kitchen, Mrs. Gruber told me, she had been able to see the sky only by craning her neck. They had had enough money to design their ideal house and to furnish it exactly as they had always wanted: everything was new. But now, having lived in it for eighteen months, they were seriously wondering whether they had done the right thing. Mr. Gruber had started off his retirement by enthusiastically planting fruit trees and growing vegetables; he had grown some fine tomatoes, but they couldn't eat them all themselves and when he tried to give them away he could find nobody who wanted them. The old trees had originally belonged to a ruined old house further down the dirt road; one of them was a walnut, and another an apple tree.

The walnuts and apples rotted on the ground because nobody wanted them. Mrs. Gruber's heart wasn't really in the few pounds of fruit she was preserving, she told me, because she couldn't really see the point when there was so much canned fruit in the shops. Besides the Grubers felt cut off from other people; that was one reason they were so pleased I had called. And the view: they were getting a little tired of that: just the empty field and the green hill. They owned the field, but couldn't think of any way to use it. Mrs. Gruber blurted out: "I would really have rather used the money to travel."

Yet outwardly—the little house, the green fields, the handy town, the peace, the sun, and the lucky break that made the move possible—here was the universal working-class dream come true.

CHAPTER 6

Protesters

> Put your bodies upon the gears and upon the
> wheels, upon the levers, upon all the apparatus
> and . . . make it stop.
>
> *Mario Savio*

EVEN if California had only had to cope with the immigrants who have swarmed into the state in recent years, its patchy social fabric would have come under considerable strain. In addition, it has been buffeted by unparalleled affluence—leading to unforeseen dissatisfactions—by exceptional mobility, by technological vertigo, and by the backwash of a brutal and unpopular war. These disruptions have been accompanied by a rising clamor of revolt—occasionally dying down, then returning with extra bitterness—which has been marked by riots, shoot-outs, arson, bombings, sit-ins, and novel mass happenings resembling the religious seizures of the Middle Ages. Those who have led or inspired the revolt have acquired international fame: Mario Savio, the leader of the Berkeley Free Speech Movement, which ignited the student revolt that subsequently roared across the Western world; Herbert Marcuse, the Marxist sage of San Diego; Allen Ginsberg, the poet; Ken Kesey, the drug booster; Eldridge Cleaver, Huey Newton, and Bobby Seale, Black Panther leaders; Angela Davis, the Communist don; Cesar Chavez, the Mexican organizer; Jane Fonda, the champion of the Indians; Jerry

112

Rubin, the showman Yippie; and Joan Baez, the beautiful pacifist folk-singer.

The peculiarity of this list is that none of its members can be classified simply as a politician, though all of them are, or have been, involved in political activity. One of the most significant points about the protest movement is that its echoes are heard only faintly among the professional politicians in Sacramento. For the protesters, the battleground is not the state capitol, but the streets, the ghettoes, the campuses, the Central Valley, the law courts. Though Governor Reagan personifies all that the protesters most hate, his official opponents are not international headline names at all, but such relatively uncolorful politicos as Jesse Unruh, the Democratic leader, or Senator John Tunney—neither of whom arouses much excitement even inside California, let alone beyond. When the heroes of protest enter the formal political arena they do so only to guy it, as when, at the 1968 Chicago Convention, the Yippies nominated a pig for the presidency.

THE VIOLENT PAST

Such antics bewilder ordinary Californians; and they are still more disturbed by acts of left-wing violence. They would perhaps be slightly comforted if they realized—as many of them do not—that California has the most vigorous left-wing tradition in the United States, and a history of protest that is both violent and radical. In the 1890s, during organized labor's struggle to make San Francisco the first closed-shop city in America, trade-unionists blew up a boardinghouse and killed eight non-unionists. Between 1908 and 1911 there were forty-three bombings at different building sites in and around San Francisco, the result of a prolonged and bitter dispute between employers and workers in the construction industry. It was an outcrop of this dispute that led to the most tragic event in Californian labor history when, on October 1, 1910, the offices of the *Los Angeles Times* were dynamited by a bomb left in a suitcase in a passageway known as Ink Alley, between the stereotyping and press rooms: the explosion killed twenty workers, and the subsequent fire gutted the building. The owner of the *Times* was Harrison Gray Otis, an exceptionally cantankerous and megalomaniacal character even for a newspaper proprietor. He himself had been a printer as a young man and had quit his first job with the Rock Island *Courier* when the owner refused to unionize his shop; but by the time he acquired control of the *Los Angeles Times* in 1886, he had become virulently anti-union. When the unions on one occasion refused to accept a twenty percent wage cut, he stormed into the composing room and bellowed, "Every man get out of here and get out— quick." It was to be expected, therefore, that Otis would blame the dynamiting on the unions; and equally natural that liberal-minded people should scoff. When two trade unionists, the McNamara brothers, were arrested for the bombing, virtually every liberal in the United States assumed that they had been framed. The American Federation of Labor collected a defense fund of nearly a quarter of a million dollars; the famous lawyer, Clarence Darrow, took on the defense. Then, on the day the trial opened, the McNamara brothers pleaded guilty. The effect on the defense that had rallied in support of the two men was devastating; and both liberalism and trade unionism were set back in southern California for decades. Even now, the triumph of Harrison Gray Otis lingers on. His bronze bust occupies a place of honor in the *Los Angeles Times* lobby; his grandson, Otis Chandler, runs the paper; and the policy of the paper remains anti-union.

Sixty years after the McNamara debacle, liberals wholeheartedly took up a comparable cause when Angela Davis, a black philosophy teacher at UCLA, was threatened with expulsion on the grounds that she was a Communist. As in the McNamara case, liberals joined the left in protest. Again, the alliance collapsed, this time when Angela Davis, to the shock of the liberals who were supporting her, was charged with supplying guns used in an attempt to kidnap a judge. Despite her acquittal, the violence that seems endemic in California once again rebounded to strengthen the right, weaken the center, and make the left angrier, more isolated, and more embattled than ever.

RADICAL THINKERS

The other characteristic of California's radical history is its left-wing thinkers who, in their day, aroused quite as much alarm and were still more influential than, say, Herbert Marcuse. The San Francisco printer and editor, Henry George, sold two million copies of his *Progress and Poverty,* published in 1879, and deeply influenced not only Bernard Shaw and Sidney Webb, two founding fathers of the British welfare state, but also Tolstoy and Sun Yat-sen, precursors, respectively, of the Russian and Chinese revolutions. George was an impetuous and strident social critic who was shocked by the gap between the wealthy Californian landowners and the penniless workers; to close the gap, he recommended a simple cure-all: the single tax. The landlords, George maintained, did little to improve their land, yet they hauled in a rich reward, as the growing prosperity of the state sent up the price of their holdings. George proposed to tax this unearned increment, arguing that the money thereby raised would lower the general burden of taxation, destroy monopoly, and restore economic equality—all at a single blow.

Not less influential than Henry George was Thorstein Veblen, the theoretician of the "leisure class," who was thrown out of Stanford by angry trustees in an episode recalling the later battles over Angela Davis. The socialist Jack London, an illegitimate son of an astrologer and a medium, was another San Franciscan, who poured out the astronomical total of fifty books—novels and socialist tracts—in seventeen years. Again, Jack London was an international influence: he was one of the mentors of Aneurin Bevan, the most uncompromising British Labor leader after World War II and the man who, in the spirit of Jack London, described the Conservative Party as "vermin."

London's patron was a rich poet called George Sterling, who

founded a literary colony at Carmel. The colony attracted both Sinclair Lewis, whose *Babbitt* remains the most wounding attack yet written on the "silent majority," and the muckraker Upton Sinclair. (The original muckraker, Lincoln Steffens, was born in Sacramento; his family home became the official residence of the state governor—until the Reagans spurned it as a firetrap.) Sinclair made his name with *The Jungle* and confirmed it with *Oil,* a blistering exposure of the oil industry.[1] Then, in 1934, at the height of the Depression, he ran for governor, with a plan to "End Poverty In California" which so alarmed the business community that it raised $10 million to fight him. Sinclair put forward twelve measures which he maintained would end the Depression, including state land colonies for the unemployed, an increase of inheritance and public-utility taxes, old age pensions, and (following Henry George) a tax on unimproved land. The campaign, even for California, was vicious, with the motion-picture industry heavily involved against Sinclair; but if the anti-Republican vote had not split (then, as now, the forces of protest had difficulty in remaining united), Sinclair would have been elected governor.

So California possesses a lurid and embattled history of protest. The question arises: why is the Californian left today so detached from this past? How is it that the left, unlike the right (as we shall see), has not held on to its traditions, but instead floats about and changes shape like an amoeba, constantly altering its aims and programs?

Part of the answer can be found by looking at the career of the most famous of all Californian left-wing leaders, Harry Bridges of the San Francisco waterfront. Bridges was born in Australia, gave up the sea in 1922 to work in the San Francisco docks, and came to prominence in 1934 as one of the leaders of a strike for more pay and a shorter week. Bridges, too, has experienced violence. The strike began on March 7, 1934. On July 5, pickets attacked police with bricks and rocks, and the police replied with tear gas and riot guns. Near Mission Street and Stuart, police fired into a crowd, killing a cook and a longshoreman. That afternoon, Governor Merriam ordered troops into the city; and by nightfall the National Guard had machineguns mounted on the waterfront piers. For the funeral march for the dead men, four days later, some 10,000 men, women, and children marched in absolute silence, controlled not by police but by the longshoremen themselves. "It was," wrote one reporter, "a stupendous and reverent procession that astounded the city."

But in the years between this traumatic event and World War II, trade unionism made vast advances, both on the waterfront and in San Francisco as a whole; even Los Angeles made progress. At the heart of these advances was Harry Bridges who, when he wasn't working with his union, was resisting attempts at deportation to Australia because of his alleged Communism.

The Communist Party has maintained more effective presence in the bay area than anywhere else in the United States. In those days, Bridges and his longshoremen were a beacon to every left-winger in the country: the union was clean, idealistic, the model of what the left wanted a union to be. Then, after World War II, the union was transformed: after years of strife and strikes, the longshoremen and their hated employers were pushed into one another's arms by the arrival of automation.

New ship design, new machinery, new methods of bulk handling of cargo faced both workers and employers alike with a waterfront revolution. New ways of handling sugar, for instance, reduced the number of men needed to unload a 10,000-ton freighter from 164 to 25, working a forty-hour week. Huge benefits were thus available both to the employers and to the waterfront workers; and eventually the deals were made. The employers were free to install any machines they liked; in return, they set up a fund of $29 million to make sure that the machines did not reduce the earnings of the employees. Today, the longshoremen can be said to have joined the prosperous middle class, often earning more than white-collar workers.[2] The union has even turned landlord, diversifying into apartment blocks. With the increase in money has come a decrease in the old idealism. The union now is exclusive, with a sharp eye out for interlopers. Its reputation as a union entirely free of corruption has faded. Nor have its members shown much enthusiasm for the two principal left-wing causes of recent years, civil rights for the blacks, and the war in Vietnam: the war, indeed, has brought a lot of business to the California waterfront, and still higher wages to the longshoremen.[3] So the union has changed, and Harry Bridges with it. Nowadays, old-style left-wing intellectuals in the bay area speak of him with sadness and, sometimes, a touch of contempt. They feel he has, in his old age, sold out. Thus the taming of the longshoremen, and of other unions, has deprived the modern protest movement of any hope of finding a base among the white working class.

A connected reason for the detached nature of the Californian left is that they have never managed to produce an intellectual theory tailored to the achievement of power. The United States has a written constitution, which guarantees basic human rights. In Europe, men have had to battle for the establishment of those rights and have been compelled to find a theory to go to war with. In America, the struggle has been over the implementation of the rights already guaranteed, for almost everyone—even Harrison Gray Otis, and certainly Ronald Reagan—has publicly agreed on the basic principles of American life; namely, liberty, fraternity, equality, and the sanctity of private property. Even Upton Sinclair, who was regarded by the establishment of his day as a socialist of the most dangerous kind, wanted to abolish all taxes on owner-occupied houses and small ranches. Those outside this mainstream—the Communist Party, the Norman Thomas socialists, the Industrial Workers of the World, who filled the jails of Fresno and San Diego on the eve of World War I and stood for a federation of industries owned by the workers—have never been able to find a doctrine that appealed to their main potential supporters, the white industrial working class. The workers have clung to the belief, first, that their rights were already established, and second, that the capitalist system would deliver—as, in the event, it has.

Lacking an anchor, today's actual or self-styled revolutionaries are fragmented and without consistent direction. For a time in the early sixties, members of the then prominent Students for a Democratic Society, which grew out of the civil-rights struggles in the south, thought that they might be able to construct a base among the black proletariat. In October, 1960, the Student Non-Violent Coordinating Committee was set up jointly by blacks and whites; they affirmed "the religious ideal of nonviolence" and announced that they sought "a social order permeated by love." Students from the University of California, including Mario Savio, were well to the fore in this movement. But in 1966 SNCC abandoned nonviolence and later on excluded whites altogether. By the end of the sixties it was plain that blacks and whites, especially white students, had different aims.

Today, the various groups are more divided than ever. Eldridge Cleaver, exiled in Algeria, has attacked other Panther leaders and announced that Angela Davis is a dupe of the Communists. Jerry Rubin, formerly a hero to students in the bay area, has been attacked by the Berkeley *Tribe,* the most unrelenting of the underground papers, as a clown on an ego-trip who cannot be taken seriously. Marcuse has become less and less read or listened to on the campuses, and he in return has firmly dissociated himself from the farther shores of student rebellion.

CESAR CHAVEZ

> And over our ill-kept, shadeless, dusty roads, where a house is an unwanted landmark, and which run frequently for miles through the same man's land, plod the tramps, with blankets on back, the laborers of the Californian farmer, looking for work, in its seasons.
>
> *Henry George, 1871*

Some individual groups, however, still retain plenty of vitality; and none more so than the Mexican agricultural workers led by Cesar Chavez. Of all the multifarious protesters in California,

Chavez is the easiest to understand. He, at least, is fighting a familiar battle—the right of workers to combine in a union to protect themselves against exploitation: and the battle goes on in the old-fashioned, sepia world of *The Grapes of Wrath,* apparently unconnected with anything else in California. Chavez's followers are victims of a system of seasonal labor whose record, the U.S. Senate's La Follette Committee concluded back in the thirties, "discloses with monotonous regularity a shocking degree of human misery."

Mexicans worked most of California's crops in the twenties; they were pushed south again to Mexico during the great Depression; with World War II, they traveled north again. The *braceros,* as they were called, became a sad feature of the Californian landscape, performing both the backbreaking "stoop" labor and the "upright" labor—pruning and thinning and irrigation. Finally, in 1964, despite the protests of the state's farmers, Congress ended the *bracero* system. And with the abolition of the cheap labor supply came the promise, for the first time in generations, of unionizing farm labor.[4]

Attempts to organize the farm workers have had a long and dreary history of failure. The huge fields of central California do not lend themselves to picketing. Workers could not be pulled out and kept out, on the traditional pattern, partly because the growers could always bring in other workers, and partly because no union ever had enough money to pay strikers a living wage. There was a further obstacle: all the local institutions, the police, and the government officials were wholly on the side of the growers and against any strikers. It was this formidable set of obstacles that Chavez overcame, in one of the most extraordinary and moving stories in American social history.

The story of his grape strike, which is also the possibly far more important story of how the Mexican-American community found a new self-respect, centers around Delano, a small town in the middle of the Great Central Valley. Unlike other grape-growing areas of the world, the terrain around Delano is flat—a dispiriting endless plain, with no fences, few trees, and little to look at except straight rows of crops stretching away forever. The place seems timeless, removed from the rest of California, flattened by the weight of the sun. From March to October, valley people rarely see a cloud.

The main feature of Delano itself is a double line of large metal sheds in which farm machinery is sold. At night, there is a constant din from the big piggyback trucks hurtling along State Highway 99 through the middle of the valley, and from the alarming whistles of the Southern Pacific freight trains, rattling between Santa Fe and San Francisco.[5] The country around Delano grows not only grapes but cotton, roses, big potatoes, oranges, and mile upon mile of almonds. The wine grapes are increasingly picked by machine, the table grapes by hand. Only one local winery is owned by a big firm; the rest are family firms or cooperatives.

Visiting Delano not long ago, I called first on the general manager of the local paper, the Delano *Record,* to discuss the grape strike. He said at once that he thought the reporting of it in the national press had been disgracefully slanted. Delano, he said, was presented as a rundown place with nothing but drab streets and mean houses, and the growers were caricatured as big, fat, rich, whip-carrying slave-drivers. It was just incredible. Most of the growers were not against the formation of a union at all, he went on, but they were worried about what it could portend. It could mean that, as a result of union action, the growers would have no control over the prices of their products, so that a bad year with low demand could wipe them out. "As for the famous grape strike," he added, "basically there hasn't been a strike. The day it is supposed to have started, back in September, 1965, it was reported that there were thousands of pickers walking off their jobs, and hundreds of pickets. But I was up there as a reporter, camera in hand, and I never found one. The whole strike is a confidence trick."

Chavez, whom I visited next, lives one block over from the *Record,* in a small frame house with worn yellow-brown paint. An old car in the drive was plastered with "Don't Buy California

Grapes" stickers; a very large bodyguard leaned against a tree on the sidewalk. Chavez's life has been threatened more than once, and the guard didn't seem too friendly until he gathered that I was a foreigner. At length, I was admitted. Chavez was in bed with a bad back, so I interviewed him in his bedroom, which few journalists and no grape growers or local Anglos see; if they did, I thought, they could hardly continue to describe him as a Communist. There was a rosary over the bed, a small Catholic shrine against the wall, and a prominent photograph of Gandhi. The books beside the bed did not seem those of a Communist, either: George Woodcock on *Civil Disobedience,* Gandhi's *All Men Are Brothers,* Bonhoeffer's *Letters and Papers from Prison,* Tolstoi on *Civil Disobedience,* and a biography of Gandhi.

Chavez is small, with jet-black hair and a gold eyetooth. To talk to, he is gentleness itself, but it became plain as we conversed that he must possess exceptional willpower. His whole cast of mind, though by no means devoid of cunning, struck me as that of a religious man. "I am a Catholic, you know," he said mildly at one point, and I did not disbelieve him.

I asked him to tell me his life story. "There's really nothing to it," he said slowly. "I come from three generations of poverty; I really don't have anything to brag about. My father was born on a hacienda in Mexico where his father was pretty much a slave. In 1887 my grandfather ran away to El Paso in Texas, and he was there working on the railroad when some politician came along and asked him for his vote. As you can understand, he was totally illiterate, both in English and Spanish, and he replied 'But I'm not a citizen,' and the politician said, 'That's okay, I'll fix it.' And he did; he made him a citizen, though I've never been able to figure out how, and he voted for this gentleman. Later on he moved from Texas to Yuma, Arizona, and there someone told him that American citizens could homestead land in Arizona. So he homesteaded in a very fertile, very small little valley, and my father grew up there, one of a family of sixteen kids, and that's where I was born.

"Then something happened; the land was taken away; it was

one of those illegal things. My family were thrown out; big companies moved in, and instead of owning a small plot of land we became migratory workers. We moved to California, traveling up and down the state, and Delano was one of the stops on our pilgrimage, where we picked cotton and grapes, usually in the fall. Then after about five years, around 1941, I guess, we decided to stay in Delano and make it our winter home, migrating north in the summer. We picked everything under the sun, except pockets, of course.

"Then came the Second World War, and I did a hitch in that [in a U.S. Navy destroyer]. I came back to Delano, married—my wife was raised here—and in 1949 we moved to San José. I had had little education, you understand. In those days it was very difficult both to get an education and to keep alive. They used to close the schools to Mexican Americans and Negroes until the cotton and grapes were in: the other kids had to go, but we were excluded.

"After the war there were several short-lived attempts to organize the workers, and my family were always the first to join, mostly because of my father. But the movements would only last for two or three days, the fever would subside, and that would be the end of that."

In 1952 Chavez was working in an apricot orchard in San José when he was approached by a local priest and urged to attend a meeting arranged by the new Community Service Organization, which had been set up to try to help the Mexican-American poor. The CSO already had some successes to its credit. It had fought and won the first school segregation case in the country. Still more impressive, it had taken on and defeated the police department of Los Angeles when, in the famous Bloody Christmas case, six drunken cops who had beaten up Mexican prisoners were sent to the state penitentiary. The CSO was now looking for volunteers to register Mexican-Americans for voting, to urge noncitizens to become citizens, and to persuade them to learn how to read and write—at least enough to vote. Chevez joined the CSO as a volunteer, lost his job, and then became a full-time organizer.

"It was a way to strike back against the poverty and the misery and the police brutality: a way to correct some of those ills."

He became executive director of the whole movement, but gradually became disenchanted by it. He had expected that the CSO, once it got going, would take on the problems of the farm workers. But it never did. "It got caught up in city problems and inaction, and became top-heavy with self-appointed leaders."

In 1957, Chavez began to agitate within the CSO for a union, by that time convinced that the main Mexican-American problem was economics, not race.

He began to investigate previous efforts to organize the farm workers, and to identify the reasons for their failure. First, he found, the activists had always tried to organize the workers and to strike at the same time. Second, the success of the strikes depended on the flow of money. If a thousand men struck, the organizers tried to pay them. "It was like pouring money down a rat hole, because the employers would simply bring in other men. Instead of a strike lasting six months, it had to fold up after six days." Third, there was the psychological problem. If the laborers struck a tomato field, the growers would harvest it with scab labor, and the strikers would find themselves striking nothing but a piece of bare ground: the very thing they were protesting about disappeared. "There was another point: the strikers would be starving, while the leaders were well fed. It was just one more thing that had to be explained." Defeat followed defeat; and the unions that supplied the money, millions of dollars, were disappointed when they didn't get results.

It was against this apparently hopeless background that Chavez went to work to form the first effective farm workers' union in American history. Early in 1962 he quit the CSO. "I thought I had a two percent chance of success. My friends in the CSO said, 'He's got eight children. He'll be back.'

"I came to Del.no, where I knew I could get people together. I thought: I have got to see this valley once more. So I started traveling, in my old car; I began up in the Tehachapis, then went from Bakersfield to Fresno, just looking at the topography and the system. I went east and west and all the way up north to Chico, and I would stop at all the chambers of commerce and pick up the histories of the little towns, and at night I would read them. Finally I came back to Delano. I got here at two in the morning, and my wife wanted to know all about my journey: did I see anything different? And I said 'You know, it's damn big. It's frighteningly big. But,' I said, 'it's got to be done,' and so we started."

The CSO offered Chavez financial help, but he refused, on the grounds that outside money had played too large a role in the past, and that if the new system was to be a success the workers themselves must finance their own union. But the trouble was that the workers did not want a union and could not be persuaded to pay for one.

"So I went to work in the fields, and spent hours winning little problems in the lives of the people. They would offer me money in return, but I would reply, 'You owe the union.' At about that time a cousin of mine arrived from Arizona and said cynically: 'There must be a gimmick, or why are you doing all this?' I replied that it must be very difficult for him to understand, because I was doing something that required a very skillful organizer to accomplish. He was a salesman, and my remark wounded his pride. I said: 'You try it. No money. No food. But St. Francis never really worried about having anything, and I'm sure his part of the world was a lot poorer than our part of the world, and *he* made it. So why couldn't we do the same thing?' And my cousin said, 'You know, you have a point.' And the movement changed his life.

"We decided we had to establish places where we could go and beg for food. I felt I would be humiliated if I were turned away by someone more prosperous than I was, so we decided to go to the poorest people. They didn't even look surprised. They didn't know who we were, or what we were doing. Sometimes we did try the better homes. From the poorer homes, we were never turned away; from the better homes, almost always."

By the fall of 1962, Chavez felt confident enough of the growing strength of his union to call a convention to discuss a program and establish a regular system of union dues. On September 30, the convention assembled, with some seventy small towns represented by some 250 people. Chavez wanted to charge one dollar a month; his cousin five dollars. At four A.M. they compromised on three-fifty, but made it a family affair, so that if one member of the family paid dues, then all the rest, even if there were twelve of them, got cards. "So the union began. We kept it quiet."

Three years later, Chavez called his strike where he had his strongest base, in Delano. The growers were bewildered and at first scornful. They knew of no union: they began to refer to the "so-called strike." And in a way they were right. As Chavez told me, "The union wasn't very large. The plan was to let everyone know that the strike was on, and get more and more and more support. It worked, thank God. Now we've got banks and railroads and God-knows-what involved against us. We will win the strike, because we've only got to do one thing, whereas the growers have to grow, sell, store, transport, and hire labor. They are a fixed target, but we don't need a rigid organization; the more fluid we are, the better. We've got nothing to lose. We're being sued now for millions of dollars, but I haven't lost a wink of sleep over that because we don't have the money."

He summed up. "Our fight has become a national issue. The church has helped, which is close to a miracle. The students have helped most: they were the first, and they've been with us ever since. The idea that farm workers have the right to collective bargaining is pretty well implanted now. But it's a constant battle. In America, everyone aspires to be a millionaire. In other countries, workers are content to be workers."

After I left Chavez, I reflected that the famous grape strike, which had attracted the support of bishops and governors and senators, to say nothing of the entire Kennedy family, had been less of a strike than a vast public-relations exercise. Unlike other union leaders, Chavez was not able to bring direct pressure on the employers, and had to resort to indirect pressure. Public opinion was crucial; what he had to do was convince the United States that an injustice was being done; and he did this largely through the device of the grape boycott, an idea that only came to him three months after the strike began. People across the U.S. slowly learned that for some reason someone didn't want them to eat California grapes. Then when they heard about Chavez and his cause, some of them supported him. In getting this support, Chavez needed ordinary people—doctors, churchmen, house-wives, students—more than politicians.

The bewilderment and irritation of the local newspaperman was understandable. There were few pickets; the union was small; production was not being seriously interrupted. The "strikers," indeed, were actually at work all through the strike, though they were not picking grapes. Yet most of the United States believed that an orthodox strike was on, and all the time Delano was get-ting a worse and worse name. The growers—by no means the brutal Wasp combines that the public imagination conjured up, but mainly the hard-working sons of Yugoslav peasants who had arrived in the Valley owning nothing—were not helped by the way the right wing, and some of the Delano police kept calling Chavez and his lieutenants Communists, when it was plain to any rational observer that they were no such thing.

Throughout the struggle, it was very important for Chavez— despite the constant provocations and even physical assaults on his supporters by agents of the growers—never to appear either as a racist or as an advocate of violence. He is not naturally either of these, but it was vital that he not move an inch in either direc-tion, lest he alienate the middle-of-the-road whites whose sup-port he had to have. He was wise to look to Gandhi, who by com-parable means aroused the conscience of Britons about India. What was obscure to me was how far Chavez himself realized fully what had happened. His men from time to time had imitated the expected features of a strike: workers would walk off; pickets would show up. But the crucial element in Chavez's success has been the aroused conscience of America.

For a union leader, Chavez is quite philosophical. "What you do in life is an accident," he told me. "Your life is determined by those who love you, and those who hate you." He also told me what he had learned about power. "It affects you; it really does. And the longer you stay in power, the more it affects you. People keep power, first, through the iron fist; and, second, through hypocrisy."

He has a dream for his union. "We want to go into housing. If a worker's storm drain gets plugged, we want to take care of it. The idea of a community is very important. But we need political power. Some day, we'll take the city on, and that day things are going to change."

It used to be said that the chicanos were a sleepy people, hard to rouse, awkward to organize, and apathetic because of their Catholicism. Few people still take that view. Chavez has surprised everyone by showing what can be done; the mistake of the growers was precisely to underrate him as "a dumb Mex." Ultimately, though, the cause for which Chavez has fought during most of his adult life is doomed; the United Farm Workers will eventually yield to machines that will pick grapes as gently as a hand.[6] The real battle of the chicanos will be fought, as Chavez says, when they "take the city on." It is to be hoped that the city, as that time steadily approaches, will show more imagination about what is involved than the rural representatives of "the authorities" who have opposed Chavez in Delano.

BLACK PANTHERS

The two main minority protest movements in California, Brown Power and Black Power, share the same root; they begin on the land. The blacks were pushed out of the rural south into the northern cities, where their frustrations boiled over and exploded. Many of the chicanos now stirring in Los Angeles or Fresno were once on the land; some of them used to be landowners (like the family of Chavez). But the two movements have developed in different ways. The blacks' new self-awareness has grown up through action in the cities; the chicanos', through action in the fields. The difference has been partly caused by the whites. Urban whites are rarely (so far) frightened by chicanos, but they are often alarmed by blacks. The Panther movement was born in the slums of Oakland, largely in response to persecution by the white Oakland police.

From the beginning, the Panthers accordingly needed a tight organization (unlike Chavez); and it is no accident that their first international headlines were stimulated by their armed march on city hall in San Francisco. They are a paramilitary outfit. Whereas Chavez's concept of leadership is first to listen carefully to the ideas of his followers and learn from them, the Panther leaders tell their followers what to do, issuing orders like officers in a regiment. Huey Newton, whatever else he may be, is first and foremost a commander; and without his authority the Panthers would not have held together for so long.

But there are other blacks, no less committed to the general cause, who think the Panthers have gone about their work in entirely the wrong way. One of their most cogent and best qualified black critics is Dr. Carlton B. Goodlett. An energetic and outspoken man, Goodlett is the Panthers' physician, editor and publisher of a black paper, the *Sun Reporter,* and a recipient of the Lenin Commemorative Medal, presented to him in San Francisco by a delegation from Moscow in the autumn of 1970, to honor his work for the world peace movement. Goodlett, when I saw him, had just been talking to a black revolutionary group at San Francisco State College that had presented the college authorities with a set of demands while at the same time saying that the demands were not negotiable. "I told them it was silly. How could they fight a battle at San Francisco State? There's no cover there: scarcely a blade of grass: and they hadn't got enough firepower to last thirty seconds. I told them it was the job of a revolutionary to survive."

Goodlett had been lecturing the Panthers themselves on the same theme, he told me. He had spoken to a group of them, including Bobby Seale, he said, and "it was so quiet you could have heard a mouse piss on damp cotton-wool. I asked them if they couldn't stop using Maoist or Marxist phrases in every third sentence: couldn't they quote the Lincoln-Douglas debates for a change? And I told them their organization was much too tight; do you know, my own son couldn't get in. They have missed a great opportunity. They could have brought together all the young blacks in the entire country, instead of just having an organization of five thousand. They could have done it. But they've gone in the wrong direction. I told them that if they didn't change their methods, they would all end up under tombstones, or in jail, in exile like Cleaver, or underground: and what would that have accomplished?"

Goodlett criticized Huey Newton, too, for his recently announced intention of getting together a group to fight for North Vietnam against the south. It was absurd, Goodlett said, so patently absurd as to discredit the movement. "Newton should be organizing the black liberation movement to keep himself out of jail." Goodlett made the same criticism of the most militant blacks that I had heard applied to the most militant whites: "They think it all started the day they themselves became aware."

Goodlett himself is up to his neck in politics; he takes the position that whites can be made to yield much more by, roughly speaking, traditional means than by the tactics adopted by the Panthers. He thought the Panthers were running into a dead end —probably literally. I found the Goodlett view of the Panthers refreshing, since most Californians regard them either as a disease in their midst that must be stamped out, or, if they are left-inclined, they are so guilty about blacks that they feel they have no right to be critical at all.

The Panthers now have invented a kind of politics of their own, drawing up their own constitution and appointing their own ministers, as if a black state could be brought into existence by such means alone. One of their weaknesses is that by keeping their proceedings so much inside a semisecret group (in the fall of 1970, I was not allowed to attend a Huey Newton speech, although I had the usual credentials of a foreign journalist working in America), the information that reaches the public is thoroughly distorted. The Panthers would argue that the media misrepresent them deliberately, which may be true of some, but not of all. The fact that the Panthers' ideas of socialism sound quite similar to those of Clement Attlee after World War II is a judgment that I had to get second-hand from a reliable reporter, Nora Sayre; the general public in California, and in the U.S. as a whole, has no real idea of where the Panthers stand on anything —even on relations with whites. One point that did strike me about Newton's published announcements (Goodlett's strictures notwithstanding) was the frequency with which he quotes the Declaration of Independence, concerning "the right of the People to alter or to abolish" a government which is destructive of their rights and "to provide new Guards for their future security." Perhaps part of the reason for the Panthers' incoherence is, as we saw earlier, that *in theory* their rights are already established under the Constitution, so that all they have to do is to fight for their implementation, and not construct a political theory. What concerns them is whether the whites will or will not give them their rights. As Huey Newton has said, "It is a fact that we will change the society. . . . It will be up to the oppressors if this is going to be a peaceful change."

WAR ON THE CAMPUS

Most Californian whites have a good idea why there are brown and black revolts. What they find inexplicable is the campus war. Californians these days are not as bullish as they used to be, however. They, like the young, lost enthusiasm long ago for the Vietnam War, and feel that society has taken a wrong turning. Student social protest, to the mass of Californian whites, would be understandable. What they cannot understand is the violence of the student revolt, its aggression, and its across-the-board rejection of all adult attitudes.

Even now, eight years after the first battle in the campus war, there is no generally agreed-on analysis of it, although some of the cleverest people in the United States—the Berkeley faculty—have had a grandstand view of the action from their office windows. To me, the most persuasive account comes from John Searle, a philosophy professor at Berkeley. At the beginning of the time of troubles, Searle was heavily engaged on the side of the student protesters; he was one of the faculty members who helped undermine the position of Clark Kerr, the president of the University of California, who was driven from office shortly after Reagan was elected governor. Later Searle found himself increasingly exasperated by, and hostile to, the way the revolt was developing, and became one of the Berkeley faculty who were officially engaged in trying to keep it within bounds.

On the flyleaf of his book, *The Campus War*, Searle puts a quotation from Crane Brinton, the historian of the French Revolution:

> The devotional language of the Jacobins, their frequent access of collective emotion, their conviction of righteousness, their assurance that their opponents are sinners, direct agents of the devil, their intolerance, their desire for martyrdom, their total want of humor—all these are unmistakable signs of the theological temperament.

Searle says he first began to notice the religious character of the student revolt during the great night march of 1965 when 14,000 of the faithful marched in solemn procession through the streets of South Berkeley in a manner that recalled Holy Week in Spain. "The liturgical style," says Searle, "was perhaps most visible in the Vietnam moratoria of 1969, with their candlelight processions and the gripping solemn roll call of the dead, an alphabetical litany, a ritual exorcism of the devil of the Establishment." The students with whom Searle battled in the months and years after the Free Speech Movement were offering their hearers, he concluded, not a set of political aims, or a program of university reform, but a chance to find a meaning in life. They preached personal fulfillment.

Looked at as a religious movement, the student revolt becomes much more comprehensible. Its opponents often ask: why do they want to tear away the thin crust of civilization that man has precariously achieved after centuries of effort and suffering, when they have no coherent ideas about what to put in its place? The answer is that religions on the march always want to transform the life around them. This aim always appears to the defenders of the status quo as sabotage. Besides, the concerns of religion—a religion taken seriously by its adherents, that is—will invariably seem outlandish to outsiders. As Searle remarks, the university administrators who have had to grapple with the student revolt as it has swept across the world have been like Roman governors confronted with the early Christians.

BERKELEY

The face of Berkeley becomes at once more understandable if, peering into it, one keeps the religious interpretation in mind. A stranger arriving at Berkeley for the first time, provided there isn't actually a riot in progress, may well be surprised by its air of sleepiness. The campus occupies one of the finest university sites in the world: big cedars, lawns with scrupulously clipped edges, a view across to the Golden Gate Bridge, an elegant student union, and the dear old campanile in the middle, playing "Widdecombe Fair" on the bells. What could be more peaceful than Berkeley on a quiet day?

Even on the most somnolent days, though, one can usually encounter some group engaged in what can be interpreted as religious activity: that is, an activity which pertains to putting the soul into contact with extraterrestial concerns. For a place that is often regarded as, in Professor J.K. Galbraith's phrase, "the most intense intellectual and political community in the world," its members spend an exceptional amount of time sitting around in silence doing nothing. On the dozens of occasions that I strolled about the campus, I invariably saw young men and girls sitting alone and gazing into space, as if in meditation. Once, out-side the student union, I came across one of the shaven-headed Hare Krishna adherents, robed in orange, wearing dirty gray socks, seated cross-legged on the ground. Around him, ten or a dozen deep, were students, some leaning on their elbows, some cross-legged in imitation of the Hare Krishna man, others hug-ging their knees, others standing. Many of them were holding books or files, as if they had stopped on their way to or from lec-tures. Absolutely nothing was happening, except that nothing was happening, which was perhaps the point. I, too, sat down, and waited for an event—music, perhaps; a statement; even a prayer. But the nothing continued, and eventually, uncomfortable and bored, I moved on, leaving the strange assembly as I had found it, still in silence. Viewed as a bunch of students sitting on their asses wasting time, the scene is incomprehensible—that is not the way students waste time. Viewed as a form of religious activity, it becomes understandable.

There is a clue here to the difference in the way student mili-tants and black militants receive question-asking strangers. The blacks are hostile. They want to put you down. They want you to understand that for once they, the blacks, are in a position to grant or refuse a white man's request. They are on top. There is no trace of this attitude with the student militants. They may not always choose to be helpful, and they may not answer your ques-tions; but they are never (in my experience) openly aggressive: they receive you with a kind of superior tolerance, much as a gathering of evangelicals might receive a known and incorrigible atheist. The blacks want their rights; the warring students want a creed.

But why did the student revolt start at Berkeley? One can only guess, but some of the reasons may be included in the following list:

1. Affluence. One reason why students now are able to ask their startled professors "What is the purpose of life?" whereas their predecessors asked "What have you got to teach me?" is sim-ply that this post-depression generation worries little about ca-

reers. They assume that the Californian cornucopia will continue to pour out its benefits without their help. I was often struck by the contrast between the appearance of the loiterers on Telegraph Avenue, who looked as if they could scarcely raise the price of a joint between them, and the sleek shops in which one could see them making purchases. The main coffee shop at Berkeley, a center of militant talk and planning, offered a wide range of high-priced coffee—Turkish, espresso, Mexican—and trays of rich and expensive cakes that would test the willpower of the most dedicated macrobiotic adherent. I bought the *Berkeley Barb* one day from a bedraggled salesman on Telegraph; I thought he would be glad, poor fellow, of the few cents' commission. Next minute he was getting behind the wheel of a new Volkswagen. Of course, some of those who look poor *are* poor; but many are not.

2. Environment. Berkeley has long been one of the two or three most left-wing congressional districts in the United States (in the 1970 election it voted for Ron Dellums, about the most radical black ever to win a seat in Congress). The causes taken up by students in the early days were directly descended from those of the thirties: race (Jews and anti-Fascism in the thirties; blacks and "antifascism" in the sixties), and the Free Speech Movement itself stirred the blood in old liberal arteries: had not Adlai Stevenson himself been forbidden to speak on the Berkeley campus in 1952? As long ago as 1957 two sociology professors from the universities of Rochester and Michigan, having studied and questioned a sample of 894 students, found that Berkeley, by comparison with the other campuses, was "very libertarian indeed." There is ample evidence that libertarianism increases with education and urbanization, and that it is stronger in the west than in any other part of the United States. Since Berkeley students come largely from urban, middle-class families, that fact alone is enough to account for a good part of their libertarianism. As they go through the university, they become more libertarian still. In the early days, at least, most of the active students were not out of line with the way their parents would have wanted them to behave.

3. Tradition. Despite a widespread assumption now that Berkeley was all sweetness and light before the sixties, apart from the Great Panty Raid (almost a riot) of 1956, the campus in fact had a tradition of protest. As long ago as the 1880s Lincoln Steffens and his friends, because they objected to being treated like schoolboys, secured a ladder, pushed one end through the president's window, and stirred it around until everything in the room was shattered: the violence was successful, for the president was replaced. From 1935 to 1941 there were campus strikes annually against "War and Fascism."

4. Size and bleakness. Founded with 167 men and 22 women in 1873, Berkeley now contains 27,500 students. Including faculty and other staff, the campus population is larger than that of Modesto. There are 86 undergraduate departments, and more than 5000 courses. Size requires efficient administration. Here is a characteristically bleak passage from the Berkeley General Catalogue, laying down some of the rules that govern a student's progress.

For each unit of credit, grade A is assigned 4 grade points; B, 3 points; C, 2 points; D, 1 point; no grade points attach to other grades or symbols. The passing grades, A, B, C, and D, may be modified by plus (+) or minus (−) suffixes. "Minus" grades carry three-tenths grade point less per unit, and "plus" grades three-tenths grade point more per unit, except for the A + which carries 4.0 grade points per unit as does the A. The numerical values, or grade points, given above are intended to provide a more exact determination of a student's scholarship. To compute the grade-point average for course work . . . the point value of each grade is mutliplied first by the unit value of the course to obtain a total of all grade points earned. That total is then divided by the total units undertaken, exclusive of courses in which P, S, NP, U, or IP were assigned. The resulting figure is the grade-point average.

Another facet of the university as factory (though not confined to Berkeley) is that the bookshops are organized not by subjects, nor by authors, but by courses—as if the purpose of books is to enable students to obtain a high grade-point average. Browsing in a Berkeley bookshop is next to impossible; it is like walking along the sleepers of a railway line. A further crude, commercial division is often adopted whereby "hardback" bookstores do not stock paperbacks. Besides, the assistants often have no idea what books are on their own shelves and rarely know anything about books in general.

5. Experimental atmosphere. The air of Berkeley encourages experiment. Traditionally, the faculty have been liberal. In retrospect, it can be seen now that for the administration to yield to militant student demands is an irrelevant response, because the militants merely switch their demands until they find an issue on which the administration cannot yield. In the early days of the Berkeley revolt, the faculty was full of good-hearted people who were in sympathy with what they supposed to be—and which to some extent were—genuine student grievances. So the place was especially vulnerable. The students pushed, and it nearly collapsed.

6. Climate. Berkeley is hospitable to hangers-on from out-of-town, people who have nothing to do with the university but are not readily distinguishable from real students. Sleeping on pavements on a warm night is no hardship.

7. Berkeley is a good place to be. Hitch-hiking is taken for granted by the local population; the city of San Francisco is an easy hitch across the Bay bridge and is tolerant.

8. The main campus entrance, and the plaza in front of Sproul Hall, is a natural stage for demos, riots, etc., offering excellent backgrounds and sites for television cameras. Demos have often been timed to suit the evening TV news bulletins. Besides, magazine editors have known that they can rely on Berkeley to produce photogenic people, with every hope of perfect weather for color pictures. The People's Park troubles produced some of the best American photography for years.

9. The Regents. The university Board of Regents, the nearest that California has to an establishment, formed a specially tempting target, especially after Reagan became governor and an ex-officio Regent. The Regents govern the university, yet few of them know a great deal about it. Some are on the board because they are rich, some because they are politicians, some because they belong to a powerful institution—Lockheed, or the Bank of America, or a union. In accordance with a convention which no doubt at one time seemed rational, but which now seems insane, the Regents hold meetings and make decisions in public. I attended one Regents' meeting on the campus at Santa Cruz, at which a crucial decision about faculty appointments was on the agenda—so crucial that the president of UC, Charles Hitch, said that it could have disastrous consequences for the university: a question, he said, of the university's survival. Even before Governor Reagan arrived, the atmosphere on campus was electric: crowds of students with banners, huddles of nervous Regents. Inside the hall, when the meeting began, there were sixty reporters and a packed audience, with the Regents' wives anxiously seated in the front row; the Regents themselves were placed on a stage, as if about to take part in a play. Leaning against the wall behind Reagan stood his public-relations man, Lyn Nofziger, with his belly sagging over his trousers, chewing gum. Also on the platform were two armed policemen, and plainclothesmen guarded the doors, which were locked against the mass of students who had been unable to reserve seats. The proceedings were constantly interrupted by the angry rattling of the doors, and, because loudspeakers had been rigged to broadcast the Regents' words to those outside, by loud shouts of approval or disapproval. When Reagan spoke, some people in the hall hissed, and those outside yelled and jeered. Twice, a student in the hall stood up and shouted "Fuck Reagan!" in loud, clear tones.

This was the atmosphere in which the Regents were required to make a decision affecting the survival of the university. For the militant students, it was a field day, for which they had long been preparing.

10. Because the blacks of Oakland, the U.S. Navy, and Governor Reagan are prominent features of local life, and because many Berkeley scientists are heavily involved in the defense program, Berkeley students feel themselves to be specially near the front line. This circumstance may have made them specially optimistic that their protests could be effective, and also correspondingly alienated and volatile when they were not. By 1971, they had become almost totally unpredictable, even to themselves.

OLD LEFT AND NEW LEFT

Californian protest is at its most spectacular on the campus, but at its most revealing among the lawyers. One might expect law offices and courtrooms to offer little scope for novelty, but it is a sign of the times that they do. The arguments between the middle-aged lawyers of the Old Left—survivors of the Communist battles of the thirties and the McCarthyite battles of the fifties—and young men of the New Left perfectly illustrate not only the divisions of the protest movement, but still more the way the new protesters are determined to approach everything, even the profession of lawyer, *de novo,* and how they decline to pay attention to any lessons the past may provide.

The struggle between Old Left and New is at its sharpest in the Lawyers Guild, the long-established left-wing national organization. The New Left are trying to take it over, and they are succeeding. The Old Left president of the Guild, an able lady named Mrs. Roberson, told me that the old-timers, no matter how distinguished their battle honors might be, are regarded by the newcomers as traitors. "We failed to make the revolution, and therefore we are responsible for the way things are now."

Mrs. Roberson said that the young radicals coming into the profession were not really interested in the law as such: "They think of it as a vehicle for theatrical performances." Their hero, she said, was William Kunstler, who made a name for himself at the trial of the Chicago Seven; and she had found it impossible to convince them that Kunstler's theatricality on that occasion had very possibly not achieved the best results for his clients. He had been presented with fine openings by Judge Hoffman's provocations, but had made the mistake of becoming provocative also: "His reaction should have been to become extraprofessional, and thereby dominate the courtroom and ultimately the whole trial." She added that a Yale professor had been so irritated by the New Left's lack of interest in the law that he had suggested starting a lawyer's branch of the Lawyers Guild.

The New Left lawyers were not, she had found, the slightest bit interested in the past. "I organized a Marxist seminar for young lawyers," she told me. "None of them did the work; they don't read. Each meeting was a bull session for people to give *their* ideas. They were incapable of using the material as a take-off point for a discussion, or of analyzing the ideas raised by the material. I think they feel they have no time to be interested in the past, with the bomb hanging over us, and the warnings of ecological doom."

Another Old Left lawyer advised me, however, that the New Left's influence on courtroom techniques had in some ways been refreshing and effective.

"During the Communist trials of the thirties in California—the biggest series of trials before the Panther trials of the sixties—the Communists used to welcome prosecutions because they thought they could use them to get their ideas across. But a trial is a very poor way of doing that. The new style of defense is partly directed, as before, toward the community, but the real hope and expectation of the defendants is that they can reach the jury on the issues; it is based on a less cynical view of juries. The Old Left became rather defeatist. New Left influence in this sense began with the sit-ins; young people who came to lawyers wanted to involve them and have the lawyers help them try their own cases.

"If the personality of the defendant comes through, it often becomes hard for the prosecution to build up a conspiracy case. In the old days, juries were convinced the Communists were conspirators because they *acted* like conspirators. For years and years people hauled before the Un-American Activities Committee would remain silent: their defense was silence. The result was that they were prosecuted anyway, and they did not get their story across. But the episode that totally undermined the Congressional committees inquiring into subversion was when they subpoenaed Rubin and Hoffman; Rubin showed up in his revolutionary army costume, and, instead of remaining silent, they both talked their heads off: the committee couldn't stop them. Instead of denying the accusations they would say, 'Of *course* I'm in favor of overthrowing the government.' The committee simply stopped holding hearings.

"Similarly, in the case of the Oakland Seven, the defendants said: 'Of *course* we organized these demonstrations.' They convinced the jury that that was a proper patriotic thing to do. It is a more imaginative use of the law."

RON DELLUMS

Between the new protesters and the old political system there is by now almost a complete cut-off; the new-style protesters gyrate in a different firmament from the professionals at Sacramento. There is one man, however, who straddles, with increasing discomfort, the two worlds: Ron Dellums, the black who was elected congressman from Berkeley in the 1970 elections. Dellums was then thirty-four—tall, groovy, highly articulate; very reasonable in tone, very radical in content. He was born in Oakland, growing up alongside some of the Panthers; he became a social worker, took a master's degree, and then plunged into local politics as a member of the Berkeley City Council. In the council, Dellums adopted all the radical causes, including immediate withdrawal from Vietnam; he appointed himself spokesman for all the minorities, especially the blacks, and often shared the point of view of the Panthers, a movement he regards as a natural outgrowth of "America's racist society." He is, however, firmly opposed to the use of violence, which enables liberals to vote for him with a clear conscience.

In the primary in June, 1970, Dellums defeated a good liberal opponent, a Democrat who had been in Congress for twelve years. In the subsequent congressional election, he relied almost entirely on voluntary help. His campaign was fierce and radical: he banked on the guess that the Berkeley electorate was in a mood to reject what one of his campaign managers described to me as "that nice nice stuff"; and the blacks of Oakland (who are not in a majority there) plus the university community around Berkeley elected him.

It is a highly unusual event in American politics for a liberal to be defeated from the left. The Dellums victory was a symptom of the liberals' steady loss of support, because of their alleged ineffectiveness. The question is whether the militant Dellums will be any more effective. With him, the "system" is more than ever on trial. The leftist students worked for him; he is the only Californian politician of whom they approved. If he should drop out, there will be a total cut-off between these students and many Oakland blacks on the one hand, and the orthodox political process on the other. Some students, I noticed, hoped that Dellums *would* fail in Washington and thereby demonstrate the bankruptcy of the system once and for all.

What, then, has a decade of revolt achieved? In terms of the actual battlefields, the campuses and the ghettos, the answer is: very little. Despite early faculty boasts about its capacity to adapt itself to student complaints, and despite the students' boasts about its vulnerability, the University of California—its structure, methods, and even its caliber—is still much the same as it was ten years ago. One key formal demand of the student protesters was that there should be more contact between students and faculty; but a study of the whole university found that professors in 1970 spent less time with their students than in 1960—9.3 hours a week with third- and fourth-year students, against 12.8 hours a week a decade earlier. Students still have no say in the appointment of teachers, and the curriculum remains much as it was. In one respect, the students' cause has actually lost ground, because the university has silently eased out some of the faculty members whom the students found most relevant and stimulating.[7]

In the ghetto, the blacks are more embattled than ever, with unemployment, especially youth unemployment, getting worse and little attention given to the admittedly profoundly difficult problem of what a society does when there are not enough jobs for unskilled workers. Even the most menial jobs for blacks are disappearing. A fellow aboard an electric sweeping cart at one motel told me that in one hour he could sweep up an area that used to provide a full-time job for a man with a broom. Government programs come and go, but the problem remains. Meanwhile, divisions among blacks grow wider, with the Panthers—themselves increasingly divided—at one extreme, and at the other, the far more numerous bourgeois-minded blacks who are unwilling to forgo the benefits of an affluent society and in fact are still struggling to join it.

Nor can it be said that the prospects for other minorities have improved. Stirrings among the urban Mexicans became noticeable around 1967–68; but little has been done by the white authorities to review their grievances, although five years ago it was clear that the whites must act quickly if they wanted to avoid a brown replay of the black uprising. The prospect now, especially following the big Mexican-American riot of August, 1970, in Los Angeles, is of rising demands from a new breed of young chicano activists, fired by dreams of the old Aztec empire, being met with rising white resistance.

Perhaps the most baleful result of the revolt has been the undermining of the center position in Californian politics. The beginnings of unrest can be traced back to April, 1960, when fifty students went to Sacramento to picket the State Capitol and present a petition urging the abolition of the death penalty and a stay of execution for Caryl Chessman. The next month, there was a massive student rally against the House Un-American Activities Committee when it met in San Francisco amid rumors that a Berkeley teacher under investigation would not be rehired. The first confrontation between police and students occurred on that occasion on the steps of City Hall: police used hoses to wash students down the steps.

These two demonstrations had the full support of all liberals. What subsequently confused matters for California liberals, and has proved their undoing, was that thereafter protest increasingly involved violence and civil disobedience. A classic statement of the point of fissure is contained in a proclamation issued by the acting chancellor of Berkeley, Martin Meyerson, in January, 1965, in the wake of the outbreak of the Free Speech Movement, which had dislodged his predecessor. "I believe civil disobedience is warranted as a last resort in our democracy—it was warranted in Boston at the famous Tea Party—it has been warranted at other times and places. But civil disobedience is warranted only when there is no recourse to reasonable deliberation."

But the militants did not want reasonable deliberation. Nor did their opponents on the right. And the center has been squeezed between the two, becoming more and more blurred and confused, like civilians trapped in no-man's-land while armies to the right and left are opening fire. One senior administrator at Berkeley told me how Eldridge Cleaver came to make his famous appearance on the Berkeley campus, when he had the students shouting "Fuck Ronald Reagan" and scandalizing the state. It happened that a new university course called for a lecture on civil rights; plenty of speakers were available who had more experience and knowledge of civil rights than Cleaver. But the students did not want information: they wanted Cleaver, and they were backed by members of the faculty who were similarly indifferent to his qualifications. Cleaver's lecture probably did more damage to the university's image in the minds of ordinary Californians than any other single event. Film of Cleaver's angry face shouting "——ck Ronald Reagan" (you could hear the "ck" but not the "f") was later heavily used to great effect in a campaign television commercial by Max Rafferty. With Cleaver and the students abusing the governor on one side, and the right wing shouting "outrage!" on the other, the voices of the liberals in the middle could not be heard saying, "He should probably not have been invited onto campus in the first place because he did not have the necessary qualifications, and it is true that he behaved badly and did not give the lecture he agreed to give; nevertheless an academic institution must possess the absolute right to ask anyone it pleases to address its students." This rigmarole stood little chance of being attended to; one of the handicaps of liberalism is that "rational deliberation" takes up a lot of words. There is no middle-of-the-road slogan with the force and brevity of either "Send in the troops" or "Off the Pigs." Already by the midsixties the revolt had made both political extremes aware that they needed each other: Rafferty needed Cleaver, just as Cleaver needed Rafferty: the militant students needed Reagan as much as he needed them to get elected and reelected. What the revolt has principally achieved is to stir up—as we shall see in the next chapter—a formidable counterrevolt of the masses.

CHAPTER 7

The New Right Wing

> The right wing's effectiveness rests, . . . I believe,
> on certain points of contact with real problems of
> domestic life and foreign policy and widespread
> and deeply rooted American ideas and impulses.
> *Professor Richard Hofstadter*

Unlike their counterparts on the left, who are not interested in ancestors, the right-wingers of California live off the past, and especially off the powerful myth of the conquest of the west. Most physical traces of the old west disappeared long ago, the trails turned into highways, the grizzlies and buffalo decimated, the prairies fenced in, and the wilderness tamed for national parks. Only the Indians, debased and mysterious, survive.

But the ideology of the old west is still going strong. The notion that rural democracy is superior to urban democracy; the idea of the individual standing on his own feet, beholden to no one; the cry of law and order; reliance on the gun; the suspicion of alien minorities: all these strands run through right-wing attitudes today. To find their source, one need go back only to the flood of nineteenth-century dime novels about the western movement. The dominating image that comes through all these westerns is of the posse riding off to get their man or, especially, the decent, straightforward hero in the empty street confronting the villain, his hand poised over his gun. As Leslie Fiedler has

146

pointed out, the pattern was set once and for all in Owen Wister's *The Virginian*, in which "the horseman, the cowpuncher, the last romantic figure upon our soil" upholds standards of behavior that have long since lapsed elsewhere, including the east. Fiedler says of this type, "If he gave his word, he kept it; Wall Street would have found him behind the times. Nor did he talk lewdly to women; Newport would have found him old-fashioned." These are words that Reagan would be proud to have as his epitaph. But, as Fiedler says, it is personal violence, taking the law into one's own hands, for which *The Virginian* primarily stands. When the posse rides out or the good man guns down the villain, the justification is always the same: extralegal violence is the only protector of true justice in a world where authority has gone to seed and savagery is close at hand. It is not pure accident that the right wing's principal hero emerged from the movie industry, which took over as western myth-maker from the dime novelists, and inherited, too, the dime novel's plots and standards.

And the movies have remained an ideological battleground. In *High Noon,* Gary Cooper, playing the sheriff, is possessed by doubts about his capacity for the job and ends up throwing his badge into the dust. John Wayne thought *High Noon* was Communist-inspired (the scriptwriter, Carl Foreman, was driven from the United States by McCarthyite harrassments). As a riposte, Wayne made *Rio Bravo,* in which the sheriff behaves in exactly the opposite way, standing firm in the time-honored manner and adopting the positive approach. Wayne these days is the only big star who still makes westerns that embody the full-blown myth. He is now Governor Reagan's most prominent supporter in the film world, just as Reagan used to be Goldwater's. Undoubtedly, there is a close link in the public mind between what Wayne represents on the screen and what Reagan stands for in politics. Occasionally, Reagan appears in public on horseback wearing a Stetson, and the role of modern governor merges into the role of old-time sheriff. It is another example of California's habit of blurring the distinction between reality and unreality.

But Reagan has shown himself to be much more than a faded

movie star, and he is harder to classify than at first appears. So are his supporters. Part of the difficulty here is the left-wing tendency to lump all Californian right-wingers together and label them fascists—in the same way that the right wing lumps left-wingers together and calls them Communists. These are dangerous practices; they not only increase mutual anger and intolerance (which is, of course, why some extremists use the labels), but also make it harder to cut through the rhetoric to the appeal of each group. As one approaches the Californian right, now riding high in the saddle there and showing little sign of toppling out, it is important to realize that many of those who now support Reagan are exactly the same people who, in the fifties, voted for the moderate Republican governor Earl Warren, and later for the Democratic governor Edmund G. Brown.

THE LUNATIC RIGHT

It is prudent first of all to separate the lunatic right from what may be called the rational right. One night in an Oakland bar a fellow-drinker advised me that the real agent of California's ills was Khrushchev—at that time long in retirement. Khrushchev, my acquaintance recalled, had visited Los Angeles and had been insulted by Mayor Yorty, who had scornfully introduced him as the man who planned to "bury America." Khrushchev had been very angry; but in San Francisco, by contrast, he had been very well received, kissed on both cheeks by Mayor Christopher, and given a golden key to the city. This, my acquaintance earnestly explained, had given Khrushchev his opportunity; using the pliant Christopher, he had arranged for California to enter a time of troubles; "Since then, we've been falling apart, with the war, and the students out of hand, and Negro pimps everywhere, and the shootings, and the streets not safe to walk on."

Besides the friendly nut, California also specializes in the crazy mimeographed pamphlet. At the Rand Corporation in Santa Monica I was given a fuzzy copy of the "Official Anti-Riot Instructions of the American Civilian Defense Committee (ACDC), issued as a public service." The man who gave it to me had gotten it from his secretary, who had been given it by someone in Pasadena. This document said that "riots and destruction were promised by Reds, their Pawns and Dupes," and that the police, "hampered by constitutionally illegal Supreme Court edicts," would not be allowed, when the destruction started, to protect law-abiding citizens. Therefore, all law-abiding citizens must organize their own defense as follows: "FOOD—keep your cupboards full. The subversives are counting on HUNGRY, PANIC-STRICKEN PEOPLE adding to the confusion. WATER—have some jugs and jars stored away (keeps six or seven months). Also there are forty or more gallons in your HOT WATER TANK. This will be a safe source of water if the supply hasn't been poisoned. Keep a LANTERN, LAMP, OR CANDLES; a Japanese Hibachi, Camp Stove, or canned heat stove; fireplace fuel; flashlight; paper plates, cups, towels, etc. Line Up Trusted Neighbors for sentries or patrol-shifts to warn of danger."

Better known than the obscure ACDC are the Minutemen, who first attracted public notice in 1962 when their southern California branch claimed that Red Chinese troops were massing over the Mexican border and preparing to invade the United States. It was after this announcement that the Minutemen were photographed, allegedly on maneuvers, with howitzers in the hills. Certainly they believe in being armed at all times. As a gun-shop owner in Stockton, who distributes Minuteman literature, put it: "The private citizen has an inalienable right to carry around his own machine gun, howitzer, or atomic device."

Not much has been heard of the Minutemen lately. Such groups come and go. While I was in San Francisco in 1969, eight members of another armed group called "The Society of Man" were arrested following an alarming series of explosions at public utility installations, including electricity towers. At the society's headquarters, the police picked up not only bomb-making equipment, Nazi flags, and photographs of Hitler, but also piles of devotional literature. "Eight Members of Bible Society held in

Bombings," read one headline.

But the largest and most significant group on the Lunatic Right is the John Birch Society, founded in 1958 by the notorious ex-candy manufacturer, Robert H. W. Welch, Jr. According to Welch, Birch was the first victim of the cold war; he was an army captain and Baptist missionary who was killed shortly after the end of World War II by the Chinese Communists. The Birchers did not start in California, but it is in the southern counties now that they have their main stronghold, with full-time organizers and a prominent role in politics. Because membership is secret, estimates of Bircher strength vary, but they are supposed to have some 15,000 supporters in southern California, organized into 1200 chapters. The Birchers are not part of the "armed" right, as are the Minutemen, and they are not racist, as are the Ku Klux Klan. Nor are they exclusive: they include Catholics (very strong), Protestants, Jews, and blacks. Their main obsession is that the United States is being undermined by a gigantic conspiracy and may at any instant succumb. They see the threat coming, not only from the Reds outside, but still more dangerously from America's own institutions—the presidency, the Supreme Court, the State Department.

In 1961, the Birchers singled out as the leading Californian conspirator Earl Warren, at that time chief justice of the Supreme Court. These attacks—preposterous as they were—provoked serious, and even national, concern. Warren's main defender was Tom Storke, the eighty-four-year-old editor of the *Santa Barbara News Press,* who went after the Birchers in a series of fierce editorials, backed up with news stories. For this "crusade" (as his autobiography calls it) he was given an award by Harvard "for outstanding work in defense of civil liberties," and a Pulitzer Prize by Columbia University. Absurd though the Birchers seem, many politicians in California are wary of their talent for character assassination; and no right-wing politician ever publicly raises his voice against them, though he may try to keep his distance. The Birchers claimed to have one hundred delegates in the Cow Palace in San Francisco when Goldwater won the Republican nomination, a striking sign of power. Does southern California attract Birchers, or does it create them? One clue to the puzzle may be that Birchers are a product of rootlessness; their tireless search for conspiracies indicates a total lack of security. And no place in America is more rootless than southern California.

RATIONAL RIGHT

I saw the sheriff's badge right across the country.
Republican Party Chairman Thurston Morton on the role of the
law and order issue in the 1970 elections.

With the lunatic right out of the way, we may turn to the "rational right"; and one key point about the rational right, which is often ignored, is that its appeal can make itself felt far beyond California. In 1966, the capture of the governorship by Reagan at first caused some hilarity as a typical aberration. In truth, as is now plain, the Reagan victory was vastly significant for the whole United States. As California went in 1966, so went the nation two years later when it elected another southern Californian, Richard Nixon, to the presidency. Nor does Reagan's relatively subtle brand of right-wingery appeal only to Americans. In 1969 he visited London to speak at the annual meeting of the British Institute of Directors; this is a businessmen's organization made up of much the same type of aspiring small businessmen who support Reagan in California. The secretary of the institute, Sir Richard Powell, told me he had been put on to Reagan by the American ambassador in London, Walter Annenberg, the right-wing newspaper owner (at that time) from Philadelphia, who owns a (very expensive) house in Reaganite country in Palm Springs. Powell's original American selection was Senator Edward Kennedy, but Kennedy had tactfully withdrawn after the Chappaquiddick incident, and Annenberg had advised Powell that the best possible substitute would be Governor Reagan. When I told Powell I was surprised that he thought it prudent to associate his institute, which practices a discreet conservatism, with a red-blooded right-winger to whom the ideas of the British Conservative Party would seem little better than socialism, Powell replied: "But he doesn't believe in hanging Jews or Negroes, does he?"

Reagan spoke in the Albert Hall, which was full. At first, the massed company directors were wary, but Reagan soon dispersed their suspicions with a joke about how he had spent twenty-five years riding off into the sunset with "the end" superimposed on his back, and a tactful quotation from Churchill. (He also fed in a quote from someone he called "Lord Thomas Macaulay"). He then served the audience his businessman's special, his theme being that businessmen had kept out of politics but politics had not kept out of business, and so businessmen must now get into politics and help run it efficiently. He next gave his own achievements a modest boost. He told them how he himself had saved California money by applying business practices: he saved a hundred thousand dollars on stamps alone by sending out notices of automobile license renewals a month early, having discovered that the Federal Government was about to raise postage rates. He ended with a ringing endorsement of freedom, and the Albert Hall filled with applause. The chairman of the meeting, a prominent brewer, was so carried away in his speech of thanks that he cried: "If you ever think of going into politics in this country, Governor, I'm sure there are a lot of people in this hall who would vote for you"—a declaration that brought many directors to their feet, clapping and shouting.

So the appeal of the Californian right is not confined to California, although it does have a special attraction there, and especially in greater Los Angeles. Any election issue that is a left-right test case invariably picks up twice as many right-wing votes in southern California as it does in the north. State Senator Milton Marks, a moderate Republican from San Francisco, told me he "just wouldn't get elected in southern California." What is the reason for this southern conservatism? The usual explanation is that the citizens down there, who mainly originate from the middle west, are trying to recreate the settled conditions they knew back home. But the midwestern migrants moved west to find something new, not to reproduce Iowa; and many of them found what they sought. Personally, I connect their conservatism with Utopianism. The new Californians wanted to leave the bad features of the old life behind them: not only the cold and the poverty, but also the problems. What the right-wingers among them wish to do now is to be rid of unpleasantness. They have yearned to get back to what they take to be the old American virtues, to enjoy the material advantages that California can offer, and to lead a quiet, private, family life. What they got instead was World War II, a black invasion, a student uprising, Vietnam, and—quite frequently—a rebellion in their very own homes by their own children.

After a number of talks with Californians who could be described as right wing, I noted down a summary of their beliefs as follows.

1. Belief in hard work. "We *worked* our way through college," said Reagan. Even if you are poor, as Reagan originally was, you can get ahead (that is, make money) by sheer application. Examples are to be found everywhere you look (say the right-wingers), despite the thirties Depression through which many of today's rich Californians lived.

2. Belief in the goodness of most people. In the same way that Communist propaganda constantly argues that the masses in capitalist democracies have the right ideas but are misled by their bosses, so at one time or another I often heard Californian right-wingers attributing the student revolt entirely to the stimulus of Mario Savio, or the black revolt to Eldridge Cleaver, or Mexican rumblings to Cesar Chavez.

3. Belief in respect. The word "respect" is constantly used by right-wingers, as in, "We were brought up to *respect* our elders," etc.

4. Belief that America's behavior abroad has been morally superior to that of other nations. Almost all Californian right-wingers, in conversing with an Englishman, make a respectful refer-

ence to Sir Winston Churchill, but at the same time they often indicate that they are smart enough to realize that he was acting wholly in support of British interests. America, on the other hand, acts in the general interest. In Vietnam, it has been protecting nations from the spread of Communism.

5. Belief in self-reliance. "Most of the foreigners who come into the state are good workers," a radio-shop owner in Stockton said to me. "My neighbor Mr. Bowler started with nothing, but now he's worth three or four million dollars, just from planting pears and walnuts. But if you walk around the streets near Berkeley at night there are half a dozen panhandlers asking for money. Why don't they get out and do something for themselves—get started? During the Depression, I didn't have a dime—like them. I used to work with a pick and shovel, alongside doctors and lawyers. Now I've got a house that's worth $60,000. It shows what you can do. But these guys [he meant the young], they don't want to do that. They rely on other people."

6. Belief that modern government is undermining traditional virtues. Welfare payments prevent a man from standing on his own feet and showing self-reliance.

One obvious pressure that pushes people to the right is fear. The Birchers live and move in irrational fear; it is their element. The bulk of the right, on the other hand, are worried for more solid reasons than middle-of-the-roaders sometimes give them credit for. In 1968, for instance, there was a rash of robberies on the Alameda County–Contra Costa buses. In six months, according to police figures, there were thirty-seven robberies and two shootings. The bus drivers demanded a token system, so that they did not have to carry change; and the right wing was up in arms about the incidents. My middle-of-the-road friends thought the outcry exaggerated, but they weren't using the buses. As it happened, I was, and to me it seemed perfectly reasonable that the public should want something done.

The right feel physically threatened by crime in the streets and are made nervous by the new self-confidence that blacks show in public—driving aggressively, behaving boisterously in shops.

They hear the Panthers' talk of uprisings, and they believe the black communities to be heavily armed. They watch the shoot-outs between blacks and police on television and wonder about their own safety. Besides, being conventional, they also feel psychologically threatened by the scornful attitudes that some blacks and most young people have for the values by which they themselves live. They think of themselves as law-abiding, hard-working citizens, who have perhaps not done a great deal for others but at least have raised a family and not done anyone any harm; and now they find themselves labeled as white racists and hypocrites, and told they have wasted their lives. The point is that not all members of the Californian right are out of their minds; many of them are responding to, and reacting against, a state of affairs that actually exists.

RONALD REAGAN

This is where Reagan comes in. He appears to be an ordinary guy, who shares the fears of other ordinary guys. He is antipolitical; he spoke of politics in his early campaigns as "playing games." At the same time, although he articulates the fears of the suburbs, his personality exudes the low-keyed confidence of the good man onto whose breast, with his slightly reluctant consent, the worried citizens have pinned a sheriff's badge.

When I interviewed him, it was his earnest, reassuring style that impressed me most. His political ancestor, Barry Goldwater, was not reassuring but harsh—he was a divider and an evident extremist. Reagan, on the contrary, appears as a conciliator, with apparently modest aims. All he wants to do, he has often said, is to apply "a little common sense" to government. His main advantage is that he is the first political master of television. Most politicians are nervous of television, aware that one wrong step can ruin them, and are haunted by the memory of Nixon's debacle in 1960. Reagan is always at ease, having spent his whole career in front of a microphone or cameras. He started as a sportscaster in

Iowa, then became a staff announcer on a radio station. By the age of twenty-six, having changed his spectacles for contact lenses (he was a pioneer of these devices), he was making films. He has been a lecturer, and an MC at Las Vegas—always in front of an audience. He was one of the first actors to switch from movies to television. Both Nixon and Goldwater have often been floored by press questioning, but Reagan has never yet had a glove laid on him, however cunning the reporters. At one of his first gubernatorial press conferences in Sacramento, in front of twelve television cameras, a reporter asked him a technical but important question about the state budget. Reagan had no idea what the reporter was talking about. Most politicians, in this plight, would have bluffed. Reagan smiled and said easily, "You guys are taking advantage of me." Again, when he was new to the governorship, he declined to commute the death penalty on Aaron Mitchell, who had been convicted of killing a policeman. At a press conference, a TV reporter asked whether the governor believed that capital punishment was a deterrent. "I believe that no case has been presented to alter the view that capital punishment is a deterrent," Reagan replied. In that case, said the reporter, why not allow the execution to be televised? I saw the governor's communications director, Lynn Nofziger, stiffen up and frown angrily. (He said to me afterward: "I never heard of such bad taste.") But Reagan did not pause: he said he thought a man being executed had the right to die in private. Then he was asked his opinion of the clergymen throughout the state who had said they would ring their church bells in protest. "I certainly am religious," Reagan replied, "and I think everyone must have a prayer in his heart for this man."

Unlike the nut right, Reagan rarely questions the sincerity of his opponents; nor indeed is he in a strong position to do so, since he supported Roosevelt in the early days and voted for Truman in 1948—the very presidents under whom things began to go wrong, according to his view now. He does not take a conspiratorial view of history. "The liberals did a good job of analysis," he told me. "But they tried the wrong solutions."

The formal principles that Reagan publicly professes are entirely unexceptional, which is why they have a wide appeal. Who could be against them? Local people in control of local affairs. Less bureaucracy. Washington to allow more freedom to the states. Less waste of public money. No government financial help to those who refuse to take a job though physically fit to do so.

Behind these simple and constantly reiterated principles, Reagan's actual policies have been a blur. He talks like a conservative, but when he senses (or his public-relations advisers tell him) that a strong right-wing line may lose him votes, he quickly swerves. He has been consistently right wing only on the student issue, where he knows he has a winner. After he sent the forces of law and order in massive strength onto the Berkeley campus in the spring of 1969—an invasion not invited by the university authorities—his support in the public-opinion polls shot up by twelve points. More subtle is his approach to race. Unlike Governor Wallace of Alabama, Reagan never campaigns against blacks as such. One of the very few times he has lost his temper in public occurred during a campaign meeting when an opponent implied that he was a racist. Reagan walked off the platform shouting, "I resent the implication there is any bigotry in my nature," and, after being persuaded with difficulty to return, apologized for losing his temper, saying, "Some things a man just can't take." He avoids racial questions as much as he can, knowing he cannot win black votes and might lose white ones. At his victory celebration in Los Angeles, when he appeared on a dais at the Century Plaza Hotel with the other victorious candidates, he deliberately reached out and drew into the position next to him Wilson C. Riles, who is black. Reagan resists state intervention in dealing with the black ghettos, but justifies this as part of his general dislike of state grants for education, welfare, etc. But he does not say that blacks should be kept in their place, and has encouraged businessmen to undertake job-training schemes for blacks. Thus the right-wing image blurs.

MAX RAFFERTY

The most voluble and clear-cut right-winger in California is not Reagan but Dr. Max Rafferty, who was for eight years the elected Superintendent of Public Instruction. Listening to Rafferty is much the best way to tune in to the authentic voice of southern California's right, and he has done more than any other man to make the unrestrained expression of right-wing thoughts respectable—much like Enoch Powell in Britain.

Rafferty is a demagogue who loves an audience. With an audience of one, he sits with his hands folded in front of him, gradually getting carried away by his own phrase-making and rhetoric. His looks, with his long face, are unremarkable; his eloquence is perhaps Irish in origin. He is like a frustrated schoolmaster who lets fly scornfully at the outside world from the security of his classroom.

He was born, he told me, in New Orleans, but raised in Iowa. His father was in the wallpaper and paint business, went broke in the Depression, and decided he might as well starve in California —"so we drove west." His father became a floor manager for Chrysler in Los Angeles and then went into the aircraft industry. Rafferty himself went to the university and then took up a teaching career in the small (and profoundly conservative) desert towns of the south.

Rafferty's strongest suit is not his political attitudes, which are commonplace, but his attacks on Californian education and culture. Arguing that the past was better than the present, the right characteristically feels obliged to pinpoint the moment at which society suddenly left the tracks. Reagan told me that things went wrong with Roosevelt. Rafferty said the villain was John Dewey, the inventor of the dread "permissiveness." "Dewey's idea was to adjust the subject matter to the child. As a result we have produced the first generation of people who know how to read but cannot discriminate when they do so."

In one way, Rafferty is a populist. He thinks that the people have lost the power to control their own institutions and, when asked for an example, refers with special contempt to the University Regents. "Those people are elected for sixteen years. They are immune to public opinion and anyway they are practically all millionaires. You are seeing the rise of an intellectual fascism, fascist because it is a center of power that public opinion does not control." But if Rafferty dislikes the university, he equally abhors the popular culture that flourishes in California. "The problem is one of leisure. More and more Californians are on a forty-hour week, and before long it will be a thirty-six-hour week. No other civilization has had to cope with a leisure problem like this, and it is growing apace. One man who supports me has invented a cleaning system whereby you press a button and vacuum cleaners come rushing out of the wall and clean the carpets. Southern California is dedicated to leisure, yet it isn't, I would say, the ideal laboratory.

"The recreation industry is dangerous. Television has planted a distorted picture of American life in the minds of Americans. Violence is exploited to the utmost. Practically everything is in bad taste, and anything good has to be put on at odd hours. In publishing, it is impossible to name anyone in the same class as Poe or Hawthorne or Mark Twain; instead we are invited to admire twentieth-century graffiti writers such as Norman Mailer and James Baldwin. The motion-picture business is employing actors and actresses to do more and more outrageous things."

I asked Rafferty who his heroes were: Theodore Roosevelt and General MacArthur, he replied. "Roosevelt is the classic example of the vigorous but moderate Republican: a great reformer—the first to come out against the great trusts of his day—and belligerent, yet the only president to get the Nobel peace prize, for fixing up peace between Russia and Japan. He was antiboss and antimachine politics: he was all that is good, clean, and honorable. As for MacArthur, I regard him as one of our great modern geniuses. He settled Korea; he made Japan. He was a great military strategist and a great proconsul."

Hearing him praise these two expansionist-minded Americans, I supposed that Rafferty himself might harbor an imperialist streak, but, on the contrary, he talked like an isolationist. America, he said, had had no business in sending a single soldier to Southeast Asia, and he drew a parallel for me between Vietnam and the Boer War. Before the Boer War, Britain was the world's great exporter of capital and expertise; after the Boer War, she was weakened and exhausted. "We cannot impose our will—as the Boer War showed you could not impose *your* will—on a country ten thousand miles away." But did he not fear the expansion of China? "We should train our missiles on China and let them get on with it. They'll change, as the Russians have changed. It'll be like the French Revolution. That was run by a madman, Robespierre; he was the craziest of all; we would have him locked up today."

Rafferty and Reagan and their supporters want a clean-up, disliking variety and confusion. Although Rafferty said he was not a prude—"it would be hard to find an Irish puritan"—he certainly gave me the impression, from the vehemence of his disgust over a play put on in a state college "in which Christ and Judas were shown as homosexuals," that he would not be averse to some form of censorship. At the heart of both Reagan and Rafferty I sensed a longing for stability and conformity—a powerful strain in American life. The snag from their point of view is that the institutions that used to encourage conformity do so no longer, especially in California. The university is an agent of diversity and change; indeed much of the scientific and sociological work of the university actively promotes and causes change. The schools busily engage in educational experiment. The churches, far from encouraging orthodoxy, try to be as unorthodox as they dare, to keep up: who could be less orthodox than the late Bishop Pike of San Francisco, with his exotic left-wing views and notions of communicating with the dead? Nor is there, especially in southern California, a social structure strong enough to guide and channel people's behavior. Where then is the source of authority for which the right wing yearns? The only source left is the police.

THE POLICE

In his book *La Technique,* the French Christian philosopher Jacques Ellul cites the police as an instance of how institutions in a technological society become distorted when they follow the example of machines and adopt efficiency as their only goal. The police task is to protect society against criminals. To do so efficiently, the police must anticipate and forestall crime. They will therefore tend to keep as many citizens as possible under surveillance, and they will tend to become independent, forming a closed, autonomous organization in order to operate by the most effective means and not be shackled by subsidiary considerations. They will "create an atmosphere, an environment, even a model of social relations." They will induce a climate of social conformity.

Things have not gone quite that far in California, but they are moving that way. Not long ago, in pursuit of better community relations, Chief Thomas J. Reddin of the Los Angeles police department officially met a group of Mexicans from the *barrios.* They presented Reddin with a petition saying that he should tell all his police in Mexican-American communities to cease name-calling, harassment, and bad treatment. "I don't receive demands," Reddin replied. "I am not susceptible to demands."

A group of young patrolmen whom I talked to in Oakland seemed to me to be very conscious of their separateness from the rest of society and of their role as the ultimate source of authority. "Police are in the front line," said one of them, a fair-haired young man in spectacles. "I hate to say it, but it is essential in any society to have respect for authority. People nowadays are shying away from accepting or asserting authority, and they are dumping the load onto us, because the men who become policemen these days are men who tend to accept and obey authority. Take me. The Department says we can have sideburns to midear; the desk sergeant says we can't. I hate the desk sergeant, I think he is stupid and senile, but I'm not going to challenge his authority.

"It all starts in the home, very early, this respect for authority. My father used to let me work at his carpenter's bench, but he always insisted when I finished that I put away the tools. Some parents won't discipline their children: either they're reluctant, or they're lazy, or they don't give a damn. By sixteen the child has developed in the way he's going to go. That's why one kid will come out of the ghetto and make good, while others succumb to their environment.

"The blacks have a basic distrust of the police, but we have got eight black police in the department. I bet they went to parochial schools. These have a different approach from the public schools: they teach the fundamental things, like reading, writing, and arithmetic, plus a certain amount of respect for authority, which the public schools, much more permissive, do not."

He sounded tired when he talked about the people he had to deal with. He had recently been tracing some young runaways. "They live in hippie pads, in a way that is really uncivilized. They come here from Oregon or Kansas and often have good homes; but the homes are sterile. They have taught the kids nothing. Combine that sterility with Marxism-Leninism, and you've got a problem." I asked if he had noticed, that day, a newspaper report of complaints about the rising number of rape cases. "That'll be women's lib," he said. "They're always bitching about something."

He said that to get into his department you had to have "a moral character that is above reproach"; you must also be five foot eight inches or more in height, with two years of college. All candidates underwent a psychiatric exam, principally to find out their boiling point under pressure. The patrolmen patrolled alone to get "more cop for the buck"; and the guns they carried had to be regular, both as to the type of bullet and the make—a .38 caliber Smith and Wesson—so that they were familiar with one another's weapons. None of the group considered that guns should be banned; "guns are in our tradition." They shot only for self-protection, they said, but they shot to kill; they aimed at the chest, since it is the biggest target. "All that stuff about shooting in the hand or leg is strictly for TV. If you only hit a guy in the leg, he could still shoot you, couldn't he?" One of their great worries, they said, was when they were chasing someone through backyards, "because some citizen may want to protect himself and shoot *us*. So we always have the radio on loud and try and show we're police." The radios they carried were made by Motorola, with a range of up to two miles to a radio car and perhaps four miles to the base, costing $850 exclusive of batteries, which cost a further $50. "You need reliability."

I thought I detected in these patrolmen a faint impatience with some of California's laws, on the ground that they hampered police work. Although none of them wished to ban guns, they evidently found it irritating that to be in possession of a concealed weapon was a misdemeanor, not a felony, carrying a sentence only up to one year. Similarly, the offense of battery was a misdemeanor, and the bail was only fifty dollars. "So you might be asked to stop a family fight in the ghetto. The obvious thing is to arrest the man who is beating up his wife. But if you do, the bail is only fifty dollars, and he'll go back down and beat her up again, only worse. So we're reluctant to intervene, and the blacks distrust us." Again, the patrolmen said they knew all the heroin pushers in the district. But a pusher would often enclose his heroin supply in a toy balloon inside his cheek. "We know it's there, but we can't do anything." Or a suspect might be carrying a "hype kick" in his pocket (an eyedropper with a hypodermic on the end). "You know what it is and where it is, but you can't prosecute him."

After his companions left, the fair-haired patrolman, becoming friendlier, showed me a "stop card"—a white form the size of a postcard. "Say I use some pretext to stop a Ford which just feels suspicious to me. I fill in a stop card, with the names of the passengers, and the number and make of the car. That information will go into the computer at Sacramento. Later, say a woman reporter says she saw a thief driving a blue Ford, we can flick through the Fords and maybe find a connection. They might have left a fingerprint. So the computer may link them with a crime which, at the time I stopped them, had not yet been committed."

One of Governor Reagan's boasted achievements is that, during his period of office, the California crime-information computer has been linked both to Washington and to other principal cities —"the first such hook-up in our nation's history." [1] Thus police technique advances hand-in-hand with the police belief that the maintenance of authority—which is none other than a synonym for the health of society—is becoming more and more loaded onto their shoulders.

THE NEW CALIFORNIA AND THE OLD WEST

As we saw at the beginning of the chapter, Californian right-wing attitudes today can be traced back to the dime novels and their imaginary account of early western life. But the right wing also has roots in a more respectable source: the celebrated frontier hypothesis of Professor Frederick Jackson Turner. Turner's achievement was to give all Americans a new way of thinking about themselves. Until the end of the nineteenth century, an American was defined usually in terms of his relation to Europe. Then, in 1893, Turner put forward his famous theory arguing that the American had been formed, not by his European connection, but by his experience of the frontier. Since then, this has become by far the most popular notion of what an American really is.

And it is, of course, an especially popular notion in California. Migration has cut people off from their old roots, and many of them seem worried by their free-floating condition. Sometimes mild efforts are made to connect modern California with her Spanish or Mexican past, but it is not easy for a Californian to feel that he has anything in common with previous Spanish tenants of the land; and most white Californians would hesitate before conceding that they are in any sense the heirs of the Mexicans. But the old American west . . . surely a link must exist there?

One right-winger has made a fortune by conveying to placid surbanites the notion that they are the legatees of a fiercely independent frontier tradition. This is Walter Knott, the owner and operator of Knott's Berry Farm and Ghost Town, "truly one of America's most unusual and enjoyable dining, shopping, and entertainment attractions," half an hour's drive from Los Angeles. It is the best place in California to study what the western inheritance really amounts to. The atmosphere is established immediately at the ticket counters, where the girls wear pink gingham bonnets and dresses, like farm-bred sweethearts in an old movie. Inside, spread out over two hundred acres, is a confusing mixture of reconstructions of the old west, shops, and propaganda for the values of old America. "You can ride an ore car through a mountain mine, pan for real gold, ride a stage coach and a narrow-gauge railroad, see trained barnyard animals at Old MacDonald's Farm, ride San Francisco cable cars, laugh at old-time melodrama, and wander through an authentically recreated Ghost Town." There are also forty-two shops selling homemade jams and jellies and candies, and a Freedom Center that features a full-scale replica of Independence Hall in Philadelphia and the Liberty Bell, "complete with the crack." The whole enterprise exudes a powerful air of old-fashioned patriotism.

Mr. Knott, founder and owner of the Berry Farm, is now well into his seventies, but he still has a firm grip on the enterprise, working long hours every day in a modest office described to visitors as being "beyond Chicken Dinner Restaurant Door Four." He is a neat, well-preserved man, gray-haired and bespectacled, with a quiet, thoughtful manner. His office furnishings include a citation from Governor Reagan, a Goldwater calendar, a shelf of books (often with the word "freedom" in the title), some miniature figures of western pioneers, and a pair of scales for weighing gold.

Mr. Knott has been hard at work building up his Berry Farm and Ghost Town since 1920. His grandparents had come from

Texas (his grandmother had a rooming house in San Bernardino) and his father was a Methodist parson, as one might have guessed from Walter's own parsonical look and air. He had a rugged upbringing, as a young man picking cantaloupes in the Imperial Valley, and later homesteading in the Mojave Desert. Then, in 1920, having made a little money as a vegetable farmer, he rented, with a cousin, twenty acres in Buena Park, where he still is, and started growing fruit and selling it from a roadside stand. In 1929, on the eve of the Depression, he bought the land, and in 1934 his wife, Cordelia, cooked and sold her first chicken dinner. The sale of meals started Knott's expansion, but it was not chicken dinners but a new fruit called the boysenberry that founded the Knott family fortune. Knott explained to me that he did not breed the boysenberry himself; it was developed by the superintendent of parks in Anaheim, a Mr. Boysen, but it was Walter who saw its possibilities, grew it on a large scale, and exploited it. (One of its properties, as a jam ingredient, is that it jells quickly, in four minutes. It still is a "fabulous seller," especially at Christmas). Knott's business expanded slowly, he told me. "We didn't go out and borrow money. Our way isn't the way to build a business quickly; but it *is* one way of owning it when you get it built."

With success, Knott has more and more turned his activities toward preserving, not only boysenberries, but what he regards as free America's basic political beliefs: first, the maintenance of property rights, "without which our whole system will collapse"; second, the freedom of the individual from interference by the state, "which has been gradually chipping away at the American idea of liberty." Third, lower taxes. In support of these beliefs, Knott has held large rallies at the Berry Farm for both Goldwater and Reagan, and has made substantial contributions to their campaign funds. His office staff, the day I visited him, were busy stuffing envelopes with campaign literature in support of Dr. Max Rafferty, who was then running for the Senate on a strongly right-wing platform.

After I left Mr. Knott and toured his enterprise—watching his employees dressed up as gold miners showing the customers how to pan gold, listening to the merry ring of the cash register in the turn-of-the-century Candy Parlor, and looking at the hideous junk in the gift shop—it struck me that there was a distinct contradiction between the present attitudes of Mr. Knott and the actual history of his life and farm.

The old west that Mr. Knott looks back to with nostalgia disappeared before he came on the scene. He reached Buena Park not by stage coach or buggy but by automobile. He learned about ghost towns not from his own experience but from the tales of his grandmother. In recreating the old west, he relies on new techniques; one of his achievements is to have saved and rebuilt the abandoned mining town of Calico, away in the desert; but he used "an Austrian specialist in aging techniques" to make the town look authentic. The adobe buildings in his Ghost Town are reinforced with steel. The profitable fruit that helped him to his fortune was developed, not by private enterprise, but by a state official; and he was told where to find the fruit by a visitor from the U.S. Department of Agriculture in Washington.

Mr. Knott gave me a copy of his biography, written by a Presbyterian minister and published in Grand Rapids, Michigan, which describes "how God has honored one of his sincere servants." From it I learned that the Knott Freedom Center, which "combats Communism and the subversion of youth," has been the subject of a dispute between Mr. Knott and the Bureau of Internal Revenue. The bureau said that the center was not part of the farm and must therefore be taxed separately. Mr. Knott argued that the center was merely an advertising medium for the farm. Most dispiriting of all, I discovered from questioning the staff that the Berry Farm, despite the homely, local image, no longer produces boysenberries; the literature says that "our menu has stayed the same since we started, complete with boysenberry pie"; but the boysenberries, alas, are now trucked in from the San Fernando Valley. Nor are the blueberries grown on the farm: they come from Canada.

I was saddened also by what I learned about the gift shop. This shop contains more elaborate junk than any I saw in California, which is the junk capital of the Western world: wall plaques of Bizet; fifth-rate reproductions of a portrait of an old man, by Rembrandt, with a cheap brass plate tacked on as if it were an original; alabaster ashtrays swinging from chains; plaster groups of singing nuns, one of them clasping a guitar. Mr. Knott told me candidly that he personally did not care for these objects, but employed a lady buyer who was more in tune with public taste than he was. He added that he had just been visited by the Duke of Bedford, England's most successful country-house showman, and that Bedford had remarked to him, after examining the gift shop: "We have one thing in common. The uglier the things are, the better they sell."

Mr. Knott symbolizes a Californian difficulty. Californians need a cultural background, as all men do, a context in which to live, and ideals to live by. But the state has grown so fast that there is no established cultural background that newcomers can latch on to, and there has not been time for the migrants to develop ideals that are appropriate to their exotic, affluent, and sometimes bewildering environment. So they are forced back on ideas and images that do not come naturally to them. Knott himself is making an effort to cling to a set of disconnected objects and ideas, linking up homemade jellies and restored desert shacks with notions about liberty and the free life of the old west. But even in his case the contradictions and absurdities are unavoidable. For all its air of authenticity and historical plausibility, Knott's Berry Farm and Ghost Town is a daydream, a recreation of images first learned in the nursery—mother at the stove, father at church, grandfather in the gold fields, the family secure and untroubled by change—spread out over two hundred acres and opened to the public. It is the plainest evidence in California that the western myth, for all its apparent potency, is, alas, as irrelevant and obsolete as the covered wagon.

RIGHT-WING SOLUTIONS

In some respects, the frontier myth has always been fraudulent, especially insofar as it has rested on the fundamental notion that, in the west, good men have stood on their own feet, beholden to none. The fact is that the west since the start has depended on Washington. Some of the founders of California were rescued from death in the Sierras by federal troops. None of the irrigation projects, which were essential to the cultivation of California, could have been undertaken without federal help. The farmers of California have been subsidized to the hilt, with eastern taxpayers' money. Reagan once said, "As an economic entity, California ranks sixth among the nations of the world." In the next sentence he continued: "For eight years prior to our administration, the government of California had been a little brother to big brother in Washington," and went on to excoriate this federal domination. Yet without Washington's defense contracts and colossal scientific subsidies the governor would not be able to boast about California standing sixth among the nations.

The western myth is fraudulent, too, when it assumes a uniformly pleasant Californian past. Referring to local right-wingers, an old fellow in Bakersfield said to me: "They want it like it was. But they don't know how it was. I tell them to go to the cemeteries and look at the dates on the graves; see how the waves of epidemics wiped out children. Do they want to cook on a wood range? They think it was placid then, with no problems about blacks or kids or Vietnam. They say it was more virtuous, but I was a police reporter for thirty years, and I see less vice now. For eight solid blocks in Bakersfield there was a red-light district. When the Barbary Coast closed down in San Francisco, the whores and pimps came here. I don't say there aren't whores here now, but my kids don't have to see them. These people haven't the slightest idea what the good old days were like. The pioneering virtues were fine—for those who had 'em. But who did? Who stood on his own two feet? If it hadn't been for the Land Grant Act, the University of California wouldn't exist. If the university hadn't existed, where would California be? Where would the farmers be? The average westerner prides himself on his independence and calls himself a rugged individualist. He hates the federal government, and he says he hates state encroachment. Yet no section of the United States has benefited as much from state aid as California. Every drop of water we get in this central valley outside the rivers, which are very inadequate, comes to us via the federal government. The cotton crop is under a federal program. The Great California Water Project: who paid for that? Without it, they wouldn't be able to farm here. These rugged individualists get loans from the government on terms you and I would be delighted to get in buying an automobile. I am amazed at their intellectual dishonesty."

So the western myth is a shaky basis on which to found a philosophy. In any case, the old remedies show little sign of producing results. "Law and order," which is the principal traditional remedy, is not silencing the ghettoes. In black ghettos and brown *barrios,* the police are enemies—pigs, *placas,* dog pack, *chortas, gabachos,* motherfuckers, *los muertes,* the Man. The prison system, once regarded as the most liberal and pioneering in the Western world, is in serious trouble. The new idea at the heart of it was to separate judgment of guilt from sentencing; the sentence was to be decided in accordance with the character of the convicted man by an Adult Authority Board, who would keep it under review and adjust it according to the needs of the individual prisoner. Instead, the board has turned into an instrument for controlling prisoners, using a carrot-and-stick mechanism that is immune from legal and public control. The prison administrators have the "power to play God with the lives of the inmates." [2] Meanwhile, the prisons have filled up with new types of malefactor—draft-card burners, political blacks—who are bringing a new intelligence and militancy to all California's prisons. Thus prison, the prime symbol of law and order, has itself become lawless and disorderly. It is another sign of a general truth: that despite the ascendency of the right in California, the conventional right-wing solutions, based on the old values, will not work.

CHAPTER 8

New Values

If I am not myself, who will be?

Thoreau

When a man has obtained those things which are necessary to life, there is another alternative than to obtain the superfluities; and that is, to adventure on life now.

Thoreau

From *Om* the music of the spheres,
From *Om* the mist of Nature's tears,
All things of earth and heav'n declare
Om! Om! resounding everywhere.

Paramahansa Yogananda

Om! Om!

Allen Ginsberg to the Chicago police, 1968.

Each step we make today toward material progress not only does not 'advance us toward the general well-being, but shows us, on the contrary, that all these technical improvements only increase our miseries.

Tolstoy

CALIFORNIA is the richest and most materialistic society in the world, but it is also the scene of an extraordinary reaction against materialism. This is not as paradoxical as it sounds. As one of the hippies' heroes, Henry David Thoreau, pointed out more than a century ago, it is only after people have secured "the necessaries of life" that they are "prepared to entertain the true problems of life." Thus the richer the Californians get, the more

172

they worry about what they are rich *for*. Nowhere outside California is there such a variety of organizations catering to people's spiritual anxiety. Most of these organizations, however wild the beliefs peddled, are of a traditional type: a group of people following a leader who is considered to have special insight into the nature of the universe, and meeting regularly at a church or its equivalent. In recent years, however, California has begun to produce spiritual centers of an entirely new kind, searching for new values; of these, Esalen is the most striking.

THE ESALEN INSTITUTE

The first time I heard the name Esalen was at a cocktail party given by a professor at Berkeley. Esalen, I gathered, was some sort of weekend seminar center where people went in search of their souls. The wife of a psychology professor had just come back. She had been in an encounter group and had been asked to get down on her hands and knees and bark like a dog, while another member of the group behaved like a cat. She had, apparently, gotten little out of the experience; and the main impression she had brought back to Berkeley was that about thirty percent of the clients had slept with someone other than their legal mate during the weekend. A professor protested: there was a lot of interesting work being done at Esalen by serious people, and to smear it as a sex center was grotesquely unfair. Later, another professor described the place to me as "a mass masturbation clinic."

Fired by these descriptions, I shortly afterward spent a weekend at Esalen myself, observing. From San Francisco, you drive south down the coast for 150 miles, along a route that, in its later stretches, becomes one of the most exhilarating coast roads in the world—U.S. Scenic Highway One: a winding, narrow (for California) road cut into the side of the mountains, with the Pacific stretching away endlessly to a mysterious, blurred horizon.

People near Esalen, I found as I approached, had as unfavorable a view of the place as the professors I had talked to. A motel owner at Big Sur, a village buried among the coastal redwoods, became distinctly hostile when I asked him the way. "You're British, aren't you? Why would you want to go to a place like that? You know what they do? They take their clothes off and rub backs to get to know one another without speaking. Nuts." Outside his motel he had put up a notice saying that no one would be admitted unless they were clean and wearing shoes. Hippies, he explained, had been streaming down the coast ever since the police started to clear them out of the Haight-Ashbury district of San Francisco. He evidently believed that Esalen was one of the magnets drawing them south, like Mecca, and he didn't like it, because they interfered with the regular family tourist and camping trade, who wanted open air, a glimpse of raccoons, and somewhere to park the trailer, and not to be offended by dirty, hairy kids who cadged lifts on the highway, slept in the hills, and made love in public.

Twenty miles beyond Big Sur, a dirt road ran steeply off the main highway down to a plateau above the ocean. A wooden sign said Esalen Institute. There was a group of long wooden bungalows, a line of trailers, a lawn, a swimming pool at the top of a fifty-foot cliff above the ocean, and, two hundred yards away, among old trees, an old house that looked as if it had been built by a man looking for quiet a long time before the coast became famous. Inside a wooden office that served as a reception center were some small pieces of jewelry and a few books for sale: *The Tibetan Book of the Dead, Finnegan's Wake,* and local poetry. A girl behind the desk was talking to an older woman, who was booking a course.

"We're trying to get away from the idea that the old should be treated in such and such a way just because they are old," the girl was saying. She was not wearing a brassiere, and you could see her nipples when she leaned forward. "Here we all work together and play together. One thing they learn from group therapy is that there's nothing wrong with body contact."

"That's what's wrong with my parents. They never hug or anything," said the older woman.

The girl behind the desk looked at me. "Are you Otto?" she asked.

"No."

"I only asked because you're the only two wearing suits. He's a lecturer we're expecting."

She sold me a ticket for dinner, costing four dollars, and handed me some literature, which I took outside and read on the edge of the cliff. No one was about.

"Esalen Institute," I read, "is a center to explore those trends in the behavioral sciences, religion, and philosophy which emphasize the potentialities and values of human existence. Its activities consist of seminars and workshops, research and consulting programs, and a resident program exploring new directions in education and the behavioral sciences."

The literature listed and described the courses being offered, together with biographical sketches of those in charge. Some of them I had heard of: Herman Kahn, the futurologist and thinker of the unthinkable about nuclear war; Professor B. F. Skinner of Harvard, the leader of the behaviorist school of psychology, which holds that pigeons and people have much in common; Ali Akbar Khan, the Indian musician; Allen Ginsberg, the bearded poet and forerunner of the hippies; [1] Alan Watts, who popularized Zen Buddhism in the United States; [2] and R. D. Laing, the London psychiatrist with the "blow-out" centers, who considers that schizophrenics may be saner than the rest of us. The people who gave the courses were a mixture of qualified academics, people from the strange institutes which abound in California—since money can be raised for almost any study, however eccentric— and free-lance practitioners of spiritual (and physical) uplift from all over.

The index of a typical month's activities at Esalen read as follows:

5-Day Workshop	Edward Maupin	Body Awareness–Encounter Group
5-Day Workshop	Hobart Thomas and Michael Murphy	Developing Inner Resources

5-Day Workshop	Robert K. Hall	Gestalt Therapy: Open Workshop
5-Day Workshop	Guild of Hands	Workshop in Crafts
Weekend Seminar	Claudio Naranjo and Michael Harner	Shamanism, Ritual, and The Psychotic
Weekend Seminar	Silverman/Laing/ Perry	Psychosis as Personal Transformation
5-Day Workshop	James S. Simkin	Gestalt Therapy: Open Workshop
Two 5-Day Workshops	George I. Brown and Research Staff	Affective Learning: Training in Teaching
4-Week Workshop	Wm. C. Schutz/ Stroud/Fuller	Intensive Workshop Training
Weekend Seminar	Maurice Friedman and Ann Dreyfuss	Confirmation: Discussion and Encounter
Weekend Workshop	Ann Halprin with Casey Sonnabend	A Dance Celebration
5-Day Workshop	James Simkin and Irma Lee Shepherd	Gestalt Therapy: Professional
Weekend Seminar	Herman Kahn and Anthony J. Wiener	Scenarios for the Year 2000
Weekend Workshop	John Heider and Steven A. Stroud	Encounter Group Techniques
5-Day Workshop	Edward Maupin and John Heider	Encounter Workshop
5-Day Workshop	James S. Simkin and Jos. J. Downing	Gestalt Therapy: Professional
2-Day Workshop	Sonia and Ed Nevis	For Married Couples: Encounter
Weekend Seminar	Bernard Gunther	Advanced Sensory Workshop
Weekend Seminar	Albert Ellis	Comprehensive Personality Change
5-Day Workshop	Robert K. Hall and Ida Rolf	Gestalt Therapy and Struc. Integ. (Open)
5-Day Workshop	Huston Smith	A Search for Relevant Philosophy

Other programs listed that struck me as original included "Hydropsychotherapy," a five-day workshop with Lily Wiener, whose main idea is that "in water, formerly unconscious movements of the body are placed under conscious control, facilitating not only bodily but emotional changes as well." My attention was also caught by a course called "Videotape Feedback: Confronting oneself requires a different set of attitudes from being confronted by

others. Videotape enables the individual to confront himself in action." This was run by H. L. Myerhoff of Camarillo State Hospital, who, it was stated, had conducted field research on the Contal Indians of the Oaxaca region of Mexico and had made field observations of middle-class gangs.

The institute evidently was looking for enlightenment both to primitive man, including Australian aborigines, and to Eastern holy men, including Tibetan lamas and Zen monks. But the main weight was on "personal awareness." The title of one seminar, "Awake, Tune In, Unfold," seemed to sum up what many of them aimed at. It also struck me that the prose describing the courses was suspiciously bad even for an organization that "concentrates on the nonverbal aspects of life," as, for instance, a sentence reading: "Most of the noise that surrounds us is not cordial to our personal growth." In places, the jargon was impenetrable. One course given by a professor of English was described as "a semantic approach to various nonverbal, nonlinear modes of symbolization in human experience." I was reminded that Leo Rosten, the author of "The Education of H*Y*M*A*N K*A*P*L*A*N," had once told a faculty dinner at Berkeley, of which he was then a member, that the solution to the problem of overcrowded Californian campuses was to exclude all professors and students who could not write a page of simple English prose —a requirement he added, that would virtually depopulate the university.

It was thus with lowered spirits that I went in to dinner in one of the wooden huts. The diners—some thirty or forty people— seemed uniformly cheerful, however. Most of them were dressed in weekend freakout gear, as if they were members of some special Californian holiday camp. Two men in standard American resort wear, Bermuda shorts, stood out as eccentrically clad. The clientele, I guessed, was predominantly well-heeled, an impression I had already gained from the cars in the driveway. The meal was self-service: the Greek dish, moussaka, for the four dollars, with wine fifty cents extra—a middle-class price. I could spot no blacks, and only one or two possible Orientals.

I sat down opposite a man who told me that he was a resident at Esalen studying Oriental religion, and he was indeed suited-up Indian style. When I asked him why California was so hung up on Eastern religion, he replied that it was so far west that it was practically *in* the East, which seemed, at the time, a good reply.

When he left, his place was taken by a plump girl in spectacles and a flowing dress who, when I asked her what she did, said solemnly: "It depends who asks." Then, apparently deciding she could trust me, she said she was studying astrology, but meanwhile, to earn money, was devising natal charts. She had first become interested in astrology at the Jung Institute in Zurich, when Jung was alive, and she drew a sharp distinction between popular astrology, which took into account only your birthday, and serious astrology, which had to take into account some three hundred factors. The movement of the stars and planets, she explained, was the only stable phenomenon in the life of primitive man, and prediction had developed naturally out of farmers' attempts to relate the prospects for their crops to the only stable thing they knew. Actually, she said firmly, astrology was not very good for prediction; what interested her was that it showed the possibilities of a person's character and could indicate whether he was realizing himself fully or not. (After I left Esalen, I heard a crisp explanation of the puzzling astrology boom in California among the otherwise skeptical young: "After you've said screw everything and everybody," another girl explained, "you begin to wonder who and what *you* are. Astrology tells you.")

After dinner, I wandered out onto the grassy cliff and looked at the stars: could there be clues up there? The night was warm and very still. The Pacific boomed below the cliff; anything seemed possible. Suddenly I became aware that I was being examined by a small man, aged about thirty, with a shaggy beard and hair in a ponytail, who seemed in the darkness to resemble Robinson Crusoe. "I used to be a little Sears Roebuck manikin like you," he said, without malice, as he saw me looking at him. He was, he went on, continuing to scrutinize me closely, on a high—induced by the beauty of the evening, not by drugs. He had recently revis-

ited San Francisco and had realized how much he disliked city
life; he had been born in Los Angeles, the ultimate city, and had
worked there as an aircraft mechanic. His only interesting experience during his San Francisco trip was the discovery that his car
radio now worked when he drove on the *lower* deck of the Bay
Bridge, whereas it used to cut out: he understood a special cable
had been fitted for this purpose. Developing his criticisms of city
life, he went on to say that he was specially exercised by the smog
problem, which he thought would eventually make life intolera-
ble in all cities, as it was already doing in Los Angeles. Did I realize that Los Angeles burned eight million gallons of gasoline
every day? Only the federal government, he was sure, could solve
the smog problem, by itself developing electric cars: private enterprise simply had too much capital invested in the gasoline engine.

Despairing of cities, he had abandoned the aircraft industry,
built himself a shack on the edge of the cliff nearby, which the
housing inspector didn't know about, and taken a job at Esalen as
a masseur. He thought massage could be an important part of life.
"If you lie like a cadaver it's no good. If I sense a person is on a
trip of his own, I don't worry. I try to get a person on a trip of his
own, and then I become the conductor. I've seen some extraordinary things happen. People often cry: I even made one man vomit,
but he *needed* to vomit."

He thought there was too much talk in the world, especially
purely social, totally meaningless talk. And he didn't plan for the
future: in fact, he was specifically against the practice. As for Esalen, he wasn't entirely sold on it. He said it had a high turnover
of staff: "People are in a rocky emotional state when they come
here."

During the next two days, my odd initial impression of Esalen
somewhat changed as I gradually got the hang of what it was
trying to do. The big house, I discovered, had been built by an
old country doctor who had moved to that part of the coast because of the natural hot springs, which he considered health-giv-
ing. (Weekend customers now bathe naked in these springs: an-

other cause of offense to the Big Sur motel owner.) The doctor had had huge bathtubs (they are still in use) hauled up the cliff by breeches buoy from boats, for the coast road had not then been built. Subsequently the old man died, and the hot springs were "taken over by a bunch of fags." Then in 1960 the doctor's grandson, Michael Murphy, who had traveled in the east and been slightly hooked by Eastern religion, decided to turn the place into some kind of cultural center specifically for the study of far-out ideas: a center that would deliberately be "on the cutting edge," out beyond what was normally thought respectable to teach or to study in universities, even Californian universities. To Murphy's surprise, his idea caught on, evidently fulfilling some urgent need. Now the place had sixty residents living in the trailers or in the hills, and a weekend clientele of another 180 people, some of whom came from as far away as British Columbia and Iowa, paying $65 per person for the weekend. Visitors at different times had included two Beatles, Arnold Toynbee, the Maharishi, and Peter Fonda. Esalen had become so busy, indeed, that they had opened a branch and administrative headquarters in San Francisco, where they did more formal work, especially lectures, some of it in connection with local churches; and the idea was spreading at an astonishing rate. In the past year, the director, Ben Weaver, told me, he had heard of no less than twenty-six Esalen-inspired places opening up all across the United States, and ripples of Esalen-type ideas, he had been told, were reaching even the uptight English.

Some of the resident staff had also begun to experiment in local society. The Ford Foundation had given them a grant for work with local elementary schoolteachers. They had run encounter groups and other experiments in Soledad Prison between convicts and wardens; "It was amazing: really bad guys were meditating in their cells, and we even had the prisoners worrying about therapy for the *guards*." Most recently they had tried an encounter group between militant blacks and white policemen, which had shown promise, with "both sides really exposing and discovering their deepest feelings, until the blacks ceased to show up."

ENCOUNTER GROUP GAMES

One of the men who has given Esalen its special far-out flavor is William C. Schutz, a Californian who has worked at the Department of Social Relations at Harvard, lectured in psychiatry at Berkeley, and also (the United States being the place it is) advised several business corporations on "group behavioral problems." The Schutz doctrine, as he explained in his book *Joy,* is that "society seems to place a premium on relationships featuring hypocrisy and superficiality, so that it is hard for an individual to learn to know himself, to like himself, or to become acquainted with his real feelings and desires." The problem, for Schutz, is how to "expand human awareness" and release a person's "human potential." You start, he thinks, by "undoing guilt, shame, embarrassment, fear of punishment, failure, success, retribution," and the techniques he uses most often are those of encounter groups, in which some six or twelve people, not technically "sick," explore their feelings under the guidance of a group leader. The leader may be silent, or tough, or aggressive, or whatever seems to help the group along.

One device Schutz uses at Esalen is "to convert feelings into a body experience": for instance, encouraging a person to release his aggression by hammering a couch until exhausted. This is how "Tom" described his experience of this technique:

"I had been feeling out of the group. I had a logjam inside. I began to talk of my feelings about my parents and the difficulty I have had in expressing my feelings toward people, especially those close to me.

"I was talking about the inability of my father to express feelings, and how angry I have gotten with him. All of a sudden I felt I wanted to slug the mattress. I put a pillow on the bed and began slowly going through a process of rising on my tiptoes and bringing both hands down on the bed. I went slowly and made noises as I did so. The rhythm became faster and I began to strike the pillow harder. I could visualize my father's head on the pillow. I beat him again and again and when I had him beaten up very badly I experienced a great surge of warmth and longing for him. Breathing heavily, I collapsed on the bed and hugged the pillow. After I had recovered from the bed-beating, Bill Schutz asked if I wanted to do it to my mother. I said I was too tired and felt too much warmth for her. I didn't want to hit her. He asked if I couldn't just begin with light tapping and see what happened, and I finally decided to try it. I put her 'head' on the pillow and was beginning to warm up when the face of my mother changed to that of *her father* and I began to belt him hard. Finally I was banging both of them pretty lustily. It was not as intense as before, but I got pretty well involved and became physically spent again. This time no surge of positive feeling came up."

As a result of this experience, Tom said, he worked out a much more realistic relationship to his parents, finding, for example, that he could now argue with his father.

One point Schutz makes about this episode is that "Tom" could not have had this experience on his own: he needed the group's support to help him break through his resistance and beat up the "mother pillow," thus realizing that his "warm" feelings about his mother weren't really so warm after all. "His relations with his parents were improved, and his feelings about himself strengthened," says Schutz.

Schutz has invented or developed a number of games or techniques all aimed, roughly speaking, at making people more alert to their own feelings and desires. There is, for instance, the "Fantasy Game," in which you imagine that two people have a conversation inside your head. One of these people tells you to volunteer for some special task; the other tells you not to. You have to imagine a dispute between these two, in which each tries to convince the other, until finally one of them wins. Then you imagine that the two of them meet without speaking, and see what happens. Some people who try this game conjure up particular individuals; others see themselves at different ages. The idea is that you get a clearer view of the way you make decisions.

Then there is "Doubling." In this, a group leader asks you to imitate the physical posture of another person in the group (arms crossed, legs entwined, for instance) with the idea that you may thereby be able to share, to some degree, the emotions of the person you are imitating. You can also imitate another person's way of talking and his facial expressions, with the same object. Another little device, again using physical means to capture an emotional state, is to write your name very slowly, barely moving the pen or pencil on the page: people who try this can often recapture the way they felt as children in school. Married women may find themselves writing their maiden name.

Or there is the "Wordless Meeting." When an encounter group first assembles, people are asked to "relate" to each other for an hour without speaking: gazing, touching, smelling, rubbing. (Esalen discourages any directly sexual touching, on the grounds that it can cause distraction). The theory of the "Wordless Meeting" is that people often use words as camouflage to prevent others getting to know them, and that the silent encounter can give you a more accurate idea of someone else than an hour's misleading chatter.

Indeed, Schutz thinks that making contact with other people is one of the main problems of modern society. "Painfully few ways of meeting others are socially acceptable, a condition that makes for much human heartbreak," he believes. "Furthermore, the discomfort in actually verbally engaging another person, in knowing what to say, or what to do to prolong and develop the association, is a serious problem for far too many people." So, to get people into contact, Schutz uses what he calls "Feeling Space," "Blind Milling," "New Names," and "The Encounter."

In "Feeling Space," a group of people sit together on the floor, close their eyes, stretch out their hands and "feel space." Gradually you become aware of other people, of touching them and of them touching you. This goes on for about five minutes. Some people who try this activity definitely prefer, in Schutz's experience, to stay in their own space, resenting any intrusion. Others feel chary of intruding into others' space, for fear they are not wanted. Others, again, seek out people and enjoy the touching. Afterward the participants discuss their behavior, which is often a way of opening up whole areas of feeling about loneliness and contact.

In "Blind Milling," everyone shuts his eyes, puts out his hands, and just mills around the room, "exploring" others (again with discretion). Slow music is used to help the mood.

In "New Names," people who have not previously met adopt new names and keep their jobs secret, the idea being that they will thus shed the restraints of their usual name and not arouse stereotyped expectations in others because of their particular job. Schutz recalls how one man took the name Pix and captivated everyone, especially women, with his pixielike behavior: it turned out that for thirty-five years he had been a Catholic priest, and he said afterward that that was the first time in all those years that anyone had treated him as an individual, not as a priest.

Finally there is "The Encounter," in which two people stand at opposite ends of the room, look into one another's eyes and, remaining silent, slowly walk toward each other. When they meet, they do whatever they feel like doing—trying to let their emotions take over and not planning what they do before they do it. It sounds simple, but it can produce unexpected, and even unsettling, results.

Schutz himself is not entirely clear why these methods seem so effective. He surmises that the problems a person develops in growing up are caused less by the actual events of his life, as is taught by traditional psychotherapy, than by the view he takes of himself as a result of these events. For instance, in Schutz's opinion it is not so much the fact of a broken home that may leave its mark on a child as the child's subsequent perception of his role in causing the breakup. "If the child is left feeling guilty, he will be debilitated. If he can feel guiltless, then the break-up may produce a feeling of strength and confidence. The place to concentrate for making useful changes is not so much on the traumatic historical events as on the individual's perception of himself."

Do these methods work? One person at Esalen whose experience has convinced her that they do is Linda Cross, a handsome, well-set-up New York girl in her midtwenties who, when I met her, was wearing a blue shirt over a blue bikini and swinging a mattock in the Esalen vegetable garden.

She had had a beautiful apartment and a good job in New York, she told me, and she went to a different restaurant every night. She was, however, frustrated; and her frustration sprang from what she called her inability to put herself on the line. "I thought I was brave enough to do things, but I didn't actually do them." She heard rumors about Esalen, but no one could tell her what it was really like, so she had simply set off. The transfer delighted her. "In New York, you're supposed to get up and *struggle* every day. There are all these nervous people and they're not able to say a thing about it. You're not supposed to act out what's inside you: that's in exact contrast to the way it is here." She had now more or less dropped out of New York, she told me, though once in a while she went back "to check out the scene at Elaine's." She had even acquired a missionary zeal about Esalen and was trying to persuade a girl friend of hers, who was high up in the Morgan Guaranty Trust, to come out and join her: "She comes on very strong and funny, but she's miserable."

Linda explained that it was now insane for her to think of living any other way. "I'm much freer not to talk to people who bore me, and to accept only those invitations I want to accept. 'No' is a very important word, and here I've learned to say it." The main thing Esalen had done for her, she said, was to give her a kind of release by making her capable of dealing honestly with people.

Encounter groups had surprised her. "They say, do some action, and to your surprise you find you know what you want to do. It comes out. They won't force you to do it, but there's a subtle pressure, and then once you start they'll go after it. Steve (one of the encounter-group leaders) is pretty rough. He'll yell, tell you what you're saying is bullshit, and do some physical stuff. John is more supportive. But either of these ways works. It's scary as hell. But one trouble is that a weekend isn't long enough really to take someone to pieces, because they have to be put together again before they leave."

Schutz, she said, had been on the Johnny Carson Show and also on a local California show, and had caused chaos by suggesting that husbands and wives should try telling each other three things apiece that they had never said before. The station was swamped with calls from people ringing in desperately, saying what do we do *now?*

Linda laughed, put down her mattock and came over and felt the muscles at the back of my neck.

"Too tight," she said. "Feel mine." Hers did seem deliciously flexible.

"There's this man who is freeing up my ribcage and muscles," she explained. "Look at these bruises." She showed me some bruises. "He lengthens your muscles too, including your mouth and throat muscles. You should never lock your knees, as it blocks energy. He puts you in touch with every bone in your spine."

She looked—for a moment—sheepish. "It would have sounded like a far-out mystery thing in New York, I know, but here it just makes so much sense."

She talked about some of the newer Esalen experiments. "There was a marathon of *forty-eight hours*. We didn't eat, and had rock and roll as loud as you can do it. You certainly go down through your levels. Then there was a bath experiment. It was very hot. You take a deep breath, your fingers curl up, your diaphragm tightens up, and the feeling may come out as crying or swearing. It's scary as you feel yourself going into it, but it was wonderful afterward when we went to this restaurant, Nepenthe, up on the hill overlooking the ocean, and drank Velvet Hammers, a mixture of creme de menthe and creme de cacao. They also do something they call a death trick, in which you go out; and they're going to experiment with sodium pentathol, a truth drug."

A strange booming sound came over the air. "That's a conch," said Linda. "One of the residents has taken to blowing it every day at sundown."

Linda liked Esalen, all right, but she didn't regard it as paradise. "It looks like a summer camp, but everyone is in turmoil. Everyone does something: if it weren't that way it would be very dull, and anyway I wouldn't want to live with a bunch of hippies. The hippies are negative; this place is positive. And there are no illegal drugs on the property: Michael Murphy says he gets much more out of his daily meditation sessions than he has ever gotten from using drugs. And have you seen the little kids? They're so clear and unafraid. There's one kid named Bernice: she just spooks me every time I talk to her. One thing about Esalen, you don't see people twitching and spilling out words nervously, the way they do in New York."

She resumed her work with the mattock, looking, as the sun went down, like a California poster girl: an ad for Human Potential.

As Linda said, at Esalen you don't see people twitching. What you do see is people doing things like this: a man is gardening; he pauses and sits on the ground; a girl sits astride him; they both rock very gently back and forth; then he gets up and starts work again. Again: a young man in swimming trunks with his hair tied back is giving Yoga lessons beside the pool to a girl with very long hair, wearing a ballet dancer's tutu, and to a bald, narrow-chested man in baggy gray trousers. In the baths, people lie naked, talking and sleeping. Outside the huts, two men stand holding hands. I noticed that all Esalen inhabitants seem to walk slowly, Arcadia-style; and they all have a very slow handshake, with plenty of touch. I thought I also noticed a wary attitude toward outsiders, which was combined, in some cases, though not in Linda's, with a faint whiff of superiority, as if the Esalen people had hit on a truth that non-Esalen people were unaware of.

I was thus pleased to meet one man who said, as soon as I started to talk to him: "My name is Abe. I smoke cigars and I chase women." Abe was a New York contractor who had happened on Esalen by chance. He was on vacation, on his way to pick up a boat in Monterey and sail it down to Mexico: a big, old, normal American, wearing plum-colored slacks and a peaked golf cap, with a battered face that was easy to imagine under a yellow helmet on a Sixth Avenue building site. Abe spent much of his time at Esalen standing with his hands in his pockets, staring with unconcealed interest at the goings-on. "They got a tough racket," he said tolerantly, "selling food and lodging and instant therapy to frustrated schoolteachers at sixty-five bucks a time. My whole life, people try to sell me things, so I'm skeptical." His skepticism had not been dented by his experience of an encounter group, which he described as "a load of bullshit," and I had put him down as a failure for increased self-awareness—perhaps he had been totally self-aware on arrival—when he remarked that he liked the naked bathing in the hot springs, which he thought would do everyone a lot of good. The "teacher," as he called the group leader, had taken them in to encourage group feeling, but Abe had noticed how people in and around the baths pulled their arms and legs in so they didn't come in contact with each other, somewhat against Esalen teaching as he understood it.

Not only did he like the baths, he also liked the massage. "Back east I belong to a golf club and I've been pounded ten thousand times by the masseur. Just a slab of meat. But this girl was really doing something for me. At the end," he paused, and the battered face looked embarrassed, "I just had to kiss her hands." He had been so moved by his experience that he had postponed his trip to Mexico and had signed on for a massage course.

Indeed, the only person I found who took a wholly detached view of the place was a blonde girl in suede boots and a red miniskirt who was working as a waitress. She had come to Esalen because her man, Gordy, was there in retreat from his father who was the head, she said, of one of the biggest corporations in the United States. Dad wanted Gordy to become head in time, too, but Gordy could not see the point: Gordy liked menial work, but not among menial people, so he was working at Esalen as a carpenter. They had expectations of money, and when it arrived they thought they might go to Peru. The blonde said the point about Esalen was that people went there to freak out, only it wasn't thought of as that. No, she did not do workshops, as she didn't want her mind blown. "I'm happy already," she said.

Leaving the happy blonde, and wondering whether she was right to regard Esalen as merely a freak-out headquarters, I walked up behind the trailers and took a narrow path leading to a canyon that runs deep into the mountains. The redwoods got taller and taller and the canyon narrower, with the rocks dripping wet and the air green. It was like walking into a pre-Raphaelite painting. Here and there, perched up among the trunks of the redwoods, I could see strange little dwellings, one of them little more than a sheet of polyethylene draped over stakes to form a crude tent. It would be hard to find a better place to freak out, I thought—especially with moussaka and California wine less than half a mile away.

As I wandered deeper into the canyon, I began to wonder whether Esalen was indeed a freak-out center, or whether its rising popularity had some real significance. Certainly, the place had its faults. The staff seemed to spend little time questioning or analyzing their work, and their pursuit of self-awareness appeared to encourage vague ideas of emotional uplift at the expense of intellectual precision. More seriously, their attitude toward the customers was, it seemed to me, a shade irresponsible: what effect might some of the tougher Esalen techniques have on a person who was unbalanced when he arrived? The staff maintained that they accepted only "normal neurotics" in the courses; but who could distinguish, at sight, a normal from an abnormal neurotic? No attempt was made, I had been told, to follow up the fate of customers after they left. Still, I had seen enough of Esalen, I thought, to know that the purely scornful attacks made on the place by outsiders were unjustified. It might have defects; but these certainly did not mean that it could be brushed aside as one of the nutty movements for which California had long been famous. The followers of Aimee Semple McPherson and her doctrine of the Shared Happiness of Kindred Souls—to take the most notorious of these movements—believed a kind of claptrap that would be too dotty for even the least sensible member of Esalen to swallow. The nut movements sprang fully fashioned from the heads of their founders; Esalen, on the contrary, was interesting partly because it possessed an intellectual ancestry—especially in its attention to the techniques and beliefs of Eastern religion.

EASTERN RELIGIONS

California's interest in Eastern religion goes back a long way. From the earliest days, California took account of Eastern culture: one of the first chairs at Berkeley was for the study of Japanese civilization, endowed by a benefactor who specifically enjoined the citizens of the new state to look up to, and learn from, the ancient wisdom of the East. The founder of Esalen, Michael Murphy, had been partly inspired in his project by the encouragement of Aldous Huxley and Gerald Heard, two European intellectuals who had established themselves in the Los Angeles region during the late thirties and took up with "nonverbal disciplines," especially with Eastern religions. Nor is Esalen alone; the same impulse to look East has produced, as I noticed elsewhere in California, an astonishing proliferation of other centers that look for spiritual enlightenment, not toward the Mediterranean and Rome or Zion, but across the Pacific to the monasteries of Kyoto or the *ashrams* of the upper Ganges.

Among the coastal redwoods, with the Pacific immediately at hand, such concerns seemed perfectly reasonable. But after I had left Esalen and the coast and was driving the freeways elsewhere in California, I began to wonder whether the growing local obsession with Eastern religion did not require more explanation than mere geography.

It struck me that the obsession has been greatly helped by the weakness, locally, of more conventional Christianity. The state was developed at the very time that Christianity was losing both its confidence and its drive: California was the last sizable chunk of the Western world to be colonized, and the first to be developed by Europeans who did not carry firm religious beliefs with them. True, the earliest footholds in California were Christian missions established by the heroic Franciscan cripple, Fr. Junipero Serra, in the late eighteenth century; but the missions were broken up after Mexico declared its independence from Spain in 1821 and their lands doled out to supporters of the new Mexican government. Before long, the chapel that Serra built at Carmel was being used to store hay, and the San Fernando mission was housing pigs. By the time the first great wave of settlers arrived, the missions were in ruins. (They have been expensively restored, in the twentieth century, less as religious than as tourist centers: points of reference on the freeway map).

The migrant waves were so huge and rolled in so fast that the churches (like the political machines) could not keep up. Much of the impulse behind the first great American migrations from Europe had been religious: on the eastern seaboard and in the midwest a religious structure still underlies the social structure, like a sinopia behind a medieval Italian fresco. But the second great American migration, across the continent, was inspired not by religion but by greed: by what *The Californian* in 1848 called the "sordid cry of gold! Gold! GOLD!!!!"

What was more, the surge into California occurred precisely when Christianity was being dealt the most serious body-blow since Galileo. While the migrants were moving through the Sierras, Charles Darwin in England was sorting out the material he had gathered on the voyage of the *Beagle* and which he published, as *The Origin of Species,* in 1858. The moment the blow landed was in June, 1860, when the formidable Bishop Wilberforce attended a meeting of the British Association in Oxford in order, as he put it, to "smash Darwin." Instead, Wilberforce himself was smashed by the scientist T. H. Huxley, who announced that he would rather be descended from an ape than from a man like Wilberforce, who prostituted his gifts to the service of falsehood: an insult from which neither Wilberforce nor Christianity ever fully recovered.

Nine years later, the two halves of the American continent were finally "joined by iron" when the final spike was driven into the Central Pacific Railway. Seventy years after that, when T. H. Huxley's grandson, Aldous, decided to settle near Los Angeles, Christianity at its most westerly outpost was represented, for the most part, by scattered, debased, and eccentric cults.

The energy of Christianity which, starting in the eastern Mediterranean, had been powerful enough to inspire all European empires, from the Holy Roman to the British, and which had still, in the eighteenth century, driven Junipero Serra up the Californian coast as far as Carmel, was not strong enough in the later nineteenth and twentieth centuries to accompany the thrust of the American empire to the shores of the Pacific. The surge dried up under the Californian sun.

This was exactly what some Americans had hoped for. Thoreau, in particular, wanted the opening up of the west to be accompanied by the abandonment of Christianity. Living in his shanty beside Walden Pond, in Concord, Massachusetts, he saw the west as the place where man could at last slough off the accumulated rubbish and materialism of centuries and acquire "a sense of possible sublimity," a source of new life and health. In his walks, he always found himself stepping westward. "Eastward I go only by force, but westward I go free . . . ," he wrote. "It is hard for me to believe that I shall find fair landscapes or sufficient wilderness and freedom behind the Eastern horizon, but I believe that the forest which I see in the Western horizon stretches uninterruptedly toward the setting sun, and there are no towns or cities in it of enough consequences to disturb me." For Thoreau, the west was the future: "I must walk toward Oregon and not toward Europe. And that way the nation is moving . . . ; we go westward as into the future, with a spirit of enterprise and adventure." Wanting to break with the old world, he thought that man should stop looking across the Atlantic even for his religion and, instead, look to Asia, as he did himself. "It so happens," he emphatically wrote, "that I am better acquainted with the scriptures of the Hindoos, the Chinese and the Persians, than of the Hebrews."

There was never much chance of Thoreau's contemporaries listening when he advised them "not to live in this restless, nervous, bustling, trivial Nineteenth Century, but stand and sit thoughtfully while it goes by." And though he was not the only nineteenth-century sage to interest himself more in the religion of the East than the West (Emerson found the Vedic scriptures of India "as sublime as heat and night and a breathless ocean," containing "every religious sentiment"), this interest was not widely shared. As late as 1939 a professor from the University of Pennsylvania was complaining in the *Bulletin* of the American Council of Learned Societies that "at present, only the sheerest accident brings India into the purview of the American college student." What changed all this was the arrival, in California itself, of Eastern holy men—Hindu St. Pauls, as it were, setting out to convert the Californians instead of the Romans.

YOGANANDA IN HOLLYWOOD

The readiness of California to take Eastern holy men seriously was first demonstrated by the extraordinary career of a flamboyant Yogi named Paramahansa Yogananda: the first "great master" of India to live for a long period in the West. During his years in California, from 1924–52, Paramahansa enjoyed a career that strikingly foreshadowed the later success of the Maharishi, the mentor of the Beatles: there is the same emphasis on the idea that the East has something special to teach the West, the same transcendental jargon, the same emphasis on meditation, and the same awkward combination of asceticism with a liking for the best hotels.

Yogananda was born in northeast India; his father worked at various times as a railway official and also organized the Calcutta Urban Bank, evidently transmitting some of this financial shrewdness to his son. Yogananda as a young man refused to accept the Western idea of a safe career on the Bengal Nagpur Railway, with a pension at the end of it, which his father wanted to arrange, and instead went off to become a monk. When he was twenty-seven, his venerable and saintly guru Sri Yukteswar Giri told him that years ago he had had a conversation with India's most holy sage who had explained that one day he would be sent a disciple who, after training, would go off and teach Yoga to the West. India, the sage had explained, "has much to learn from the West in material development; in return, India can teach the universal methods by which the West will be able to base its religious beliefs on the unshakable foundations of yogic science. I perceive potential saints in America and Europe, waiting to be awakened." At that point in his story, the guru looked at Yogananda: "My son," he said, smiling in the moonlight, "you are the disciple that, years ago, Babaji promised to send me."

It might be an exaggeration to identify that 1920 conversation (reported later by Yogananda) [3] as the start of the hippie movement, but it undoubtedly had astonishing consequences. Yogananda traveled first to the east coast, where he drew an audience of a thousand to a Yoga lecture in Washington; [4] but it was not until he transferred to California that his career really blossomed. With his long curly hair, parted in the middle and falling over his shoulders, and his open, feminine good looks, he was in his youth an attractive figure (in middle age he found, to his distress, that he put on weight easily: on one return trip to India he put on fifty pounds). He soon had the good luck to attract the attention first of Luther Burbank, the Santa Rosa horticulturalist, and later of an extremely rich Californian businessman named James J. Lynn, with interests in oil and insurance. By the end of 1925, Yogananda had set up the spacious headquarters of what he called the Self-Realization Fellowship on the Mount Washington Estate in Los Angeles; and before long, Mr. Lynn had built the fellowship a self-realization *ashram* on a well-groomed bluff beside the Pacific twenty-five miles north of San Diego, in Encinitas, with two meditation caves built into the cliff, verandas, special sunbathing places, an orchard, and a private beach. Thereafter Yogananda divided his life between Los Angeles and Encinitas, conducting Sunrise Services and classes in Hindu, and pushing out a stream of lectures and magazine articles.

As time went on, Yogananda adapted his teaching more and

more to the imprecise Californian taste, enlarging his doctrine until it miraculously embraced every major religion. In 1942 he set up a blue, white, and gold structure in Hollywood called the Church of All Religions, containing statues of, among others, Krishna, Buddha, Confucius, and Moses, and featuring a mother-of-pearl reproduction of Christ at the Last Supper. He founded a similar church at San Diego, overlooking San Diego Bay, and another at Long Beach (next to the City Auditorium) in the architectural style of the Normans. Finally, in 1950, he opened a Lake Shrine and Mahatma Gandhi World Peace Memorial in Pacific Palisades, with a two-acre lake, a windmill, a Mississippi-style houseboat, a sarcophagus containing ashes of Gandhi, and a life-size, golden-robed statue of Jesus, which, illuminated at night, symbolically beckons—in the words of the fellowship—"the passing motorists to Come Unto Me, to discover the inner Christ peace." The opening ceremony at the shrine was performed by Goodwin Knight, lieutenant-governor (and later governor) of California.

Extraordinary though Yogananda's success was in life, his greatest achievement was in death—if indeed he can be said to have died at all, which his followers doubt. On March 7, 1952, he finished a speech at a Los Angeles banquet for the Indian ambassador, was suddenly taken ill and, shortly afterward, "merged in the Cosmic *Om*." For the next twenty days his body was closely observed, before it was finally buried, by Mr. Harry T. Rowe, the mortuary director of Forest Lawn Memorial Park, who subsequently sent the Self-Realization Fellowship a notarized letter:

> The absence of any visual signs of decay in the dead body of Paramahansa Yogananda offers the most extraordinary case in our experience . . . No physical disintegration was visible in his body even twenty days after his death . . . . No indication of mold was visible on his skin, and no visible desiccation took place in the bodily tissues. This state of perfect preservation is, so far as we know from mortuary annals, an unparalleled one.

At the time of receiving Yogananda's body, the mortuary personnel expected to observe, through the glass lid of the casket, the usual signs of progressive bodily decay. Our astonishment increased as day followed day without bringing any visible change in the body under observation. He looked, on March 27, as fresh and unravaged by decay as he had looked on the night of his death.

This professional testimony from Forest Lawn naturally confirmed the Yogi's followers in their conviction that he was indeed a saint. Many of them formed the idea that he was not far short of a Messiah; and it cannot be said that Yogananda, during his life, tried very hard to persuade them otherwise. He had had visions, he reported, all his life, and they grew more and more remarkable as he grew older. Even before leaving India he had had visions about the United States: at an ancient temple in Kashmir, he fell into an ecstatic trance and envisioned a mansion on top of a hill that perfectly accorded with the headquarters he later established in Los Angeles. Again in India, and still before he had been to the United States, he saw a panorama of Western faces moving across his line of sight; many of those faces, according to his own account, he later saw in California and instantly recognized. But his most stunning vision was in 1938, at Encinitas, when he not only saw Jesus—who appeared to him as a young man of about twenty-five, with a sparse beard and moustache and long black hair parted in the middle (a hairstyle resembling Yogananda's own)—but was actually spoken to by Him, though Yogananda told inquirers later that the words were so personal that he preferred not to disclose them.

Yogananda was the most exotic of the Californian holy men. The most influential is Swami Prabahavananda, a Hindu monk who lives in Los Angeles and became involved in the thirties with both Huxley and Heard and later, more closely, with the novelist Christopher Isherwood. Isherwood left England in 1938 with his boyhood friend, the poet W. H. Auden; he went west to California while Auden stayed in New York, and their subsequent histories may reflect the way their different environments have affected their different temperaments. Both are now over sixty, but Auden, with his amazing lined face like an aged coelacanth, is a Christian and still deeply involved in the mainstream of Western cultural life, spending part of the year in a house in Austria and translating poetry from Swedish and Russian. Isherwood, however, still has the manner and boyishness of an undergraduate, rarely visits Europe, and has translated Hindu scriptures.

Q: You've taken a great interest in Hindu philosophy, haven't you?

ISHERWOOD: I would never, never, never have taken even an *interest* in it, let alone been able to understand it, if it hadn't been that I met this very remarkable man who's a monk here in Los Angeles, Swami Prabahavananda. First of all either Gerald Heard or Aldous Huxley met him, but anyway then they both met him, and so I got introduced to him. This was one of the major experiences of my life, and I have remained a very close friend of his, a student, ever since.

Q: You said it was a profound experience: can you explain?

ISHERWOOD: Well, what anything like that means, if it *really* means anything, is simply that it provides you with an ultimate resource—some kind of thing which you can turn to when what one calls one's own resources are exhausted. It provides a reassurance that you won't just go screaming mad or flip under pressure, or that even if one does flip it is sort of irrelevant: that there's still something behind you even after you've flipped. It's all part of this thing that I'm eternally telling people, I'm sorry I'm not that sort of person, the concept that my life is intentional. My life is not consciously intentional. People say: why did you decide this? Why did you decide that? It was decided for me by circumstances, is how I feel. Now you may say that's just a kind of affectation, but it's how I feel, and I don't know any other way of describing my experiences except by saying that they happen to me.

ALDOUS HUXLEY

> People should use their common sense, act with decency, cultivate love, and extend and intensify their awareness—then ask themselves if they know a little more than they did about the Unknown God.
>
> *Aldous Huxley*

In the spread of curiosity about Eastern religion, World War II was a watershed. Huxley and Heard arrived in Los Angeles toward the end of 1937; soon afterward, the Vedanta Society of southern California began to publish its magazine, *Vedanta and the West,* to which Huxley contributed regularly, and whose anthologies, edited by Isherwood, were a means of spreading the new interest of these European expatriates far outside their immediate circle. In 1942, Heard established a monastery on an estate of 360 acres behind Laguna, in "very beautiful, rather English countryside"; and in 1943, Swami Prabahavananda set up another monastery under the auspices of the Vedanta Society. In 1944, Isherwood published his translation of the *Bhagavad Gita.* The boom was on.

Of all those concerned, Huxley's interest was the most crucial, for he gave a gilt-edged guarantee of intellectual seriousness to what might otherwise have seemed one more manifestation of Californian eccentricity. Huxley came from an English background of formidable brainpower; T. H. Huxley was his grandfather on his father's side, and in his mother's ancestry were Dr. Arnold of Rugby, who invented the English public-school system, and Matthew Arnold. At Oxford, during World War I, Huxley had been the star of his generation (his elder brother, the distinguished biologist Sir Julian Huxley, has always conceded that Aldous gave him an intellectual inferiority complex); and soon afterward he established himself as the most brilliant young novelist of the day, the friend of H. G. Wells, Lytton Strachey, T. S. Eliot, Arnold Bennett, D. H. Lawrence, and Bertrand Russell.

Huxley arrived in California by accident; while he was staying with Lawrence's widow in Mexico, a Hollywood agent persuaded him that his novels could be sold to make films. With his wife and son, Huxley drove in an old Ford car from Mexico to Hollywood in September, 1937, to look into the possibilities. There he was offered a job writing a script for the *Forsyte Saga,* which he turned down; met Charlie Chaplin and Anita Loos; liked the place and found the climate suited his wife's health; wrote *Madame Curie* for Garbo in eight weeks, giving him enough ($15,000) to live on for a year; and remained based in the Los Angeles area for the rest of his life (he died in 1963). From Huxley's letters, the nearest we have to an autobiography, it seems plain that a change came over him when he migrated to the west. In Europe, his friends had all been high-powered literary figures; in Los Angeles, his circle became much less literary and far more medical and scientific, until it embraced, by the end of his life, an amazing range of academics, psychiatrists, the inventor of LSD, astrophysicists from Mount Wilson Observatory, a man at Stanford with a Tibetan ghost-trap in his office, the parapsychologist J. B. Rhine, the chief of the Suez Canal Company's hospital at Ismailia, Egypt (a Hellenic scholar and heart specialist who made extensive use of psychiatry, whom Huxley was put on to by Jung)—indeed anyone who could contribute to what in middle life became Huxley's consuming interest: the true nature, both physical and psychological, of man. As the years went by, Huxley's life became as surrealist as one of his fantastic novels, for he combined a highly disciplined, single-minded combing of people, institutions, and books that bore on his main interest with spasmodic involvement in what he called the "lunatic industry." He worked on a musical of *Brave New World,* wrote a script for the cartoon character Mr. Magoo, shopped at the Largest Drug Store in the World (he was fascinated by the oddities and absurdities of southern California), kept his valuables, after his house burned down, in a filling-station safe on Sunset Boulevard, and married his second wife at a drive-in wedding chapel.

His interest in Eastern religion developed slowly. He had been raised in a defiantly rationalist household, where the ghost of Darwin was almost one of the family (his father had had Aldous baptized with extreme reluctance), and his first known reference to Oriental philosophy was in 1918 when he wrote: "How much I disapprove of the Wisdom of the East." When he traveled in India in the late twenties, he was chiefly struck, not by the holiness of the Indians but by the beastliness of the British. It seems to have been only after his arrival in California that he started to read Oriental religious literature consistently—*Time Must Have a Stop,* published in 1942, is closely linked with the Tibetan Book of the Dead.

The more Huxley looked into it, the more Eastern religion seemed to him to have clear advantages over Christianity. Any religion, he conceded, was bound to create objects of worship: gods, defunct saints, etc. But Christianity persisted in regarding its deities, not as projections of the minds of generations of worshipers, but as independent realities. The Oriental philosophers, on the other hand, were perfectly clear that all deities are projections of the mind and ultimately unreal. Reading the mystics of both East and West, Huxley concluded that all of them had had much the same kinds of experience; but whereas the Eastern mystics had known that their experience of the Clear Light of the Void represented the final reality, the Christian mystics had never been able to push their argument to its logical conclusion, since they had had to fit their experiences into an unreal framework in which God and Christ existed independently of their visions. For the Oriental philosophers, the vision *was* the ultimate reality—as it became for Huxley. The Western mystic seeks to know God, he said, but the Eastern, to *be* God.

He saw another "great merit" in Oriental systems of philosophy:

> Their metaphysics and their theology are devised in order to explain certain types of immediate experience. Christianity, Judaism, and Islam have been unduly preoccupied with concepts and symbols. They have spent too much time and energy

manipulating symbols—in ritual and sacrament, in creeds and theologies. . . . A sensible and realistic religion should be one which is based upon a set of psycho-physiological operations, designed to help individuals to realize their potentialities to the greatest possible extent (we normally live at about twenty percent of capacity), and to heighten their awareness so that they become fully conscious of the Unconscious and at the same time fully conscious of other human beings ("mutual forgiveness of each vice," in Blake's words).

Thus he came to advocate a purely mystical religion:

Christianity as such can never hope to become the religion of this new technologically and perhaps militaristically unified world we are moving into —it can never hope to become the world religion, because it has become associated, in the eyes of all non-European peoples, with the beastlinesses of our political and economic imperialism. But there is in all religions a highest common factor of mysticism, on which everyone can agree, because it depends on experience and not on revelation or history. Mysticism also has the further enormous advantage that it is concerned with the eternal present. The moment you get a religion which thinks primarily about the bigger and better future—as do all the political religions from Communism and Nazism up to the, at present, harmless, because unorganized and powerless, forms of Utopianism and Humanism—it runs the risk of becoming ruthless, of liquidating the people it happens to find inconvenient now for the sake of the people who are going, hypothetically, to be so much better and happier and more intelligent in the year 2000, of sacrificing the present to the future.

With these beliefs about mysticism, it was to be expected that Huxley would be excited about drugs and the kind of experience they offered; his crucial importance seems to be that he was the forerunner who popularized the connection between Oriental religion and drugs. He first took mescalin—at his home at 740 Kings Road, Los Angeles—in May, 1953, and soon afterward wrote to a friend: "It is without any question the most extraordinary and significant experience available to human beings this side of the Beatific Vision." In 1954, he expanded his ideas into a book, *The Doors of Perception*. "He regards mescalin as a 'gratuitous grace,' " wrote Professor G. M. Carstairs of Edinburgh University, "which facilitates the sort of mystical experience which he finds chastening and rewarding, in much the same way as Brahmins and Saddhus regard *bhang* (Indian hemp) as an aid to contemplation." (Carstairs had conducted a field survey into *bhang* in 1951, in northern India.) A year later, just before Christmas, 1955, Huxley took LSD, finding the physical symptoms more potent than mescalin (it produced feelings of intense cold), but observing that the psychological effect was the same: "transfiguration of the external world, and the understanding, through a realization involving the whole man, that Love is the One—and that, in spite of everything, the universe is all right." [5]

Huxley's experiments had a far wider audience and a much greater impact than he ever expected: *The Doors of Perception* became a best seller with "a quite stupendous circulation"; he wrote articles in *Life, Readers Digest,* and the *Saturday Evening Post,* and appeared on TV. Later on, he seemed to change his mind about publicizing drugs: "Mescalin, it seems to me, and the odder aspects of the mind are matters to be written about for a small public, not discussed on television. All that television can do is to increase the number of misunderstanders by many thousandfold." However, by that time the word was out; and there is little doubt that Huxley's enormous prestige, as well as his talents as a popularizer (his essays used to appear among the sexy pictures in *Esquire* in the days when *Esquire* was experimenting with the potent mixture of sex and serious articles later used by *Playboy*) gave the idea of drug-taking a special excitement and respectability. "How odd it is," he once exclaimed, "that writers like Belloc and Chesterton may sing the praises of alcohol (which is responsible for about two-thirds of the car accidents and three-quarters of the crimes of violence) and be regarded as good Christians and noble fellows, whereas anyone who ventures to suggest that there may be other and less harmful shortcuts to self-transcendence is treated as a dangerous drug fiend and wicked perverter of weak-minded humanity!" This argument, used by Huxley in the fifties, has been precisely the argument of those in America and Europe who have campaigned for legalizing marijuana.

At this same time, Huxley was in contact with people who played an important propagandizing role themselves in spreading Zen Buddhism—for instance, Professor Suzuki and Alan Watts (another Englishman, who became dean of the American Academy of Asian Studies in San Francisco)—as well as with the most celebrated of all advocates of "psychedelic materials," Dr. Timothy Leary.[6] And Huxley practiced what he preached. As his first wife lay dying, he whispered mystical phrases into her ear; and when he himself was on his deathbed, his second wife gave him LSD to help him die.

Huxley's last novel, *Island,* is about a Utopia, Pala, in which Western know-how and Eastern religion are finally blended "to make the best of both worlds—the Oriental and the European, the ancient and the modern." The Palanese help themselves to attain knowledge of the Infinite by the use of a drug they refer to as "the reality revealer" or the "truth-and-beauty pill." Huxley had no doubt that he himself had had a glimpse, by means of drugs, of the nature of ultimate reality. And surprisingly, since he was always profoundly pessimistic about everything that concerned man's behavior in the world, his drug experiences continually reminded him of what he called "the fundamental All Rightness" of the universe.

The interest generated by Huxley spread out, before he died, to the beats. Allen Ginsberg, the most durable beat prophet, was born in New Jersey; but it was in California that he converted himself into an American version of an Eastern *guru,* with his shoulder-length hair, holy man's beard, and posters of himself naked, as if about to enter the waters of the Ganges. After the beats came the hippies, draped with beads and tinkling with bells manufactured in India; and since then the movement's shock waves have resounded across the Western world: linking up with the student revolt and connecting with the spread of drug culture. What began as an apparently harmless fashion has thus expanded until the whole aim of Western society has been questioned. Occasionally, the bearers of the new message have been relatively old—a Ken Kesey with the drug gospel, or a Maharishi —but the real carriers seem to be the young.

In 1966, I was surprised to see circles of Berkeley students sitting on the campus in the cross-legged posture of the Buddha; in 1967, I saw a fellow in the same position perched on the hood of an automobile, also at Berkeley. By the summer of 1969, students of the University of Sussex were sitting under the trees in the same posture: a gesture to the East while boning up on the textbooks of the West.

By no means all those Californians involved in experiments in modern living—hippies, drug-takers, mind-awareness fans, mobile community groups (such as the Hog Farm, a strange assembly some seventy-five strong, who were last heard of heading into New Mexico in old buses with babies inside and belongings crammed on the roof)—are interested in religion. What does unite them, however, is their antimaterialism. This is the context, it seems to me, in which Esalen acquires significance.

Ever since the first cry of gold on the streets of San Francisco, Californians have been inspired by the notion of creating a paradise on earth. They set about this aim with a matchless enthusiasm for material goods, and now in California, for the first time, man has solved his production problem. The historic preoccupations of man—food, shelter, work—need preoccupy Californians no longer.

Now it is precisely toward the Californian goal that the rest of the world is doggedly heading. Both capitalist and, increasingly, Communist societies take it for granted that material prosperity is the high road to happiness. Meanwhile in California, where the citizens have, by and large, reached the end of the road, some of them are beginning to suspect that all along they may have been on the wrong track. They see that Californian Man can do anything: build capsules for moon landings, prepare to grow babies like cuttings from plants. At the same time, the local scientists are constantly making discoveries that seem to reduce man's significance: whether by interpreting human characteristics, such as memory, fear, or sexuality, according to molecular structures and interactions, or in pinning down the age of the universe. Man thus seems to possess unimaginable power and yet at the same time to be unimaginably insignificant. Man knows everything and can do everything: yet he is nothing.

Such anxieties are nowadays being felt increasingly everywhere, but they are felt with special acuteness in California. Elsewhere, men may briefly raise their heads and wonder what it is all for, but then they have to lower their heads again and go back to work. Californians have the time, the money, and the assurance of future comfort that leaves them with no alternative except to confront their anxieties. Hitherto, only a tiny élite in any society has ever asked itself the question: what am I? The rest have either been too busy staying alive, or have been ready to accept a system of belief handed down by the élite. In California, not only is there no general system of belief, but millions of people have the opportunity—and many of them the education—to worry about that dreadful void.

This preoccupation is inducing a vast self-consciousness. Deprived of anything external in which to believe, people in California are plunging inward in the hope that the search for themselves will somehow provide a new code of values to live by.

CHAPTER 9

The Experimenters

> We live in a world of transgressions and selfishness, and no pictures that represent us otherwise can be true; though, happily for human nature, gleamings of that pure Spirit in whose likeness man has been fashioned are to be seen relieving its deformities, and mitigating, if not excusing, its crimes.
>
> *James Fenimore Cooper*

HOWEVER well-disposed toward California a traveler may be, there are bound to be times these days when he approaches despair. At such moments I have sharply reminded myself that Americans possess a tradition of resilience and experiment, and a proven ability to produce novel solutions when required. Despite the state's unhappy condition, and predictions of worse to follow, I did spot what, to me, were signs of hope, like snowdrops in February. Just as the clues to universal troubles seem to sprout first in California, so also, one may conclude, does the search for new and possibly fruitful ways of setting about things, either in the field of social action or in private life. I sometimes noted these hopeful signs among groups of which many Californians profoundly disapprove—for instance, the flagrant homosexuals of San Francisco; the idealistic conservationists, who are often detested as trouble-makers by big business; and—most hated of all —the hairy producers of the underground press. To many Californians, such people are precisely the cause of the trouble in which the state finds itself. Believing that the trouble has deeper causes, I, on the contrary, thought that they were treating California as it should have been treated from the beginning: as a place that offers exceptional opportunities for experiment, perhaps for the ultimate benefit not only of Californians but of the rest of us as well. Their activities struck me as proof, too, that western adherents of rugged individualism need not always end up in a narrow cul-de-sac, with each rugged individual defending his own lush patch against outsiders. Instead, they could also stand in the open, showing true independence, inventing new methods to suit changing circumstances instead of sticking to old rules from motives of self-interest.

DAVID BROWER

One new positive concern in which Californians have lately been followed by the rest of the industrialized world is the "environment issue"; and the man who more than anyone else has brought it to the forefront of public anxiety is David Brower, formerly of the Sierra Club and now of Friends of the Earth. In his photographs on Friends of the Earth propaganda, Brower looks a little too good to be true: strong features, white hair ruffled by the breeze, shirt open at the neck, eyes lifted upward. In real life he is less pious and more humorous, but for a man approaching sixty he does look remarkably unpolluted, a fine advertisement for the conservationist life, as if he has just come down from the mountains and is shocked to discover what automobiles, oil companies, and Pacific Gas and Electricity have done to the place in his absence.

Brower was born in Berkeley in 1912 and has lived there ever since. During his childhood, he often went camping with his parents, and one ingredient in his distress now at the way California is being wrecked is a feeling that his boyhood is being destroyed by bulldozers. As a youth, he collected butterflies, and he still gets excited when he talks about those days.

"I had a butterfly named after me. It was an orange tip, and I really knew I had something when I got it, because there was no orange, and some of the greenish overcast on the underparts was not there. It was named *Anthocharis sara Reakirti* transition form *browerii,* and that's my only claim to fame. It's forty years since I abandoned that pastime, but I still see them, and I'm quietly proud of being able to identify a butterfly from a little flicker way off in the air. But there aren't very many now. There's been almost a wipe-out, and I don't like it. You get some of these unique little ecosystems, these little habitats, and along comes the developer who didn't know what was there, didn't know it had gone, never missed it, and then says 'Look what I've done to improve this place,' when really he has been just totally destructive."

Nostalgia is one of Brower's conscious drives. When he was born, the population of California was two million, a tenth of what it is now. When he graduated from high school, the population of the earth was half what it is now. "I watched what growth did around me. I watched the air get worse, the beauty blotted out. As a Navajo recently said, 'The air has lost its light. There was a lot added, but too much taken away. The Yosemite streams I used to drink out of reek of chlorine now." He is not ashamed of his nostalgia, believing it to be a human requirement, not a false sentiment or a quirk. Everyone, he considers, ought to have the sustaining memory of a wilderness somewhere in the back of his mind, as Brower has the Sierra and the vanished butterflies. "You know you need it, because you are fashioned to fit it. If you take the wilderness away, the world is a cage."

In seeking to preserve this essential human resource, Brower has been working in an old tradition, for California may be regarded as the seed bed of modern environmental concerns. The first conservation battle was fought here in the last century to save the sequoias; and the first American park to be set aside for the nation, which set the pattern for the rest of the country, was Yosemite. The founder in 1892 of the Sierra Club, of which Brower was executive director for seventeen years, and which he built up from 7,000 to 77,000, was the Scottish naturalist John Muir, who converted both Ralph Waldo Emerson and President Theodore Roosevelt to his own militantly conservationist views.

Brower has been continuing Muir's battles. Roosevelt's Chief Forester, Gifford Pinchot, could see no reason why resources should not be sold off and fully exploited, provided they were also well managed. Muir, on the other hand, and Brower after him, thought that man should leave tracts of nature untouched, allowing whatever happened naturally in them to happen and keeping man's sticky fingers out of it. Brower's most celebrated and successful campaign, which stopped dams being built in the Grand Canyon, was a replay of John Muir's resistance to the building of reservoirs in the Hetch Hetchy area in 1908, to provide water for San Francisco.

As threats to California have grown, Brower has widened his activities. Before he took over the running of the Sierra Club full-time in 1952, it had been mainly concerned with helping its members, hikers and campers, to appreciate the Californian landscape. Brower increasingly found himself taking the club into the ring against timber merchants, developers, the Bureau of Reclamation, the Internal Revenue Service. Finally, his militancy was too much for the club. He vehemently opposed a PG&E plan to construct a nuclear-reactor complex on an unspoiled stretch of coastline south of San Luis Obispo, and some of the club's directors were not wholeheartedly behind him in the fight; indeed, one or two were supposed to have unspecified connections with PG&E. At all events, Brower says he was pushed out. Undaunted, he started in 1969 a much more directly political organization, Friends of the Earth: "a nonprofit membership organization streamlined for activity in the U.S. and abroad aimed at restoring the environment misused by man and at preserving remaining wilderness." The advisory council includes Arlo Guthrie, Duke Ellington, Professor Paul Ehrlich, Professor Barry Commoner, C. P. Snow, Norman Cousins, and Arthur Godfrey. By 1971, Brower had a headquarters in a back street of San Francisco and branches in New York, Honolulu, Washington, Alaska, London,

Paris, Zurich, and Stockholm. The political arm of Friends of the Earth, the League of Conservation Voters, in 1970 added a new ingredient to American election campaigns—the candidate's record on rescuing the environment. In at least three instances—in Maryland, Indiana, and Idaho—the league was held by *The New York Times* to have been "a major factor" in the results, especially in the non-reelection of Governor Samuelson of Idaho, who was eager to turn the White Cloud Mountains over to the American Smelting and Refinery Company.

To the task of spreading his environmental gospel, Brower brings burning evangelism, which has sustained him through twenty years of lecturing and other inspirational work, and a talent for dramatizing issues. He has a regular description of the history of the world, designed to point up what man has done to it, which he always uses in lectures and which he broke into, when I talked to him, halfway through a beer in a San Francisco bar.

"If the creation of the world began last Sunday at midnight, the age of reptiles does not begin until four on Saturday afternoon. Then five hours later come the redwoods and the pelicans; then at ten at night the whales and the porpoises go back to sea, and there are sixty-five million years of that; and then, just three minutes before midnight, Man. A second and a half before midnight, formal agriculture—when we began to upset ecosystems. A quarter of a second to midnight. Christianity. And then, in the last fortieth of a second before midnight, the Industrial Revolution. We cannot go on behaving as we have behaved in that last fortieth of a second," says Brower. "Our demands on the earth's resources keep doubling; we cannot afford another doubling. It's becoming quite apparent what the last doubling of our demands has done to us. For all the Pollyanna thinking that goes on, and the attempts to reassure us, we see all around us, in any direction that we look, that we're in trouble—with the water, with the air, with space, with temper, with patience: we're running out of everything. We must think not only of ourselves but of our descendants." Using his extended personal timetable, Brower considers we should try to plan for the next thousand years—not such an outlandish period of time, he says, when you consider that 1066 was a mere thousand years ago, and that we are creating highly radioactive wastes that must be kept isolated for at least a thousand years. "We've got to budget something for the people who are going to be minding our garbage."

It is nearly ten years now since Brower urged the Ford Foundation to finance studies into what he called "The Economics of Peaceful Stability"—meaning the study of getting by economically without trying to grow forever in a finite environment. This has now become a fashionable and urgent theme. Brower long ago asked Professor J. K. Galbraith to give it his attention; in 1971, in England, Galbraith finally did so, delivering a series of lectures criticizing the dogma of growth.

What is most original about Brower is not so much his evangelism, but his constant prodding of people into action, like a sleepless sergeant-major kicking the troops awake to tell them the enemy is coming over the hill. When he addresses campus audiences (and the number of students who go to hear him has grown enormously in the past couple of years) he will ask, for instance, who among them wrote to President Nixon to congratulate him on his strong warnings about population growth. No one raises his hand. Then he asks if anyone present thinks we have a population problem. Everyone raises his hand. "The moral is clear: get lobbying; send telegrams; write letters to congressmen; put ads in the papers. It is amazing what one person can do. Remember Rachel Carson. You don't need to remember Ralph Nader because Detroit does. The Timber Supply Act was backed by the construction industry, the logging industry, the Forest Service, the Department of Agriculture, the pulp industry, and the president: just a few opponents beat all of those people. The moral is: it doesn't take everybody. Not everyone has to worry about everything all the time. Pick one or two issues and worry about those. If you don't like working alone, get a friend. If you can't spare the time, join an organization. Don't underestimate yourself, because you really can make the difference."

Nor is Brower merely urging people to try to stop things from happening. He points out how generously the oil industry is subsidized, and the highways; how everyone loves a subsidy. "So let's not stop subsidies, but let's subsidize the things we want: let's use our genius and technology and humanity to heal and restore the environment, for instance. How about pulling down some of the high-rises? Repairing some of the hills whose tops were lopped off for development? Restoring some of the industrial wastelands?"

Judging by the increased response to Brower, people are beginning to realize what action they can take to improve the circumstances of their lives, besides putting a piece of paper in a ballot box on a given Tuesday once every other year. "Politics has got to stop being an obscenity and become part of everybody's life," he told me. "I decry the feeling of futility people have. You can make the difference! Just get in there and hit one of these subjects. Goddammit! Stop feeling futile!"

BICYCLE BOOM

One minor, but by no means insignificant, sign of the new environmentally conscious spirit is the bicycle boom. In Washington, D.C., a few Sunday cyclists have long been in the habit of taking a trip along the towpath of the Chesapeake and Ohio Canal, knowing that they appear quaintly old-fashioned to other people. In New York, for several years Central Park has been closed to cars on Sundays (and on Saturdays in summer) and open for bicycling. But in California, people are turning to the bicycle not simply as a pastime, but as an alternative form of transportation; and there is no doubt in the minds of those at the center of the boom that the principal cause is revulsion against the automobile. Californian cyclists regard themselves not as old-fashioned, but as travel pioneers.[1]

Evidence of the boom is everywhere. The proprietor of a bicycle shop in Oakland told me he had sold 700 bikes in 1968, 3000 in 1969, and would have topped 15,000 in 1970 if he had had the machines to sell. Cycling magazines and clubs are prospering.

The Great Western Bicycle Rally, started eight years ago by a physician in La Jolla, becomes annually a bigger and bigger event. Around San Francisco, some 50,000 people now commute to work daily by bicycle—a vast increase over a few years ago.

The demand these days is for the ten-speed bicycle, which a decade ago was used only for racing. Prices range from $90 for a good serviceable machine to $500 for something extra-special— perhaps with British tubing, an Italian saddle, and a Californian frame. The modern bicycle has a narrower saddle than formerly, a narrower tire requiring higher air pressure, and a wheel that is one inch larger.

The owner of the Oakland bicycle shop called Velo-Sport Cyclery, which was spacious and gleaming, with dozens of new bicycles and a busy repair section at the back, was a round-faced, quiet thirty-year-old named Peter Rich. When he opened his first shop, Rich chose a street much used by pedestrians, but discovered that they were merely a nuisance; they wandered in, but did not buy. Then he moved to his present site "with a lot of driver-by exposure," which was the right place to be, because the impulse to buy a bike overtook automobile drivers when they were actually at the wheel; they suddenly felt an urge to liberate themselves. Buyers were often moved by the thought that exercising by bicycle might avert a heart attack, said Rich, "but the ecological theme is the big reason. It's so bad it's finally shocking people into doing something. *Some* people still enjoy driving, but less and less. A big proportion of car polluters are people who travel less than five miles; we could cut pollution in half if, for those short trips, people used alternative forms of transportation."

Rich was eloquent about the joys of cycling. He had spotted, as he rode around the state, a white stag, horned owls and, near Bakersfield, a condor; but he wondered how long such creatures would survive. Constantly he was shocked at the way little lanes had been turned into four-lane highways. A pleasant feature of bicycling was the fraternity among cyclists; they were a community and helpful to one another, in a way that automobile drivers were not.

However, the cyclists feel discriminated against. Highway restrictions abound. They are forbidden to ride on freeways; there is no legal way for a cyclist to ride either into or out of Sausalito (there is no way to walk in or out, either). The west side of the Golden Gate Bridge, reserved for bicycles when it was built, has since been closed to them (the closing was part of an attempt to cut down on suicides: for some reason, perhaps connected with the westward urge, suicides, over 400 since the bridge was built, invariably jump west). In the master plan for the new Bay Area Rapid Transit scheme, no provision whatever was made at the stations for bicycle parking, though massive lots were reserved for automobiles. Nor are the police sympathetic. Rich himself used to be a policeman, and he urges them constantly to take action about the growing number of bicycle thefts; but the police claim they do not have the manpower to bother about what they privately regard as toys. "I'm ashamed to say I came here in a car today," he said, with a guilty smile. "But I really am ashamed." A healthy short-haired Californian who was ashamed of driving an automobile: that, I reflected, was indeed a new phenomenon.

DUSKIN *V*. CITY HALL

As Brower says, many Californians feel futile as the eyeless juggernauts plunge forward, ripping out the redwoods, laying pipelines across the Alaskan tundra, storing oil in giant tin cans on the hillsides. They feel even more helpless and cut off from the process of governing. Yet few places have tried harder than California to give citizens control over their affairs: its government institutions consist of 58 counties, about 400 city authorities, 1650 school districts, and 3500 special districts.[2]

Los Angeles is hamstrung by its system of government. It prides itself on being a twentieth-century city, but its form of government follows that which other American cities had before the Civil War, and have long since abolished. It has a mayor "almost too weak to cut ribbons,"[3] a large elected council that is supposed not only to legislate but to administer, and a shoal of more-or-less independent departments run by citizens part-time. The city of Los Angeles overlaps the county of Los Angeles, both in area and in jurisdiction. Other cities are contained inside Los Angeles: as you drive into Beverly Hills, for instance, the billboards vanish: Beverly Hills is a city, with its own amenity laws, and its own police, fire, and highway departments. The city of Los Angeles tackles virtually none of the tasks it would perform in a rational system—urban renewal, for instance, or planning the advance of the suburbs. "Don't tell me what to do," said one frustrated city councilor. "Tell me how to do it."

One Californian who is trying to cut through the undergrowth and invent a new mode of civic action is a successful and earnest young Jewish garment manufacturer named Alvin Duskin. He is a San Franciscan by birth, who was involved with the student-protest movement in the early sixties before taking to the road as a salesman; since then he has prospered as a reluctant capitalist. Duskin maintains that neither the state nor the city machine is working properly. The state is crippled because by far the largest part of the taxes collected in the state goes to the federal government in Washington; on an income of $10,000, for example, a man may pay between $600 or $1000 in income tax to the federal government, but only $60 to the state. "So the hospitals are like prisons, and the welfare services are a disgrace."

The cities are not working either, in Duskin's opinion. Because the governmental machinery and the tax system are inadequate, "San Francisco is spiraling downhill. Everyone is scratching each other's eyes out. Police, blacks, unions: everybody has his back to the wall. The whole idea of cooperation has gone."

And the capitalist system is beginning to seize up, because it is changing over from being labor-intensive to being capital-intensive, and the machines are putting people out of work. On Duskin's sewing machines, one girl now does the work formerly done by two. Unemployment in the state rises, yet productivity does not really decline. "And far more could be produced if the corporations were really run for the benefit of the community instead of being caught up in the pursuit of maximized profit. My factory could produce six or ten times as much as it does, if I was engaged simply in making *clothing*, but what I'm really doing is to bring money in and turn it around, and send it out as profit. If we could find a way of freeing independent businesses from this pursuit of larger and larger profit, we could create instant utopia. As it is, a corporation's basic dynamism is growth—an impersonal mechanism geared to increased earnings, which rides roughshod over every human value."

Against this background, Duskin senses that people are becoming more and more frustrated by their powerlessness. "Everyone's talking and everyone's listening; and everyone wants to take part in the decision making. But no matter how much information you have pouring in, it doesn't help you to do anything. That's how I see the crisis."

Duskin's own method of doing something is very direct. Working with one of San Francisco's leading advertising men, he inserts full-page ads in the local papers on topics that bother him. The ads are detailed and specific, crammed with fact, graphs, and argument. Then he waits for the row. He has fought one successful campaign to stop an absurd civic monument from being erected on Telegraph Hill. In his factory, he has fed three thousand people a week who weren't getting enough to eat because, despite a federal program designed to feed them and despite federal surplus food sitting in warehouses, City Hall wouldn't operate the program.

These and similar activities have not made Duskin popular with the civic authorities. Tax men have taken an exceptionally close interest in his firm's books and have chopped out items on his personal expense account. Official harassment, however, has not deterred him from taking on U.S. Steel, City Hall, the building unions, and the longshoremen's union over a proposal by U.S. Steel to build a very tall skyscraper on a plum site near the San Francisco waterfront; the scheme also features a "Ferryport Plaza," which will stick out 1200 feet into San Francisco Bay and form both a new superterminal for passenger ships and a high density development with a hotel, shops, and offices. Duskin's full-page advertisements opposing this grandiose scheme had an instant impact. During the subsequent uproar, angry construction workers and longshoremen demonstrated outside and even inside City Hall, their argument being that the new building would provide the unions with jobs for a year or two, which, as Duskin was quick to point out to his readers, was not a rational basis on which to plan the future of the most beautiful city in the United States.

One absurdity revealed by the U.S. Steel building battle was that Duskin was doing the job supposed to be done by the San Francisco Department of City Planning. Before the storm broke, the department published a beautifully produced document called Urban Design Plans, Preliminary Report No. 8, which explained how the character of San Francisco must be preserved by keeping new development projects down in bulk and height. No notice whatever was taken by the city's power structures of these sensible notions; instead, the mayor aligned himself with the real-estate people, the unions, and U.S. Steel. Plainly, to me, the public interest would not be served by either the U.S. Steel building or by Ferryport Plaza. But the only uninvolved citizen who could see a way of getting into the argument and opposing the very strong interests who were in favor of it was Duskin. He has invented the instant pamphlet, which judiciously used in a relatively small city like San Francisco, (in New York, issues are buried as fast as they are raised, under another truckload of crises) can at least help to make citizens aware of the difference between the city as a commodity to be exploited and the city as a place to live.

THE COMMUNES

One innovation that is often said to be Californian, and which has certainly been taken up there with special enthusiasm, is the commune. So far as I could discover, the first communes were invented by rock groups who needed to be close together in order to practice and therefore found it convenient to live under the same roof. The arrangement was catching: there are now at least two hundred communes in Berkeley alone. Many Californians complain about loneliness, and for that disease a communal life offers, at least in the abstract, a certain cure. It also suits perfectly the new stop-go earning methods often practiced by the young; if you haven't made enough money this month to pay the rent, someone else in the commune probably has.

As time has gone by, the communes, like most other segments of Californian life, have become much more political. One San Francisco commune, the Red Family, issues statements and invents revolutionary songs. Economically, too, they have become more organized. Nowadays several individual communes will group themselves into a self-help collective, trying to detach themselves as far as possible from the capitalist economy. A collective may dispose of a pickup truck, a carpenter, a photographer, and an electrician, and trade these services with other collectives. If one collective bakes bread and another puts out a paper (the *Berkeley Tribe* is a collective), the bread bakers may barter loaves for free ads. During 1970, there was a sudden fashion for Women's Lib communes: "Women for the Free Future," one of them was called. When I asked if I might pay a visit, I was indignantly refused, but my female agent investigated one such pad (which contained eighteen women, six children, and one man) and reported that "it was falling apart because of ego-trips, with a sloppy atmosphere and bitter, bitter vibes." She failed to report what the man was doing in there.

But the most exotic commune that I heard of or visited was in Haight-Ashbury—a group of young homosexual actors called The Cockettes, after the (so far) more celebrated Radio City Rockettes. They live in a large run-down house and put on their shows at a rented theater in North Beach; for licensing reasons, these shows have to start at one o'clock in the morning, but in spite of this apparent disadvantage the Cockettes have had an astonishing, fashionable success with their camp song-and-dance shows and imitations of Mick Jagger, Pola Negri, and (a special favorite) Mae West. By the beginning of 1971 they had expanded to no less than sixty-five members, not all of whom lived in the commune, but all of whom were young and almost all of whom were openly homosexual. When I visited them they were involved with their first home-grown musical, a twenties-style piece about the adventures of an American tourist and her daughter in old Shanghai. The Cockettes are professional in the sense that they live by the money they take at the box office, but they also cultivate the amateur flavor of a high-school show that hasn't quite been got together. San Francisco talent-spotters think that one or two of them might make the grade in the movies.

In this commune, the decor of individual rooms can be wild, with early Edwardian prevailing: elaborate wallpapers, stuffed birds, sepia photographs, ostrich feathers. Since the Cockettes rehearse in the house, it is not always easy for a visitor to tell whether a particular Cockette is dressed for the street or the stage. Some go in for straight drag and are hard to distinguish from girls. Others go in for what might be called counter-drag, and turn out in a tremendously masculine manner with beards and frontier hats, like Buffalo Bill. Others again—and this is the most interesting style—combine the two, wearing, for example, a long twenties garden-party frock of floating chiffon and appearing in all respects female, aside from a big (real) beard.

The Cockettes are not political; many of them are articulate and intelligent, however, and they struck me as less self-absorbed than most actors. Behind the makeup, a quite precise point is being made. They are one step ahead of the Gay Liberation Movement, which wants homosexuals to be given their rights. The Cockettes think that the sharp traditional distinction between men and women is simply a mistake, and they especially want to blow to smithereens the (to them) phony stereotype of the husky American male. To further this end, some of them delight in confusing the issue by being entirely feminine but, instead of dressing as girls, come on as supernormal men, in denims, belts, and heavy boots, as if they spent every day handling bulk sugar consignments on the waterfront.

MIDDLE-CLASS COMMUNES

From hippiedom, the commune idea is spreading to the non-hippie middle class. In Berkeley one evening I attended an informal meeting of some fifteen or twenty people who had met to set up a commune.

The convener was an unmarried English girl, Sheila, in her midthirties, who worked at the University School of Environmental Design. Her life was already agreeable. She had a well-paid job; she could walk to work; her pleasant apartment looked toward the bay. But recent attendance at awareness groups had made her feel that she would get more out of life if she stopped living alone. She had no intention of getting married, but would "enjoy" being around children and old people. At the same time, she certainly did not want to be plunged into a middle-aged fraternity house. She must have several private rooms of her own. Since none of the houses she had looked at seemed suitable, she had concluded that the kind of building needed for a middle-class, middle-aged commune would have to be built specially, a prospect which did not daunt her, possibly because her working life is spent among architects and planners.

Sheila had been encouraged in her idea by a semi-drop-out Catholic priest, also in his thirties, who had left a monastery because he felt too remote from the lay world. He now wanted to be a priest in a small community—a way of life halfway between solitariness and a monastery.

The prospective communards met at eight o'clock in Claire's apartment. Wine circulated.

CLAIRE: The idea is that we might build a new kind of commune: an environment for single, older people. It would need to have a lot of private space. We might use a computer to match people with people, and people with the new environment. Personally, I am unwilling to compromise on any of my wants, which is why I think we will have to build something specially. An apartment structure, for instance, is unsuitable because it is built for privacy and mitigates against communal living.

ESTHER, *a brunette:* I've heard of such a place in Los Angeles. It's on a beautiful hillside, a series of small houses with flexible interiors. A brook runs through the settlement, and in the middle is a rise, with a pool and a large communal building with a dining room. The only convenient way to get from one house to another—but not the only way—is via the center house. This design forces interaction and reduces exclusivity.

CLAIRE: A central building would be too far away for me. I want to open my door and find people.

ESTHER: That's too close. I lived in a task-oriented commune, and there was a lot of friction over the work. We had great big living rooms for all of us, and our own rooms opened off the communal space. We were very close. It was terrible.

BLONDE, *in her midthirties:* I like the idea of "forced interaction."

PRIEST: I have lived in a community, and one of the main problems is the way it relates to outsiders. A community shouldn't guard itself against outsiders, but at the same time a division is liable to occur between those who want to entertain outsiders in the communal space and those who think it should be kept for members of the community.

BEARD, *wearing jeans:* Why do we want communal living, exactly?

PRIEST: Life in a suburb can be pleasant, but it can be artificial. Neighborliness can be artificial. In a commune you could hope to make real contact with people.

MAN *in yellow shirt:* We need to distinguish between sharing an apartment and sharing a commune. Sharing an apartment is a matter of temporary convenience. The point of a commune is to create a common shared goal. You cannot care for all mankind; but perhaps, in a commune, care can be engendered for all its members.

BLONDE: I like to be close to my good friends. Also I'd like the security: so someone is around in case the house burns down. And I'd like a place so I can exercise my care and be cared for in return. That's very important. Everyone lives in communes of friends already, but they're spread out all over town. It takes an hour to get to a friend. What I want from a commune is what I get from encounter groups.

ESTHER: I can think of nothing worse than living all the time in the forced intensity of an encounter group.

BLONDE: I went to one group six weekends running, and it turned into a very relaxed relationship. It was a free-floating commune. In ordinary life, everyone has to live behind a front in order to cope. People in a commune would be those who are unwilling to put up with superficialities.

SOCIOLOGIST: Berkeley communes are almost cell-like structures, heavily political or ideological. In the rural scene, it's more people living together as friends; ideology comes second.

SHEILA: Perhaps one should think of a commune as an extended family: it shouldn't be a failure if people move out. The cast of characters could change, but the commune would continue.

ESTHER: People who leave a commune do so in anger or bitterness.

BLONDE: A group therapy session rather than an extended family should be the model.

BLUE JEANS: At the Golden Toad Commune in Cloverdale all the communards are musicians, all of them farm, and all are licensed to be beggars. They play at Sacramento State Fair [laughter]. They have a four-acre plot and work as organic farmers; it's a very comfortable existence.

BLONDE: I am attracted by the notion that a commune might have an ethical basis. It would conserve space and resources.

JEANS: Society is increasingly fragmented. I would like to identify with a group. I would like land, a room, a fireplace, and a studio. Given the rise in land values, I have to search for an alternative to a third of an acre in Moraga, which I shall never be able to afford. So I am pushed into my search for a commune by (a) my own desires and (b) outside pressures. I lived on a commune in New Mexico, but it wasn't quite the answer. I want some of the urban life-style.

BLONDE: I saw a house in Piedmont, six acres, with fifteen bedrooms, and four fireplaces, lived in by one couple with two kids. I thought: this would do nicely for a commune of fifteen people with three cars who shopped at Safeways. Let's get into the ecology trip.

SOCIOLOGIST: There is no one definitive commune style.

SHEILA: As things are, the builders are telling everyone how to live. They build houses for families and apartments for singles; and that's how we are all implicitly told how to live.

YOUNG MAN: Yes. If you live alone now, you have to put up with that landlord stuff.

BLONDE: In the last six months, I've had several talks like this and never done anything. Shouldn't we start by creating a community of people who meet regularly with the expressed intention of establishing a commune?

NERVOUS WOMAN: There's a "non-place-orientated" community of people now; and what they do is migrate. It might be out-of-date to settle in a particular *place*.

JEANS: It might be best to have no ties at all. A person into Eastern religion might say that a community can be built without all that *arranging*. I picked up a girl hitchhiker who had been on the road for two years; she said the real community in California is among the hitchhikers.

MAN: What's this got to do with setting up a commune?

JEANS: Well, we're here to talk about alternative life-styles.

YOUNG MAN: I've been into an Oakland commune of teachers. All the decorating effort goes into the bedrooms, and the communal living rooms are terribly dull. They can't find a common taste that suits twelve people, so the rooms stay dull.

LADY: Right. In communes, all communal areas are a mess.

MAN: What's a mess?

SHEILA: We should be searching for a sustained transformation of consciousness, so that we don't think of ourselves so much.

YOUNG GIRL: I'm doing sociology. I've been reading studies made in 1960 and 1964 and at that time it was all nuclear families, married and living in the suburbs. But it's so different now; it's all changing.

BEARD: I want children, but I want more freedom . . .

LADY: . . . than being a father [laughter].

BLONDE: The nearest things to what we want are the new leisure homes for the aged.

ARCHITECT: One of the troubles is that the building codes make it very difficult for experimental things to happen. I can feel the yearnings being expressed here, but the world is so organized that they are not easily fulfilled.

ESTHER: I'm not sure what *my* yearnings are. I am both attracted to and at the same time repelled by privacy.

ARCHITECT: That's the criterion! The privacy has got to be there when you want it. Perhaps drawbridges are the answer.

PRIEST: The trick is that there is in fact no physical structure that will produce the community.

Around midnight, the group drifted off into the Berkeley night. Would they ever set up a commune? The drive seemed to be there. They wanted a new mode of living so they could be more "honest" and not have to wear masks; for security if they got sick (no one admitted to loneliness); to combat a feeling of social disintegration; to get general "support" from like-minded people; to "experience" a wider range of people, especially children and the old (there was no mention of blacks); a vague feeling that it might ease the demands of children and endless meals; to break away from landlords' tyranny; and as an alternative to the suburban third of an acre.

THE UNDERGROUND PRESS

Our first papers made a quite different appearance from any before printed in the province. . . .

some spirited remarks of my writing occasioned the paper and the manager of it to be much talked of, and in a few weeks brought them all to be our subscribers.

Benjamin Franklin

Of all recent Californian innovations, none has been more instantly successful than the so-called underground newspaper. While traditional papers have been floundering and wondering anxiously about their usefulness and financial stability in a communications industry dominated by television, the underground papers have tapped a large new market that the rest of the media was failing to satisfy or even interest, and at the same time developed a novel system of newspaper economics.

Before 1965, there were two papers in the United States which might be said to have had underground characteristics: the New York *Village Voice* and the Los Angeles *Free Press*. The *Voice* was left-wing, produced by a part-time staff, and put together without too much pedantry over professional standards of production. But it was also well inside the tradition of local papers: it provided consistent coverage of local events, offered a complete entertainment guide, put news on the front page, and ran letters to the editor, a regular cartoon, reviews, and other familiar features. Besides, the *Voice* was not then, and is not now, totally antiestablishment, which is a prime underground characteristic. Many *Voice* readers, indeed, were prosperous and contented New York residents, forming the nucleus of a fine advertising medium, so that the editorial part of the paper was enclosed by the busy hum of commerce. The L.A. *Free Press* was more like the later underground papers, but with a fundamental difference: it backed particular political parties.

For these reasons, the credit for being the first underground paper must go to the *Berkeley Barb*. Its first issue, in August, 1965, was plainly amateur, produced on a shoestring, and execrably printed. The paper owned no offices, had no staff, and had no commitment to any existing political group; it stood instead for revolution, and it opened its pages to anyone who felt as out of tune with straight society as its originator, and who would write a piece for a very small fee.

The *Barb* was conceived and produced in 105 hours flat by a drop-out named Max Scherr, then in his late forties. Scherr was born in Baltimore, Maryland, and briefly practiced law there before being seized by a compulsion to travel west. He went west, then to Mexico; but he first showed his originality by his military behavior in World War II, as a rifleman in the Twenty-ninth Division. Having a powerful dislike of Nazis, he volunteered to go to the front line during one of the fiercest phases of the invasion of Europe. When he got there, however, though his hostility to Germans remained intense, he discovered that he had no desire to kill them. "So I refused to fire my rifle. I threw rocks instead."

After the war, Scherr returned for a spell to Mexico and then drifted up to Berkeley, where he read for a Ph.D. in sociology. It was the season of the struggle over the loyalty oath for faculty, which Scherr declined to take. He worked in the law library, drove a cab, wrote a law encyclopedia, and then, having decided that the academic life did not suit his temperament, opened the Steppenwolf Bar.

In his bar, in August, 1965, he one day idly remarked to some customers that in his opinion the publishers of the forthcoming Co-Op paper did not know their business. They had accumulated $40,000 and talked about the paper for months; but where was it? "Look," he said, "if you're going to put out a paper, you don't wait around. You put it out next week."

The customers were mocking. If he knew so much about starting papers, why didn't he try? To make good his boast, Scherr accordingly made inquiries about newspaper production costs. Next he approached the student leaders of the Free Speech Movement, then in full swing, for help, which they declined, on the ground that he was out of his mind. At that, he borrowed an IBM typewriter and set to work himself. During the next week he slept only six hours, but at the end of it he had a paper. Much of it was his own prose, but there were a few contributions by others, which he secured by visiting the local coffee shops and calling for volunteers.

"Two thousand copies were printed, and when I saw them I sat down and cried," he told me. "It was so ugly. I hadn't mastered the electric typewriter, and every page was full of mistakes. Then I realized I had made no plans for distribution or anything. How was the paper to be sold? So I went straight out and sold it on the street. I sold 1200 copies. Then I had to produce another paper, and again I went out and sold it myself. It's been a rat race ever since."

When Scherr started the *Barb,* he had $55 in the bank. In 1968, his most prosperous year, he paid taxes on $130,000. (The paper sells for fifteen cents in Berkeley and twenty-five cents in the bay area, with a total circulation of some 40,000.) Not that Scherr is interested in the profits. For years he paid maximum taxes because he was unaware that he could reduce his liabilities if he arranged his business affairs differently. He buys his clothes second hand. He lives with his pretty wife Jane Scherr in a quiet Berkeley residential street, in a house with big pillars like a run-down Southern mansion; but inside there is scarcely any furniture or belongings, apart from posters and children's toys, and a kitchen piled high with unwashed dishes and canned food. Scherr shuffles about in slippers, wearing jeans, looking vaguely reminiscent of another pioneer journalist, a woolly Benjamin Franklin. He has a straggly beard, with the left fork longer than the right, and he wears round, silver-rimmed spectacles; his voice is slow and soft, and his nature humorous and gentle.

Scherr's extraordinary success is partly due, undoubtedly, to his exceptional understanding of the young, who form the main underground audience. Like them, he is out of tune with the kind of events and views that figure in regular papers. "We just couldn't see things the same way as straight people, and so we were forced to express ourselves differently." In the first issue, the paper referred to the "amorphous but thick-hided establishment"; it also referred—a year before the birth of the Black Panthers— to the need for black self-defense.

His solution to the complexities of newspaper finance has been straightforward; he hit on a brilliantly simple method of tackling the distribution problem by getting the readers to sell the product to one another; students or other hard-pressed locals peddled it in the streets on commission. Another economical device is to allow almost anyone to write for the paper, provided they are ready to accept rates of pay that Hearst at his stingiest would have hesitated to offer. When the paper was grossing $200,000 a year, the writers were getting twenty-five cents a column inch.

Scherr has also been a pioneer of small ads, admitting a species of sexual self-advertisement, mainly homosexual, that no regular paper would dare to publish. Undoubtedly, the *Barb* ads have pulling power. One man, after he was rejected by his girl, inserted an ad describing her physique, announcing her availability to all comers, and giving her telephone number. The girl received two hundred calls and sued the *Barb*. Recently Scherr has been in trouble with Women's Lib, who particularly objected to an ad that began: "Ladies! Be Multi-Orgasmic!" Scherr was indignant. "I told them that's not a sexist ad. That's a *pro-women* ad."

Despite his success, Scherr remains a revolutionary, but has become increasingly out of sympathy with the way the movement has developed. He believes that "a revolution should be a gentle thing," and he finds himself—never "a movement person"— repelled by the exclusiveness and rigidity of the new revolutionary left, and by its authoritarianism. There is, he feels, a new dividing line in the underground. On one side are those who believe in coercion. On the other, majority side, are those who say, "Okay, so we win this revolution, but it will just produce another establishment; maybe we'll be able to smoke dope legally, but the decisions won't be ours any more than they are now."

Because he declines to believe that revolutionaries are free to adopt any methods they think necessary in order to bring about the revolution, Scherr and his paper have attracted the scorn of the new hard-liners. He draws a comparison with America on the eve of the Civil War. John Brown led the raid on Harper's Ferry intending, with his band of abolitionists, to seize the government arsenal, arm the slaves, and provoke a general insurrection.

Brown was captured by the south and hanged. Three days later, when the Thirty-Sixth Congress assembled, a Senator wrote: "Both sides are armed with deadly weapons, and it is said that the friends of each are armed in the galleries." The abolitionists, Scherr recalls, thought that any necessary means should be used to abolish slavery. But, he points out, a lot of people who were anti-slavery supported neither the south nor the abolitionists. He feels himself to be in a comparable situation today.

Scherr's claim to national celebrity is that his experiment with the *Barb* stimulated first a handful and then scores of others to start similar sheets, often after consulting Scherr. "They said, 'Wow! What a crappy paper! *Anyone* could put out a better paper than that.' And now the whole country abounds in underground papers." One does not have to approve everything the *Barb* does to regard Scherr (as the right and the left do not) not only as an original but also as a useful citizen.

None of the people or activities I have touched on in this chapter belongs, of course, to the American mainstream or even to the Californian mainstream. They are on the fringes, loosening things up, leavening the loaf. For decades, the pressure of American life has been toward conformity, often of a blinkered and self-regarding kind that shies away from what is not immediately understood, or worse, wishes to crush it, as the early settlers and soldiers crushed—a central fact of American and western history—the fearful Indians. A sort of rude and manly intolerance has been a persistent theme of western life, and Chinese, Japanese, and other minorities have suffered from it. There are special reasons now why the majority should again feel threatened: the nonconformists are not only numerous and articulate, but are often white, possessing an intimate knowledge of the world they criticize or reject. Intolerance these days, however, could extract a higher price than the bad conscience which is the legacy of past repressions. It could smother the experimental attitude and alertness to new possibilities; and these new possibilities alone will get California, where the old trails all lead to dead ends, out of its impasse and onto a new route forward into the future.

CHAPTER 10

Things to Come

We have no idea where we are going, and sweeping, confident articles on the future seem to me, intellectually, the most disreputable of all forms of public utterance.

Kenneth Clark, CIVILISATION

The future is not what it used to be.

Restroom graffito

During the past decade, a new breed of serious-minded men has begun to study the future consistently and professionally. These futurologists, or "futurists" as they generally prefer to be called—perhaps because "futurology" sounds too much like "astrology" for comfort—are now to be found all over the Western world, but especially in the United States and still more commonly in California—in universities, in corporations, and in the state's many privately financed think-tanks.

For man to peer ahead and wonder where he is going is, of course, an essential part of his nature; but our generation is showing a degree of concern about the terrestial future that is entirely new. In antiquity, when Aristotle thought of the future, "he apparently expected nothing more of it than had happened already." [1] The same was true of the philosophers of the Middle Ages. It was only in the eighteenth century that people began to think of the future in terms of change; and the cause of the shift was the Industrial Revolution. The notion that conditions of life alter; the idea of progress; the invention of the word "technology"; the first predictive fantasies: all these date from the second half of the eighteenth century. The word "technology" was coined in the 1770s by Johann Beckmann as the title of a series of lectures he delivered at Göttingen University on agriculture, mineralogy, market research, and financial administration; in 1777 he published a book on these subjects that became a best seller.[2] The first English-language future book was written in 1763, entitled *The Reign of George VI, 1900–1925.* Seven years later, a Frenchman wrote *L'an 2400,* in which he predicted "optical cabinets" with shifting scenes, machines for imitating the human voice, cities lit by street lamps, and a new religion featuring a "first communion," in which the communicant would inspect the stars through a telescope and animal life through a microscope.[3]

As technology speeded up, so did the predictions. H. G. Wells, in a story called "The World Set Free," published in 1913, predicted and named the atomic bomb; Aldous Huxley foresaw the drug cult; George Orwell described, in *1984,* the spread of authoritarian governments, the division of the world into three blocs, and a state of perpetual war. Since World War II, envisaging the long-range future has ceased to be an imaginative exercise alone and has become an integral part of certain human activities. The first group to find consistent forecasting essential as part of their jobs were the U.S. military, who were compelled to take a quite precise view of the future in planning weapons systems; because the gap between the time a missile or aircraft was put on the drawing board and the time it became operational was at least ten and often fifteen years, the planning process itself had to try to foresee and make allowances for changes during that period which might affect strategy. Rand, the think-tank in Santa Monica, was involved in such weapons studies soon after World War II; one of its earliest tasks was a "futures study," required for defense purposes, of the likely course of the Russian economy. Then, during the sixties, technological forecasting came into fashion in the big corporations as a management discipline—

sometimes with successful results, sometimes not. Overestimates of the growth of jet-passenger traffic worked out during the sixties landed all American airlines in serious financial trouble in the seventies. Underestimates by AT&T of the growth of demand for telephones caused havoc, both inside AT&T and on the nation's telephones. On the other hand, American computer companies predicted the growth rate of computer use much more successfully than their European rivals, which was one important reason why the United States came to dominate the world's computer markets.

Besides this technological forecasting, the early sixties saw the beginning, with Betrand de Jouvenel in France, of what might be called philosophical future studies. De Jouvenel argued that the world must set long-term goals for itself; if it did not, galloping technology would decide man's fate by default. These ideas struck a chord in the United States, and before long the American Academy of Arts and Sciences had established a "Commission on the Year 2000," Herman Kahn had produced his superconfident and much-discussed book, *The Year 2000,* and the boom in future studies had begun.

Today, it is fair to say, man is more obsessed with his future on earth than he has ever been before. The obsession is understandable. Man is having to confront the fact that he may not have a future at all unless he takes special pains; besides, even if he has a future, he can be absolutely sure, for the first time in history, that it will be dramatically different from the present. If radical changes are *certain* in your own lifetime, it becomes prudent to worry about what those changes will be.

What, then, do the Californian futurists think is in store, for California and the rest of us? Naturally, as I found during a series of talks with these men, they do not all come up with the same ideas. Some of them, like Professor Melvin Webber, a Berkeley sociologist, confine themselves to down-to-earth, relatively short-range forecasts, in Webber's case, the prediction that the familiar automobile is on the way out, and that "we are at the same stage with the car as the Wright Brothers were with their airplane."

Webber told me that before long we would all be getting into an "automobilelike vehicle," probably powered by electricity, and dialing our destination instead of driving, whereupon we would go shooting at high speed through a system of guideways. He thought that this transportation revolution would produce dramatic social changes, because for the first time it would enable everyone—not merely the relatively affluent, the adult, and the physically competent—to enjoy complete personal mobility.

Interesting though these and other technological speculations were, I was looking for more general predictions about possible futures, and I found what I was searching for at the celebrated Stanford Research Institute. The man I saw there was Norman McEachron, and, like many of the most stimulating futurists I met, he was not a historian or a sociologist with a few vague notions about extrapolating present trends for the next twenty or thirty years, but a scientist—and a high-powered one at that. He had a trim beard and a high quiff of hair, and he told me that he was an electrical engineer, like his father and grandfather before him. I knew he was high-powered when he told me he had spent a year at Cambridge University as a Churchill Fellow and had found the electrical engineering there "about thirty years behind the times." He was working at Stanford, he told me, partly as an astrophysicist and partly as a member of a group of futurists who were involved in nothing less than an attempt to work out what alternative futures were available to the United States. This research was financed by the U.S. government.

McEachron explained that his own task was a small part of the whole project, yet grand in scope, nevertheless. He was trying to answer the question: what is the social situation in the U.S.? To this end he had drawn a number of graphs "measuring" the social scene, and they were leading him to conclude that the U.S. was in a crisis "in the medical sense: the patient may collapse."

"Since 1960," he said, "the curves on my graphs are exponentially different. By whichever measure I take, the trend is up; illegitimate births, production and import of handguns, the rate of inflation, loss of worktime through strikes, divorce, juvenile drug arrests, adult drug arrests, assaults on policemen, incidence of adult and juvenile crime—all of them." He showed me his graphs, several of which used Californian data; the line always rose, and in some cases shot up alarmingly toward the top right-hand corner of the paper. "Rates of pollution would probably show the same trend. And there's the ecological crisis."

He expanded his theme of crisis, and said that its central cause was a conflict of values. "A society works when there is a correspondence between the values of its citizens, the social structure, and the environment surrounding the society. But now they don't correspond."

He talked of the clash of values among the young, the hard-hats, the blacks, and the Middle-America whites. "We have a system whose values developed in response to a given situation. Now we have a changed situation, and the values are no longer appropriate. We have to change. Mainstream culture simply doesn't have the answers to our problems. In fact, the old value system actually increases the problems—the notion that the pride of families and the power of nations are to be furthered, as in the past, by population increase; the notion that any technology that can be applied should be; a system of economics based on an ever-increasing GNP and expenditure of irreplaceable resources; the belief that experts know best.

"And a shift in the value system does seem to be emerging. There's a really strong movement toward religion and drugs, though the actual word 'religion' is not often used. There is, for instance, a move toward seeing life more as a Christian vocation than as a job; that switch is really fundamental, more fundamental for the person who makes it than getting rid of a wife. People seem to be striving for a kind of revitalization of themselves and the culture, to try to find a new basis for progress."

Not all these ideas were new to me, but I had never heard them so neatly fitted together. Before McEachron appeared, I had picked up a house magazine advertising a show called *On A Clear Day You Can See Forever*. He seemed to be having a clear day.

"We simply have to change direction, but no one has any idea of which direction to go in, therefore everyone has to be listened to. What's most dangerous is the increasing tendency of different groups not to listen to the others. They can't even agree to disagree. They regard each other as inhuman. It's like primitive man who, as soon as he hears a growl outside his cage, says 'Give me my club.' I end up my work thinking: if we don't listen, we won't make it. The chances of our survival may have passed: who can ever tell?"

He showed me a chart his group had drawn up, showing "alternative futures" for the U.S. It was like a tree, with the present as the roots and the possible futures as the tips of a dozen branches. Each branch, when it reached the year 2000, had been given a label, ranging from the desirable goal of "exuberant democracy" to increasingly gloomy and appalling alternatives, ending up bleakly with "Caesarism" and "collapse."

"The easiest paths to take," said McEachron, "all head into what we've called a 'slough of despond': recession, confusion, apathy. It turns out that, so far as we can see, it will be very hard to get to the desirable future, which we've called 'exuberant democracy,' and much easier to get to an authoritarian form of state concentrating on social control, which we've called 'Caesarism.' "

Driving back down the freeway from Palo Alto to San Francisco, among the solid shoals of cars and the neon signs, I reflected on the report that McEachron and his colleagues had sent to Washington. The report said bluntly that desirable future histories were scarce and that it was "paramount" for the developed world to change its values.

Not all the future studies going on in California concern the far future. Some of the futurists, thinking that it is barely intellectually respectable to be looking ahead as far as the year 2000, since such speculations, by their nature, can be little better than random guesswork, concentrate instead on searching out new developments which they believe are certain to spread. It was in pursuit of one of these futurological germs, to which I had been tipped off by a communications expert at Stanford, that I visited Sunnyvale, a city of 100,000 people a couple of hours' drive south of San Francisco.

The place lived up to its name. I had chosen a Saturday morning for my visit, and the town center was bubbling with station wagons and cheerful families. There was a drugstore selling emerald-green nylon fur rugs in the shape of a huge human foot ("Everybody needs one!" called the druggist, when he saw me examining them). There was Farrell's Ice Cream Parlor ("I Made A Pig Of Myself At Farrell's"), where the young waiters were dressed riverboat-style in red waistcoats and straw hats.

The place I was looking for—Sunnyvale Cablevision—was between the ice-cream parlor and the drugstore. In the window stood a line of gray machines, like big filing cabinets, with dials on the front.

Inside, I found George Lang, the man in charge, aged twenty-one. He was fair and chunky, and wore an orange sweater. What they were doing, he told me, was to pick up the output of TV stations outside Sunnyvale by means of an antenna in the hills, bring the signals into the gray modulators in the window, clean up the signals until they were perfect, and then send them out again, by underground cable, to their 30,000 subscribers in the town. Reception of these channels—all in color, of course—was thus made perfect. They also added five channels themselves, in the Sunnyvale studio, so that each subscriber had a choice of twenty-four channels in all.

Mr. Lang took me into a viewing room and turned the dial on a television set. On one channel, a continuous "community calendar." On other channels, a high-school football game, and a "public safety" talk—"Public safety is what they call the police here," said Lang. He went on switching and up came a continous time-and-weather program, with background music; and then the twenty-four-hour news program: a continuous Associated Press wire-service tape—exactly the same tape that newspapers get much of their news from. While I watched, the tape spelled out news of a murder in London, in clear type readable from six yards away. My back prickled. The end of newspapers, I thought.

There was scarcely any technical limit to the number of channels you could put out through cable television, said Lang. London could have a hundred studios, each pushing out a hundred different programs.

But there was much more to Sunnyvale Cablevision than that. "We can tell at any time what Mrs. Smith is watching," said Lang. He added that they would soon have a "two-way capability," which would mean that subscribers could communicate with the studio and answer questions that the studio put to them. "In the future," Lang went on, "we'll be able to put cameras in the homes of the subscribers, so that everyone can be linked into the community."

I discussed what was happening at Sunnyvale with the futurologist at Stanford University who had put me on to it. His name was Dr. Donald Dunn, a quiet, self-assured engineer whose approach to future studies, he said, was that you couldn't do anything really useful unless you knew everything about a particular subject. He himself was concentrating on knowing everything about telecommunications.

"A very big shift is on the way," he said. "Television will move from a stage of tremendous scarcity to tremendous abundance—and the big shift will be to cable television."

Once you knew the technology, he said, you began to see the vast social implications. "We have the possibility of remaking our society. Local communities will be talking just to themselves. But who gets access? And on what terms? It's a hot topic. Already there are 2000 cable systems in the United States, though they don't yet have the capacity to put out local programs like Sunnyvale, or the capacity to talk to the subscribers."

I began to see the implications. Sunnyvale Cablevision was run by a big New York advertising agency, Foote Cone and Belding. Its license to operate in Sunnyvale came from the city authorities. Citizens of Sunnyvale could scarcely avoid becoming subscribers to the system; the cost was a mere five dollars a month, and the advantages were almost irresistible.

I had asked Mr. Lang who got access to his system. "Anyone with anything constructive to say," he replied. "Of course, we wouldn't tolerate the radical weirdos who want to jump all over everybody." He gave me the impression that his definition of "radical weirdos" might be fairly wide. So: to join the community, you would need to subscribe to the system; and the system would put enormous new power into the hands of the present establishment.

What seemed suddenly to be looming up was the shadow of a new Big Brother in unexpected guise. If the studio knew what Mrs. Smith watched, they could keep computer records. They could then feed in information from her credit company: income, what she owned. Advertisers could be offered a row of sitting ducks. And the data banks could compose, in time, a map of the whole community. To say nothing of the implications of a camera in every home. You could be in charge of Sunnyvale TV and dominate the community, all the while really believing you were doing the right thing by the citizens.

Sunnyvale and its cable television was an example of a new and powerful branch of technology coming into use before society had realized what was at stake and certainly before a social mechanism had been invented to cope with it. Dr. Dunn was evidently concerned lest the new device became an instrument under the control of city authorities and the existing broadcasting companies. The Federal Communications Commission had been unimaginative about cable TV, he said, failing to comprehend its full possibilities, and needed to be prodded into taking steps to insure broader access to the system.

But cable TV is only one of the technologies coming along for which California, and by extension the rest of us, is unprepared. From talks with other futurists, I gathered that all of them—and many, as I have said, were scientists of standing in their own fields—felt certain that a series of big new technological waves was bearing down on us: not only communications technology, but biological engineering, the whole information explosion connected with data banks and computers, and new possibilities in social engineering. Yet we were still reeling from the last buffeting: from the nuclear bomb, which threatened us permanently;

from the population explosion caused by medical technology; from the mess in the cities caused by automotive technology; from the rural revolution caused by agricultural technology: and the ecologists were full of warnings and alarms about dozens of technological practices, ranging from the atmospheric disturbances that might be caused by supersonic aircraft to the hazards of enzymes in detergents. If the long-range sociological view taken by McEachron and his colleagues was gloomy, so also was the shorter-range outlook of those concerned with more technical studies.

THE END OF PROGRESS

> Progress sometimes sets you backward.
> *San Diego airline clerk referring to his losing battle against*
> *a computerized booking system.*

I did get a more cheerful, and at the same time highly dramatic, vision of the future from a distinguished professor of molecular biology and bacteriology—even though there were parts of the professor's world-picture that had their gloomy side. Gunther Stent was raised in Berlin but has been at Berkeley now for nearly twenty years—a highly respected person. Stent is a bald man who wears glasses, brushes his hair forward over his bald patch, and has an agreeable way of sprinkling his conversation with American phrases delivered in a strong German accent. I saw him in a room sandwiched between two virus laboratories, with a fine view across the bay to the Golden Gate Bridge—a room, I thought, conducive to calm but wide-screen speculation. Broadly, his startling theory is that progress is coming to an end, and that an age is fast approaching when man will have no more artistic or intellectual pursuits as we have known them. Material affluence, coupled with a declining Protestant ethic, will make any sort of struggle irrelevant, and we will return to the static way of life associated with primitive cultures.

"I first started thinking on these lines at the time of the Free Speech Movement in 1964," the professor told me. "That was a deep shock to some of us. Until then, like most people, I had considered myself a good guy. I took pride in my work; I thought that what I was doing was useful—investigating the structure of DNA; I published papers; I hoped one day for some sort of recognition—perhaps a Nobel Prize; and at the least I looked for the respect of my colleagues and students.

"With the Free Speech Movement, it became apparent that everything I stood for, and everything I was doing, was rejected by my best and brightest students. The Free Speech Movement had little to do with free speech: it was a revolt against the ethical system, not simply of rednecks, but of all liberal and reasonable people. The students declared that none of the old jazz had any validity: they rejected the whole idea of success and striving; even success as an artist or a scientist had no meaning for them any more. The notion of doing anything, whether in a laboratory or on the stock market, had ceased to have any meaning for them; all this was rubbish.

"It seemed to some of us even then that what was happening was of cosmic significance. Our colleagues accused us of parochial paranoia, but subsequent events have only reinforced our view, for the same phenomenon has appeared all across the Western industrialized world. Even in China I have a feeling that the 'cultural revolution' was not really a revolution at all, but a largely destructive activity. The Red Guards were all kids. China for the first time in her history has a high degree of security, and already it seems to have produced kids who don't give a damn.

"That is guesswork, of course, and there are plainer developments here at home. The Free Speech Movement marked the matriculation of the beatniks in the university, and the point of the beats was that they stood for the abnegation of success. But the hippies now are a stage further on from the beats. The beats rejected all notions of success and were trying for some sort of inner realization, some sort of inner communion with nature. But they were still in contact with the world; they were interested in sex and food, poetry, music, and so on. For the hippies, however, there is little difference between the real and the unreal world. It makes little difference to a hippie if he actually sleeps with a girl or if he takes a drug and imagines he sleeps with a girl. The mere fact that young people are behaving in this way shows how far we have gone. People don't appreciate how far things *have* gone. I gave a lecture in Kansas, and a boy afterward asked me about hippies. Surely, he said, if a boy sleeps with a different girl from his regular girl, then his regular girl gets jealous? He couldn't believe that she didn't. But I said, 'That's exactly the way it is with the hippies.' What we are evidently seeing is the decline of Faustian man—Faust being the epitome of struggling man who is never satisfied because he is always striving for the infinite.

"Many people say, of course, that the hippies are simply alienated from society in the same way that the Bohemians were alienated from French nineteenth-century society. The Bohemians, it is said, eventually became integrated into society and the phenomenon disappeared. But Bohemianism—by no means only a French phenomenon—disappeared precisely because society itself changed. Montmartre prefigured what happened elsewhere.

"The hippie doctrine is spreading. When the beats first appeared, people were horrified. Now the hippies are accepted in all our big cities. Many people are beat who do not wear long hair, and hippie attitudes are reflected among the faculty. I think there are two correlations here: age and sensitivity. There are a lot of engineers or chemists, say, who simply won't get the message and will continue as before. But the whole curve has been shifted. Most are not remotely affected; nevertheless, they are by no means as gung-ho as their counterparts were twenty years ago. For instance, it is extremely difficult in the university now to get someone to be head of a department. Twenty years ago, being a department head was a big deal: there used to be tremendous politicking and campaigning for votes, and terrific prestige attached to the job. Now, no one wants to be a department head; it doesn't give the same satisfaction. This is true even in the chemistry department. We have here two of the leading bacterial geneticists in the world. Thousands of students will turn out to listen to a black-power speaker, but only four students have signed on for the genetics course. That must mean something. It is, of course, very damaging to the ego of the old-timers: you have worked very hard; you have become a great world expert; and now nobody wants to listen to you. That's rough. The generals must be feeling the same about the intake into the army."

Stent was developing a theme I have since heard from Professor Daniel Bell at Harvard. Bell wondered what would happen to American society as the social structure, primarily the economy and technology, become increasingly organized on the principle of functional rationality—meritocratic, technocratic—while the culture becomes increasingly apocalyptic, anti-intellectual, intuitive, and sensuous. Never in history, Bell said, had there been this intense adversary relationship in a society before.

Stent told me that it looked to him as if man is at a new stage. "It has some similarities with the early stages of Greek mythology, in which everyone had all he needed. Read Hesiod's description of the first age of man, and you will find it surprisingly close to life today in California. There is a painting of mythological life in the Munich museum which looks exactly like a summer's day in Golden Gate Park: in fact, it was seeing this picture that started me thinking—it had such a close relationship to the scene in San Francisco.

"Now let me present my argument. My first proposition is that the decline of Faustian man coincides with the end of progress. Let us say that for 100,000 years there has been some kind of progress. The *idea* of progress, however, originates only in the eighteenth century. Why? Because it was only then that the rate of change became fast enough for people to notice it. But toward the end of the nineteenth century, people already began to suspect that progress might be ending. Take Henry Adams and his law of acceleration; his proposition was that progress goes faster and faster. But the accelerated dynamics of progress—which I define as "gaining dominion over nature"—contains a contradiction. Progress must have a limit. It cannot go on and on.

"As progress speeds up, man acquires more dominion over nature. More dominion over nature brings more economic security, and thus easier living. But here is another contradiction. The more that progress succeeds, the harder it becomes to propagate the drive to success. Nietzsche's will to power, his will to dominion, is not, I think, part of human nature. It is transmitted from parents to children, but it is much harder to pass on the drive to success to a child when he doesn't encounter the need to succeed —the need to dominate nature—in his own life. I think English public schools in the last century must have grasped this point, unconsciously or consciously, which was why they created such spartan living conditions for the boys. Here in California we have had many progressive schools, and many children were fed an idea of antisuccess. The greater the progress, the harder it is to pass on the idea of success. And the faster the rate of change, the wider the generation gap. In the old days, both parents and children faced the same problems, so parental ideas seemed relevant to the children and were accepted. Now, as everyone knows, even siblings separated by five or six years are not on the same wavelength.

"Progress thus contains the seeds of the contradictions that will end it. What other evidence is there that the limits of progress are being reached? Well, the most important indices of progress are the arts and sciences. Art describes the inner world; science describes the outer world. And the interesting thing is that, quite independently of anything I have said so far, it turns out that both art and science are coming to an end. Since art is trying to describe the inner world, there must be some meaning in art, something which is being communicated. Music is the purest of the arts, because it depends least on natural models; good music is really only about the inner world. Now: how does music acquire meaning? Let us take a tone sequence. A tone sequence arouses uncertainty in the listener's mind about how it will go on. He hears the notes, and as he does so he constantly reviews his expectations of what notes will follow. Thus some kind of structure develops. In making these structures, you invoke your entire musical experience. If you hear a piece of Bach for the first time, you invoke your experience of other pieces of Bach. If you have heard no Bach before, you invoke, let us say, Mozart. As you listen, you divine the rules under which the composer is operating.

"Now what is the evolution of music? The composer of primitive music operated under the strictest possible rules. To start with, perhaps he simply imitated bird calls. But there is just so much you can do with bird calls, so by and by these strict rules become exhausted. Next, a genius appears and he has a new style. An advance in music has always involved the abandonment of one or more of the previous rules; and the first people who hear the new music always find it weird, because some rule to which they are accustomed has been overthrown. After the genius, his followers take it up; the sophisticated audience gets to understand it; and by and by the rules of this new sort of music are exhausted. So we can trace a constant process of greater and greater liberation from strict rules. There is a new style, an efflorescence, a late phase, and then—finish. That is the process that has been going on in all history. Schönberg represents a late phase in this process. He overthrows tone; there are no more keys; melody is dethroned. *But* there are still rules, though they are very free. For the listener, understanding is already extremely difficult. Audiences took a long time to appreciate and comprehend what Schönberg was doing, but finally there was an understanding in the upper reaches of musical appreciation and now his music is accepted.

"Now twelve-tone music was still perfectly conventional in the sense that it was still operating within a framework of rules, even though these were very flexible. But that set of rules in its turn became exhausted. Today, with composers like John Cage, all rules are overthrown. You have music composed at random by a computer; you have a performer who is at liberty to improvise, so that the performer himself is producing random music. At this stage, the uncertainty in the mind of the listener has become enormous, because the number of possibilities is so vast. So much information is needed in the mind of the listener that it exceeds his channel capacity. It exceeds his capacity to perceive what is going to happen next—and indeed in real chance music there is nothing to perceive. When you reach random music, you have come to the end. There is nowhere to go. That is what has taken place in music."

Stent paused. The musical stage he was talking about has certainly deeply concerned the most articulate modern composer, Pierre Boulez, who has been trying to find ways of incorporating chance techniques into more traditional forms, fearing that purely chance music will become totally meaningless. In his work "Pli Selon Pli," the sections of the piece can be played in several different sequences. The conductor makes the decision, and his decision is based on which sections of the score allow improvisation by the players. Thus the work does not require instrumental or electronic gimmicks in order to get the chance element—as those pieces do, for instance, which use transistor radios. However, Boulez has found the way ahead very hard to find. He has taken over the BBC Symphony Orchestra as a conductor, interpreting the work of others, instead of concentrating on composing himself.

"Look at other art forms," Stent went on, "and you will see that the same thing has happened. Action painting is a purely random activity. You don't know what the painter had in mind; and actually the painter had nothing in mind. In the theater, the same sort of thing has happened: the language has been used up. This is what Ionesco realized: all things have been communicated already, all situations have been explored, and all emotions have been explained, so his characters mouth meaningless words. After the theater of the absurd, there is nowhere to go. Of course, there will still be plays. There are people like Hochhuth who produce a sort of atavistic latter-day morality play." Stent here might have instanced a recent play of the Nobel prizewinner Samuel Beckett; the curtain went up on a pile of rubbish, and nothing whatever happened until the curtain descended.

"The artistic process is a constant drift to randomness. The link between the artist and the audience is finally broken. There is a connection between the speed at which art develops and progress in technology: music, for instance, started by being notated so that it could be repeated; then it could be printed and so disseminated, and then the speed of dissemination increased with the phonograph, television, tape recorders—dissemination goes faster and faster, and so music itself is used up faster. The element of communication in music has been disappearing for twenty years, until the listener now is completely on his own. Henceforward an artist's view of what he is doing must differ radically from that of his predecessors. Artists will continue, but an artist's activities will have no connection with what art has been doing hitherto."

Here again I remembered an artist: Francis Bacon. He once told me that the only thing that interested him in his painting was the random element—the unforeseen accident that happened as he applied the paint to the canvas. He was not in the least interested in communicating anything and indeed could not understand why other people wanted to buy his products.

"If you say 'art is at end,' people may well agree with you, since they cannot understand what is going on in art," Stent continued. "But if you say 'science is at an end,' people refuse to accept it. Yet developments in science parallel developments in art. Take my own field of molecular biology. Interest in the subject dates back to high antiquity: Aristotle asked 'What is heredity?' Nothing happened for a long time, until an explosion of interest and information in the nineteenth century. Today, my field is dead. All that remains to be done is to straighten out a few details. You cannot go on and on in a particular field; there is a limit to creative activity. Finally, everything has been done.[4]

"The same is true of chemistry and astronomy. People say 'Very well; but what about the social sciences? Can't we make the social sciences like the natural sciences, so that we can understand our society and clean up the mess in the world?' But it is vain to hope that social scientists can ever approach the physical scientists in understanding of their subject or in being able to predict. Here I follow the argument of the French mathematician Mandelbrot, who is a friend of mine. It is a rather technical argument. The reason why the social sciences cannot possibly make any further advance lies in the statistical nature of the phenomena that they study. At the end of the nineteenth century, the natural sciences were deterministic. You studied your set of conditions, and they led to one result. That is deterministic or causal science—which is easy science. Science is essentially a statistical study: you perceive an ensemble of events and try to make order of them. Uniqueness cannot be the subject of scientific study.

"There are some fields of study in which the uniqueness, the unique element, though present, is not so important. In planetary astronomy, for instance, the uniqueness is relatively unimportant. Planetary astronomers may study only one planet, but it always comes back to the same position and they can therefore make causal laws. The phenomena can therefore be fathomed by deterministic science.

"There are other fields of study in which you cannot be absolutely certain how phenomena will behave, but you can be ninety percent certain. This is true with the pressures of gases, for instance. You cannot make an absolutely certain prediction, but you can predict for all practical purposes.

"At the end of the nineteenth century Tyndall and people like that—Lord Kelvin, for instance—said that physics was coming to an end. When I was young, Tyndall was pointed out to me as an example of how wrong you can be, because physics was obviously not coming to an end but flourishing. But Tyndall was in fact partly right. In the twentieth century what you have had is quantum mechanics and atomic physics and the uncertainty principle of Heisenberg. Modern physics is largely of an indeterminate kind.

"Mandelbrot says we are now on the threshold of the second stage of indeterminate physics. What is the difference between the first and the second stages? It is that the element of uniqueness has now become of tremendous underlying importance. If you take an ensemble of events and study them to determine more events, the thing eventually converges in some kind of an average. You operate with this average as if it were determinate. But of the phenomena that are now left to explain, this simply is not true. You can watch as long as you want, but the thing never converges to anything. Take meteorology. You simply cannot make observations that mean anything. Take the wind velocity at Berkeley. There is no such thing. There is no average, because the fluctuations are so large. No matter how long you study it, there are so many variables, so many unique factors—of cycles, winter and summer, and so forth—that you simply don't get anything.

"In the social field, almost everything that we wish to study is in this second indeterminate stage. Mandelbrot examined the fluctuations of meat prices, trying to extract some law and meaning from their movement. But the figures don't converge on anything. Here is a similarity with art: you can measure and watch to your heart's content but you can never be sure of the meaning. There is no test you can make because the phenomena are so erratic. Nature is a chance composer. The student can never be sure he can predict what is going to happen next. The fields that we most want to understand, the remaining fields of study, are precisely of that kind.

"Thus both art and science have undergone the same kind of parallel evolution. The facts for the perceiver are finally meaningless: the semantic element has been broken. At the very time that progress was starting to kill off Faustian man, the kind of man who would want to do things, it turns out that there is nothing for him to do."

Stent gazed out of the window toward the Golden Gate Bridge. "Where will this state of affairs lead?" he went on. "Possibly Polynesia can serve as an example of the process. Some 2000 years before Christ, people from somewhere in southeast Asia launched themselves into the infinite Pacific: they must have been truly driven Faustian men, because the feats achieved by these guys are beyond belief. They settled the Polynesian Islands, and then there came a change. They introduced some form of birth control; population was stabilized; worry about the next meal became unknown; they achieved a steady-state society. The European discoverers found a beat society. But it was not the same on all islands. Cook found that the more lush the conditions, the more beat the people. On Tahiti, for instance, they were taking dope almost all the time; they had overthrown all conventional ideas of sex: it was a typical hippie scene. In New Zealand, on the other hand, a temperate zone with larger and more challenging islands, the Maoris were still pretty rugged (though not by comparison with the Europeans), and they were the only islanders with artistic forms. In Tahiti, although it is known that the original invaders had brought knowledge of pottery, for instance, with them to central Polynesia, by the time the Europeans arrived all that had been forgotten.

"In California we have an affluent society with no intellectual problems left to be solved and we also have these characters up and down the coast leading the lives of Polynesians. Assuming there is no nuclear war, I think that for all industrial nations some kind of Polynesia is ahead. Of course, I don't think the whole world can turn into hippies. Some people will manage to pick up some kind of drive. Might these people be black? Might the blacks turn into the Faustian element among us, and take over? I doubt it. Until recently they had no picture of themselves, no sense of identity. Now they are acquiring a sense of identity, but I doubt whether there will be time for them to turn into Fausts; they are faced not so much with economic insecurity as with indignity. Once that is overcome, they will be ready to join the rest of us.

"Probably horrible things will happen in the next decade: violence, perhaps some form of fascism. But the Negro leaders do not talk like Faustian men. In fact, they talk against it. Even the Panther leaders speak of some kind of togetherness, though of course they must be partly Faustian. The most outstanding student leaders must be very driven people—Mario Savio, Cohn-Bendit. Nevertheless, their *ideas* are anti-Faustian.

"One must try to think about these matters in a long perspective. My hope is that when the present younger generation's kids grow up, in twenty or thirty years' time, the black-white problem will diffuse."

I said goodbye to Stent and wandered out into the bright noon sunlight of the campus. Students were hurrying to and fro in what appeared to be Faustian activity. But it was then that I came across the strange scene I described earlier: the absolutely silent students sitting around a shaven-headed guru wearing dirty gray socks. It was certainly hard to imagine earlier members of the university—Professor J. K. Galbraith or Lincoln Steffens, or Robert McNamara or Glenn T. Seaborg, John W. Gardner or Norton Simon—so engaged.

Perhaps Professor Stent was right. Perhaps the silent and peaceful circle was indeed an intimation of a Polynesian future. I remembered a member of the distinguished staff at the Salk Institute at La Jolla, Dr. Melvin Cohen, saying: "We can do anything. We can even extend man's life span, maybe to one hundred. It should be a golden age. The next age should not need to accomplish anything."

Perhaps Stent was right, too, in believing that man had reached a new stage in his history. The modern idea of progress had arisen in Europe during the eighteenth century, when man first began to believe that his knowledge and power over nature would increase indefinitely and bring him worldly happiness.[5] Now, two centuries later, the limits of possible knowledge were beginning to appear. At the same time, serious and respected ecologists were saying with growing insistence that man must learn to cooperate with nature and stop trying to subdue it, if the world was to keep going. Furthermore, in the very part of the globe where there is the greatest concentration of knowledge and the most power over nature—namely California—many people had begun to doubt whether knowledge and power really did bring worldly happiness. The economic and technological machine was grinding on, but fewer and fewer people thought that its whirrings were a prelude to a better future.

The fact is, however, that we have no idea what is going to happen, or what will be required of us. Despite the futurists, we have a less clear idea of what may be in store than any generation of our predecessors. The reason, it seemed to me after my futurological conversations, is not simply that we are confronted by new technologies bringing new problems. True, the technologies sound as if they will need some handling; true again, the problems that face California itself now seem specially intractable. A man at Rand listed three such problems for me, and to none of them does even the glimmering of a solution exist. How are blacks and other minorities to be given skills and brought into the labor market? How can the quality of the civil service be improved, given the certainty that (despite the efforts of right-wing politicians) the role of government is going to become more and more crucial, and given also the fact that the civil service can never hope (as things are organized at present) to pay competitive salaries with the universities or still less with business? A third problem: how is the rocketing cost of higher education to be met? By 1975, the University of California enrollment will be about 145,000 students; by the year 2000 it will have risen (the university's own figure) to 275,000. Yet already the taxpayers are in revolt and, as the university lobbyist in Sacramento told me, every year the legislators look more and more suspiciously at the budget. The university dean, E. F. Cheit, said he found the university's rising costs a more worrying problem than the student revolt: California gets younger and younger, and the tax base of citizens available to finance the university gets, every year, comparatively smaller and much angrier.

But it is not problems of this type, extremely awkward though they may be, that are at the root of those profound anxieties about the future that I came across among the best and most thoughtful Californians. There is a sense in which such problems at least sound familar. But behind them is a much deeper and more shadowy malaise: a disturbing feeling that out here on the Pacific coast man has inadvertently turned a corner and gotten onto an unfamiliar road that leads into peculiar terrain, with strange shapes lurking in the undergrowth. There are the sudden freak events, like the Sharon Tate massacre; the spreading doubts among the comfortably-off about the way they have ordered their lives; the feeling that affluence creates more problems than it solves; the fact that the blacks and young are not merely not understood by outsiders, but positively do not *want* to be understood; the feeling that drug-taking, wife-swapping, and other novel social experiments are symptoms of people's inability to cope with the new leisure; a sensation, in short, that society is not holding together.

I noticed also, in my Californian travels, a symptom which I cannot find any other way to describe except as "a loss of faith." Of all Americans, Californians have been the most practical. Like the old Spanish mission stations, the campuses of the university have been dotted up and down the state to form centers of learning and civilization, but the impact of these campuses on the world outside has been mainly practical. They have been generally esteemed for their links with massive and complex defense programs or with scientific agriculture or with technological industries; the campuses have been geared to getting things done. Strangers until recently to doubt and uncertainty, Californians have instinctively believed that even the toughest problems have practical solutions, that their destiny as citizens of the state and of the United States was sure to be desirable and good, and that the ancient system would work. Now, it seems to me, this practical approach has run out of steam. Few of the people I talked to— whether in labor unions, universities, banks, the government, corporations, the churches, or the media—were sure that their institutions were adequate to the times. On the contrary, most people seemed to feel that the institutions had been created to serve a society that has now virtually disappeared, and that the institutions are not appropriately structured to tackle the problems now on hand, let alone those in the offing. I found a school of thought that maintains, with the support of plenty of examples, that institutions, by their nature, cannot adapt to meet the needs thrown up by rapid social change.[6] Certainly none of the traditional Californian institutions is coming to grips seriously with the population question, or racism, or drugs, or pollution, or the alienated young, or crime, or even with the chronic shortage of low-cost housing.

What, then, is to be done? The first step (I was often told) is to recognize that we cannot go on as we are. But where is the initiative for change to come from? Professor Richard Meier of Berkeley, a futurist specializing in urban studies, told me that the makers of the future, in his view, will be the spreading urban areas and the corporations. The big urban areas have acquired an influence and momentum of their own. The giant multinational corporations, too, increasingly ignore political boundaries and grow in power and scope: unlike politicians, who can see no further ahead than the next election, corporations can plan five, ten, or fifteen years into the future—and possess the clout and the capital to make their decisions effective.

Among corporations, I did discover uneasy flickerings of an awareness that their role in society is changing and that they must think about behaving in a new way. McKinsey, the management consultants, have been running courses on the environment for their bright and ruthless young men, whose attitudes will no doubt penetrate the firms they are called in to investigate. One futurologist told me that many middle-rank executives had confided to him that the days when firms had a single, overriding aim—the maximization of profits—were coming to an end; firms, he said, were beginning to realize that unless they began to take account of social goals, there was little chance that anyone else would—and in that case what would happen to the markets in which they were selling? To my surprise, I heard one day on my car radio that the president of Wells Fargo Bank, whose branches and billboards cover California, had made a speech urging firms to think about goals other than sheer profit. Especially among young businessmen I found this notion of social goals becoming fashionable. At Stanford Business School, it had taken particular hold. The students there had been so abused by other Stanford students for going into business that they had issued a statement protesting that they were misunderstood: they explained that they were as concerned about the ills of society as anyone else and said that it was precisely from inside the business community that most could be done to correct those ills. They set up a Corporate

Social Responsibility Index to rate corporations "on their social responsiveness and concern," and announced that, in the future, corporate social behavior must be given the same importance as profits.

Six months after the president of Wells Fargo made his speech, First National City Bank, one of the world's largest, sent a questionnaire to the beneficiaries of the personal trusts it handles, asking whether it should encourage the companies whose shares it held to spend more on pollution control, product safety, and training programs, even if the expenditures reduced profit. The questionnaire was inspired by the executive vice president in charge of investment, aged thirty-three.

That businessmen are suffering from an incipient social conscience is timely, no doubt, but scarcely all that is required. What some of the most intelligent and (it seemed to me) far-sighted Californians are advocating is the necessity of some form of long-term planning. The computer revolution, I was told, has scarcely begun; in the next phase, the machines will be able to handle untold quantities of information; and this capacity should make long-range planning much more feasible.

Some of those who talked in this way also said that the world had enough technology already. "We have all we need," said Dr. Dunn, the Stanford engineer. "We know how to do all the things necessary to rebuild our environment if we want to. We know how to build rapid-transit systems, we know how to get smog out of the air, we know how to build electric power systems that don't pollute. We don't have to imagine or predict new technologies in order to imagine a new type of city; it just needs someone to make up his mind to build it. The only thing no one knows how to do is education, and—who can tell?—the knowledge even about that might come along one day.

"What is not understood is how you fit the fields of knowledge together. Urban studies, for instance, don't include water resources or electric power, which are thought of as state problems. How do you put these things together? How do you then throw in national defense and international relations? Everyone is working in fragments: but you can't do anything individually. Even on our cable-television project we work as a group, with an electrical engineer, a systems analyst who is also an engineer, two lawyers, an economist, and a social psychologist. A regional plan, to make any sense, would need ten really good people working on it over a long period. But the way things are organized at present it's hard enough to get good people together even for short-term projects. This is the real problem that's emerging, though that doesn't make it any easier to do. We must be modest. The fact that the problem is there doesn't mean we'll be able to solve it. But at least it's clear what we have to work on."

I took Dunn's point, but I couldn't see how long-range planning was going to fit into short-range politics. Besides, new planning techniques, even if they can be developed, take a long time to filter into government. I had learned from Rand that they perfected their technique of program planning and budgeting systems (PPBS) a full fifteen years before President Johnson, on August 25, 1965, issued a directive to most of the executive agencies in the U.S. government instructing them to use the new method (and it is still not clear how well it works).

More fundamental than any of the technological or technical questions, I ended up thinking, was the conundrum underlying so many of the Californian phenomena I had encountered: what is it that holds Californian society together? De Tocqueville in the 1830s confronted the paradox of an American society that was fragmented by self-interest and self-seeking, yet nevertheless seemed to have found a principle of inner order. His answer to the paradox was the binding force of the religious principle. "Patriotism and religion are the only things which will make the whole body of citizens go persistently forward towards the same goal." Tocqueville saw religion—"the first of American political institutions"—as the glue in a democratic society no longer held together by authority.

But patriotism has been weakened by the Vietnam War; even before that war, the notion of Americanism was losing its power. Religion, especially in California, can no longer be regarded as cohesive. So what is it that holds Californian society together? For a time, perhaps it was a shared goal of material prosperity; but now that many citizens have reached this goal, it has turned out to be bleak and rocky.

Undoubtedly, Californians will have to find some other shared purpose; and it is conceivable, I suppose, that it might emerge from the mishmash of Esalen-type thinking, revolutionary chatter, Huxleyan mysticism, and hippie daydreams. An outsider, at least, may well feel that the underlying Californian turmoil is most readily explicable in terms of a search for a new religion. Tocqueville referred to the American capacity to make mistakes and then retrieve them. This capacity for recovery, he thought, went beyond social or technological tinkering. The American nation had acquired an identity from "marching through wildernesses, drying up marshes, diverting rivers, peopling the wilds and subduing nature": it thereby acquired "a hidden sinew giving strength to the whole frame." The direction in which the American nation marched was west. Possibly the new stirrings out there do mean something. The important thing, as the wisest futurologist I met implied, is not to jump to conclusions, one way or the other. "All we can be sure of," said Professor Donald Michael, "is that we are in for a time of turmoil." A friend of mine added: "Our margin of error is very small." Professor Michael added: "We must be poised to learn and to admit error. Rigidity and dogmatism are the handmaidens of disaster. In other words, we must live in the future now."

Notes

CHAPTER 1

1. Hutchings' *California Magazine,* November, 1857.
2. George R. Stewart, *Ordeal by Hunger* (Boston: Houghton Mifflin Co., 1960).
3. For Keseberg's account of his sufferings and "the unutterable repugnance with which I tasted the first mouthful of flesh," see C. F. McGlashan, *History of the Donner Party: A Tragedy of the Sierra* (Stanford: Stanford University Press, 1947).
4. A Louis Harris poll, taken in May, 1971, found that the number of "independents" in the U.S. had risen to 23 percent of the electorate.
5. *Le France Observateur,* July, 1971.
6. Pollution also first became a serious subject of scientific concern in California. At the University of California, nearly one hundred people are conducting fundamental research on air pollution—half the basic research capacity of the whole country on this subject.
7. The first documented instance of insects' genetic resistance to insecticides was recorded in the San Jose Valley as long ago as 1906.

CHAPTER 2

1. James H. Perkins in the *North American Review* (January, 1846), quoted by Henry Nash Smith, *Virgin Land* (Cambridge: Harvard University Press, 1950). My debt to Professor Nash Smith will be plain to all readers of his wise and expert writings.
2. Henry George, *Our Land and Land Policy, National and State* (San Francisco, 1871), p. 34.
3. But the old distinction between playground and schoolroom is evi-

dently becoming blurred. An intellectual couple were recently startled to learn that their five-year-old daughter, who goes to school in Malibu, had "flunked play."

4. In 1948, the U.S. Public Health Service estimated that the average American threw away two pounds of trash a day. In 1968, he threw away five. In Fresno, which has made a two-year study of garbage problems, 396,000 people generate 2.5 million tons of solid waste a year. By the year 2000, the figure is expected to be 5.5 million tons. To avoid being buried under garbage, Fresno is planning a novel system of storing refuse in underground conduits and removing it be sucking it into collection trucks. San Francisco is hauling its daily garbage thirty-two miles, to help build a park. One weird device under scrutiny is a technique of bombarding garbage with radioactive isotopes, which makes it odorless and reduces its volume by a third.

CHAPTER 3

1. Daniel S. Greenberg, *The Politics of American Science* (London: Penguin Books, 1969), p. 174.

2. Seaborg was born in Michigan but did his graduate work at Berkeley; he married Lawrence's secretary.

3. In fiscal 1970, total defense expenditures in California were estimated at $10.8 billion, with an additional $1.3 billion for NASA programs, according to Seymour Milman, ed., *The War Economy of the United States* (New York: St. Martin's Press, 1971), p. 187. Milman (p. 232) quotes a *U.S. News and World Report* estimate that 767,400 jobs in California in 1970 were "defense-generated."

4. "California's boast about being the 'society of the future' is not mere hyperbole, and the severe blow to the confidence of the middle classes of the latest recession may be something which will become apparent on a wider geographic basis in economic downturns in the future. It appears that the United States is evolving toward an economy in which white-collar and professional workers have as much reason to fear a recession as blue-collar and service ones. The long-term implications are political dynamite." The *Times* (London), March, 1971.

5. Mr. Cruse, like most Californians, did not mention earthquakes when discussing nature's contribution to the state. In 1970, seismologists recorded 130 tremors that were strong enough to be noticed in various parts of California. Over the last hundred years, twenty "severe" earthquakes have been recorded. The tremor of February,

1971, in the San Fernando Valley was officially described by the U.S. Geological Survey as "moderate," though it killed 64 people, started more than 1000 landslides, released methane gas from the ocean floor near Malibu Point, and caused damage estimated at $1 billion.

6. Venice was invented half a century ago by a midwest industrialist named Albert Kinney, who attempted to recreate the Italian city, with gondolas and matching architecture. Sarah Bernhardt came out of retirement to play *La Dame aux Camelias* at the end of the pier, but almost no one turned up to watch her.

7. In L.A. County, where there are currently 325 miles of freeways, a further 1127 miles of freeway are planned, at a cost of $5 billion.

8. *The Education of Henry Adams* (Boston and New York: Houghton Mifflin, 1918), p. 421.

9. It is true that the nature of the technological revolution and its implications was first discussed (or so its organizers claimed) at an *Encyclopaedia Britannica* conference in Santa Barbara in March, 1962. But the point of departure was a paper prepared by a Frenchman, Jacques Ellul of the University of Bordeaux, who was introduced to the conference by an Englishman, or ex-Englishman, Aldous Huxley. Of the twenty or so participants in the conference, fewer than half a dozen were Californians.

CHAPTER 4

1. Even by 1980, it is expected that 15 percent of all households in Los Angeles County will still not own a car, meaning that 450,000 households will be dependent on other forms of transportation. Today more than a million people depend at one time or another on the virtually nonexistent public-transportation system, according to a Bank of America booklet, *California* (1970).

2. "Industry is looking now to Orange County and beyond for new sites—away from the heavily urbanized and costly regions of Los Angeles County," Bank of America booklet. A survey of business firms by L.A. County showed that the cost of providing parking for their employees was a powerful stimulus in making them think of moving out of the county.

3. That is, plenty of cars. It is my impression that, possibly throughout the United States, and certainly in California, language is becoming less and less precise. Phrases and sentences are often blurred, like the horizon between the sky and the Pacific.

A radio announcer said: "The audio portion can be heard . . ."

A coffee-shop waitress in Santa Monica said: "I've put your glass in your cup because of the space factor."

An associate professor of Business Administration at the University of California wrote the following sentence: "Higher income provides the necessary purchasing power not only to make the appropriate purchases but also to make more of such purchases."

A plaque in the new university art museum at Berkeley, signed by the director, reads: "This is a time in the history of our country which is wrought with prodigious problems."

The Matterhorn bobsled at Disneyland has a notice beginning: "For expediency in loading . . ."

Dr. Max Rafferty, who had just finished telling me that he had held perhaps the most important educational job in California, said in reply to a question: "I can't project that kind of speculation."

CHAPTER 5

1. Henry James, *The American Scene* (London: Rupert Hart-Davis, 1968), p. 103.
2. Daniel Bell, "The Cultural Contradictions of Capitalism," *The Public Interest,* No. 21 (Fall, 1970), pp. 189 ff.
3. The "butcher," as the lady curator disdainfully called him, was named Henry Miller. When he died, the "kingdom" of Miller and Lux, his firm, owned a million acres and controlled half a million more. The kingdom has been broken up, but the company store survives, thirteen miles east of Los Banos.

CHAPTER 6

1. *The Jungle,* an exposure of the meat-packing industry, was published in 1906. Sixty-one years later, Upton Sinclair, in a wheelchair, was present in the White House when President Johnson signed the Wholesale Meat Act, a measure designed to stop the kind of practices that Sinclair had described.
2. A similar shift is under way in Britain; the ninety-odd dockers at the Overseas Containers Terminal in the London docks—who struck against containers for fourteen months in 1969—broke the 3000-pounds-a-year barrier in 1971, which put them well inside the middle-class income bracket.
3. "Military shipments from Pacific Coast ports—about 55 percent of all that is going to Vietnam—have more than tripled since 1965," Milman, *War Economy of the United States,* p. 192.

4. David F. Selvin, *Sky Full of Storm* (Berkeley and Los Angeles: University of California Press, 1966), p. 69.

5. Delano began as a railway station on the Central Pacific Railroad. It was named, not after a Spanish *ranchero,* but after Columbus Delano, then secretary of the interior.

6. By 1974, the Fresno County Economic Opportunities Commission predicts, 65 percent of the wine and raisin grapes in the San Joaquin Valley will be picked mechanically. "It is estimated that mechanical pickers will cost Fresno County farm workers nearly $2 million in wages during 1971 and that by 1973 some 4500 heads of families will be displaced by machine." John Gregory Dunne, "To Die Standing: Cesar Chavez and the Chicanos," *The Atlantic* (June, 1971).

7. The American Council of Education, in its five-year review published in 1970, still put Berkeley at the top of its list of American universities, one place ahead of Harvard, as "the best-balanced distinguished university in the nation."

CHAPTER 7

1. The California Highway Patrol's IBM 7740 was the first link attached to the FBI's IBM system in April, 1967, and it provided 270 local terminals. This computer link occurred almost exactly one hundred years after the east and west of the United States were first "linked with iron" by the transcontinental railroad.

2. Jessica Mitford, "Kind and Usual Punishment in California," *The Atlantic* (March, 1971).

CHAPTER 8

1. Ginsberg thinks we must all start thinking in a new way "if we want to cope with the increasing complexity of our civilization, with its overpopulation, threat of atomic annihilation, and power to leave the earth." He thinks a new "aware" attitude to the world has already started to appear among the young from Prague to Calcutta. "The consciousness-expanding drugs occupy attention in the highest intellectual circles of the West, as well as among the great mass of youth. The odd perceptions of Zen, Tibetan Yoga, Mantra Yoga, and indigenous American shamanism affect the consciousness of a universal generation, children who can recognize each other by hairstyle, tone of voice, attitude to nature, and attitude to civilization. The airwaves are filled with song of hitherto unheard-of frank-

ness and beauty." Allen Ginsberg in *The Marijuana Papers,* David Solomon, ed. (London: Panther, 1969), p. 277.

(Ginsberg, a flamboyant fellow, wrote the first half of the essay of which these are the concluding words, "while smoking marijuana.")

2. In 1956, when he was living in San Francisco, Alan Watts gave the following explanation of the "extraordinary growth of interest in Zen Buddhism since the Second World War . . . which has increased so much that it seems to be becoming a considerable force in the intellectual and artistic world of the West." He wrote:

> Western thought has changed so rapidly in this century that we are in a state of considerable confusion. Not only are there serious difficulties of communication between the intellectual and the general public, but the course of our thinking and of our very history has seriously undermined the common-sense assumptions which lie at the root of our social conventions and institutions. Familiar concepts of space, time, and motion, of nature and natural law, of history and social change, and of human personality itself have dissolved, and we find ourselves adrift in a universe which more and more resembles the Buddhist principle of the "Great Void." The various wisdoms of the West, religious, philosophical and scientific, do not offer much guidance to the art of living in such a universe, and we find the prospects of making our way in so trackless an ocean of relativity rather frightening. For we are used to absolutes, to firm principles and laws to which we can cling for spiritual and psychological security. This is why, I think, there is so much interest in a culturally productive way of life which, for some fifteen hundred years, has felt thoroughly at home in "the Void," and which not only feels no terror for it but rather a positive delight.

Alan W. Watts, Preface to *The Way of Zen* (New York: Pantheon Books, 1957).

3. Paramahansa Yogananda, *Autobiography of a Yogi,* 10th ed. (Los Angeles: Self Realization Fellowship, 1969).

4. One of those to whom Yogananda taught Yoga techniques was Margaret Woodrow Wilson, the president's eldest daughter, who subsequently spent the last five years of her life pursuing Indian wisdom in Pondicherry, India, at the Ashram of the Mother.

5. In 1956, the psychiatrist under whose supervision Huxley had first

taken mescalin, Dr. Humphry Osmond, had an exchange of letters with Huxley about what the new mind-changing drugs should be called. Osmond mentioned the word "psychedelic":

> To fathom Hell or soar angelic
> Just take a pinch of psychedelic.

To which Huxley replied with his own invention, "phanerothyme":

> To make this trivial world sublime
> Take half a gram of phanerothyme.

6. In 1962, Huxley sent Leary a reading list of books about the Tantric Buddhism of medieval India, pointing out that "Tantric exercises in awareness anticipated the whole of Gestalt therapy"—the therapy practiced at Esalen by one of its principal American exponents, the late Dr. Fritz Perls.

CHAPTER 9

1. "Bicycles are becoming an increasingly important form of modern urban transportation. Bicycles do not contribute to air pollution or to noise pollution and help to alleviate urban automobile congestion by serving as a convenient and practical alternative to the automobile." Petition addressed to the Board of Directors, San Francisco Bay Area Rapid Transit District, demanding "safe and legal access by bicycle to and across the San Francisco-Oakland Bay Bridge."
2. Any Californian community of more than five hundred people can ask to be incorporated as a "city." The "special districts" are formed by people pursuing special interests. A group wants street lighting or a park or roads; they get the approval of a majority of residents, and a special district is then set up, which has tax-collecting powers. The districts pile up, a critic has said, like "an uneven set of pancakes." One citizen may pay taxes to half a dozen special districts, as well as to the county. He gets none of the benefits of coherent local government, and he gets local control only in theory, for the vote in special-district elections is invariably extremely low—often under 5 percent of those eligible.
3. Edward C. Banfield, *Big City Politics: A Comparative Guide to the Political Systems of Nine American Cities* (New York: Random House, 1965).

CHAPTER 10

1. John Plamenatz, *Man and Society,* vol. 2 (London: Longman, 1963), p. 409.
2. W. H. Armytage, *The Rise of the Technocrats: A Social History* (Toronto: University of Toronto Press, 1965), p. 37. The word "technology" first appeared in America in *The Elements of Technology* (1829) by Jacob Bigelow, the Harvard botanist. The book consisted of a series of lectures on the application of science to the useful arts.
3. Armytage, pp. 340–1.
4. For a supporting view from a highly distinguished source, see F. Macfarlane Burnet, *Genes, Dreams, and Realities* (London: in press August, 1972). "The contribution of laboratory science to medicine has virtually come to an end. The biomedical sciences all continue to provide fascinating employment for those active in research, and sometimes enthralling reading for those who are no longer at the bench but can still appreciate a fine piece of work. But the detail of RNA phage's chemical structure, the place of cyclostomes in the evolution of immunity, or the production of antibody in test tubes are typical of today's topics in biological research. Almost none of modern basic research in the medical sciences has any direct or indirect bearing on the prevention of disease or on the improvement of medical care." (Sir Macfarlane Burnet, O.M., F.R.S., Nobel prizewinner for medicine, 1960, was formerly director of the Walter and Eliza Hall Institute for Medical Research in Melbourne, Australia.)
5. Plamenatz, p. 410.
6. Cf. Donald A. Schon, *Beyond the Stable State* (New York: Random House, 1971), an expanded version of the BBC Reith Lectures that Professor Schon delivered in 1970.

Index